Democracy In One School?

Progressive Education and Restructuring

Tuula Gordon

 The Falmer Press

(A member of the Taylor & Francis Group)
London, New York and Philadelphia

UK	The Falmer Press, Falmer House, Barcombe, Lewes, East Sussex, BN8 5DL
USA	The Falmer Press, Taylor & Francis Inc., 242 Cherry Street, Philadelphia, PA 19106-1906

First published 1986

Library of Congress Cataloging in Publication Data

Gordon, Tuula.
  Democracy in one school?

  1. Education and state—Great Britain—Case studies.
2. School management and organization—Social aspects—
Great Britain—Case studies. 3. Progressive education—
Great Britain—Case studies. 4. Politics and education
—Great Britain—Case studies. 5. Radicalism—Great
Britain—Case studies. I. Title.
LC93.G7G67 1986   379.41   86-13431
ISBN 1-85000-104-9
ISBN 1-85000-105-7 (pbk.)

Jacket design by Caroline Archer

Typeset in 10/12 Bembo by
Imago Publishing Ltd, Thame, Oxon

*Printed in Great Britain by Taylor & Francis (Printers) Ltd,
Basingstoke*

Contents

Acknowledgements   viii

Introduction   1

PART ONE: The Theory   5

1   Formal Education as State Apparatus   6

2   Restructuring, Resistance and Development of Schooling   12

3   Progressive Education   26

PART TWO: The Case Study   51

4   The Paradox — Progressive Education in a
    Conservative Local Authority   52

5   The School   60

6   The Teachers   85

7   The Students   111

PART THREE: Mediations   141

8   Individualization   142

9   Professionalism   159

PART FOUR: Greenfield — Social Relations Considered   177

10   Student Careers   178

11   Sex-gender and Sexism   205

12   Vertical Teams   223

13   The Challenge of the Eighties   240

Contents

Methodological Appendix   249

Bibliography   261

Indexes   271

To
Dougie
Mikko
Janne

Acknowledgements

This book has arisen out of research conducted for a PhD thesis (University of London Institute of Education, 1985), supported by a Social Science and Research Council award. I want to thank the teachers, students and staff of 'Greenfield College' for participating in the research, and for making the fieldwork period so interesting. I particularly thank teachers and students of the team that provided my 'home-base', and those teachers who have read and commented on my work. Tony Green in his role as my supervisor maintained a keen interest in the research. Other people have discussed aspects of the work, have provided support, have proof-read etc: Shane Blackman, Lesley Caldwell, Margo Clark, Dougie Gordon, Brian Hackland, John Hayes, Janet Holland, Doug Holly, Gerry Lander, Saila Sainomaa and Michael Young. Ivor Goodson provided encouragement for me to write this book. Last, but not least, I would like to thank my family, Dougie, Mikko and Janne. The children, born during my research work, have remained sane and good-natured. A high standard of care was provided for them in Camden Staff Day Nursery. The active role assumed by Dougie in child-care and domestic maintenance has made the completion of this book possible.

Introduction

The research that this book is based on arose out of an interest in 'progressive' education, the debate around it, and its 'crisis' in the seventies. These issues were symbolically condensed in the events surrounding William Tyndale school in the mid-seventies, culminating in the dismissal of the teachers involved amidst considerable media attention. The following quotations with differentiated criticisms stem appropriately from the debate on Tyndale. Walker argued that progressive education 'is now in grave danger of providing the soft underbelly where surely and insidiously the enemies of democracy can attack and destroy our democratic society'.[1] But Hadow and Ellis did not agree; for them 'progressive education now is a pretty way of imposing the political status quo on children, so that they are trained to take up preconceived positions within society'.[2] I shall try to understand and explain these contradictory conceptions through a theoretical, historical and empirical study of progressivism on macro- and micro-levels. I attempt to answer two questions: first, how can we explain the almost diametrically opposed critiques of progressivism by the left and the right, and second, how can we understand the 'crisis'[3] of progressivism?

The answers are sought on two levels: first, there is a study of formal state education in the context of an analysis of the development of social relations in Britain over the past two decades; second, there is an empirical study of progressivism focussing on possibilities and limitations for radicalization[4] within it. An attempt to consider articulations between 'levels' of analysis is framed within a neo-Marxist discourse question and amplified by feminist analysis. The limited range of questions addressed by 'old' sociology of education has been noted by many authors[5] — concern was mainly for 'access' in education. Interactionist 'new' sociology of education raised the content of schooling as a problematic issue, whilst abstract Marxism led to theoretical discussions divorced from the school context. Recent developments have included the Foucauldian critique of the usefulness of general theories, and feminist critique of all mainstream sociology for remaining uninterested in crucial questions of sex and gender within schooling.

Here a general theoretical framework is developed, but it is combined with empirical fieldwork drawing on the interactionist tradition. There is an attempt to conceptualize bridges between the two levels, and thus to take into account challenges met by analyses within the Marxist framework — such challenges centre on questions of mediation between schools and society. The importance of the feminist critique is noted, and questions about the relationship between Marxist and feminist analyses are addressed; capitalism and patriarchy are argued to be analytically independent. Thus the aim is to utilize a general theory fruitful in terms of empirical research, and to conduct such research in a way which enables it to be focussed by theoretical considerations. Though the necessity of such an undertaking could hardly be questioned, a survey of literature indicates the paucity of attempts to do so; production of coherent, precise, clearly outlined studies is difficult, when the area of concern is not clearly delimited. Because of the importance of the task, both theoretically and practically, I shall address such problems here.

In Part One general theoretical concepts are developed focussing on capital-labour relations and the distinction between state form and state apparatus. A historical consideration of restructuring and resistance introduces dynamic elements to the analysis through a discussion of the shifting relationship between form and apparatus. Against that background an analysis of progressivism is possible; development of its disintegration is understood through a consideration of expansion and crisis of the sixties and seventies. It is suggested that restructuring addressed progressivism specifically. The elusiveness of progressive education and contradictions within it are embodied in a discussion of the different strands it contains.

In Part Two there is an in-depth study of Greenfield College.[6] The framework of restructuring provides a dynamic element for the study, drawing attention to contradictions and tensions in a progressive school during a period of forging of changes in social relations, involving changes in the relationship between state form and apparatus, manifested in centralization and standardization in the sphere of formal education. Though the case study is contextualized, there is also an attempt to focus on the uniqueness of one particular school, and it is possible for a reader interested in education to concentrate on Greenfield College as an example of progressivism.

In order to understand the contradictions and tensions, and implications of problems considered here — that is, the 'crisis' of progressive education, the left and right critiques of it, and radical possibilities and limitations within it — analytical tools to link the theoretical and descriptive parts, and to consider mediations between macro- and micro-levels, are developed. This task is undertaken in Part Three where articulations between individualization as a form, professionalism as a mode, and practices in Greenfield College are discussed.

In Part Four different instances of the school are analyzed: student careers, sex-gender system and the organization of vertical teams. The usefulness of the perspective adopted in illuminating contradictory complexities of an institution during restructuring is considered with an attempt to specify teacher/student perceptions as thinking subject/objects and as institutional subject/objects, with their particular structural and cultural locations, and their interpretations of these locations, culminating in particular actions and out-comes which are rendered intelligible as a negotiated condensation of broader social relations.

The title of this book *Democracy in One School?* refers to the theme of restructuring and the question of the 'survival' of Greenfield which opened in 1970 and had to contend with an educational climate increasingly hostile to its aims; the longitudinal perspective adopted has given poignancy to this focus. In 1978, though there were difficulties, I nevertheless entered a thriving democratic school. In 1985, in an attempt to survive and develop in the context of centralization, standardization and public expenditure cuts the democratic structures were suspended and during an 'impasse' new structures were negotiated and struggled over, in the context of the national trade union action by teachers.

Notes

1 WALKER (1977) p. 41.
2 HADOW, B. and ELLIS, T. in *Socialist Teacher*, 4, p. 20.
3 This 'crisis' is manifested notably in the critique contained in the Great Debate of 1976, and in the Black Papers, as well as in the moves to reorganize the state education sector.
4 Radicalism is, throughout this text, used as a term covering a range of critiques, ideology, policies and activity of the left spectrum of politics, aimed at general or specific social change; it does not refer to radicalism of the right spectrum of politics. Radicalization refers to a process of assuming such a political orientation.
5 For example GREEN (1975), YOUNG (1971) and FINN *et. al.* (1977).
6 The name is invented to preserve anonymity.

Part One: The Theory

Chapter 1

Formal Education as State Apparatus

The study[1] of the emergence of free, compulsory schooling[2] indicates dis-agreements among the dominant classes about the education of the 'lower orders', and the uneven, discontinuous development of popular education. An analysis which takes into account such complexities is needed. The struggles within schooling make it a microcosm of social relationships in society, stamped by conflicts and negotiated outcomes, not a reflection of 'wider society', 'economy' etc. Historical study illustrates shifting alliances, balances of struggle, upsurgence and decrease of militancy and search for solutions forged out of debating conflicting interests and perceptions. The patterns of schooling are the patterns of social relations of and in capitalist society; the socio-economic conjuncture is condensed within formal education as Donald notes.[3]

The usefulness of neo-Marxist discourse in analyzing formal education in its complexity is considered. But Marxist categories are 'sex-blind' (Hartmann, 1979). Structured inequalities in terms of sex-gender have implications for the study of schooling. A 'dual analysis'[4] is adopted here; the concept of patriarchy is utilized to analyze sex-gender divisions (chapter 11).

Some Analyses of Formal Education

American revisionists such as Spring[5] have analyzed schooling as education for the corporate state. These writers focus largely on the development of progressivism and liberal educational theory, which are seen as intellectual justification for repression through their encouragement for integration; the fragile facade of social engineering is noted.

Bowles and Gintis (1976) analyze the way in which schools *produce* workers. The social relationships of education replicate the hierarchical division of labour in production — this is called the 'correspondence principle'. Liberal progressive reforms were unsuccessful as they did not call into question basic social and economic structures, but worked on the level of the individual.

In these analyses it is not clear what the mediations between economy and education are. A central role is accorded to the state in reproducing the capitalist order, but its role is not developed further, and no theory of the state is referred to.

The Education Group of the Centre for Contemporary Cultural Studies set out in *Unpopular Education* (1981) to overcome the problems of many Marxist analyses which are seen as unhistorical, pessimistic, and unable to inform political practice. The authors are interested in the failure of social democratic ideology. The 1960 'settlement' is analyzed in terms of the making of social democratic hegemony over education policies. The limits of reform are discussed: inadequate policies, DES power to deflect, LEA control, teacher control over curriculum, cultures within the classroom. The central problem, the authors emphasize, lay in 'the political balance of forces'. The focus on politics and policies belies, to an extent, broader statements by the authors such as that the 'breaking' of social democracy occurred

> through the weaknesses of social democratic policies and the 1960s alliance; through the accurate exploitation of these weaknesses by a new populist Toryism; and through the *more subterranean determinations of economic failure* and of the sustained reproduction of class and gender relations. (my emphasis)[6]

The authors start by emphasizing the complexity of the needs of capital, and the impossibility of understanding political processes as a response to 'one-dimensional "economic" imperative'. A consideration of social relations in a capitalist society (including age and gender relations) is seen as a necessary context for the study of the limits of educational reform. Yet despite these theoretical developments in the course of the analysis crude notions of economy take over. The analysis of 'movements of capital' is considered necessary, but is reduced to a brief consideration of the crisis of capital accumulation in terms of growth rates, shares of world market etc, and the work of economists such as Bacon and Eltis. The authors ask 'what are the limits of educational reform under capitalist and patriarchal conditions?', but the answer cannot be found in growth rates — to say that 'the educational settlement was put into jeopardy by the economic movements and economic ideologies of the late 1960s and early 1970s'[7] tells us very little about capitalist and patriarchal conditions. The authors have lapsed into a mechanical analysis they wanted to avoid. Similar problems relate to the theory of the state that is relied upon — or a lack of any real definition of the term, which allows references to negotiations 'chaired by the state', implying a peculiar personification, the crudity of which cannot be excused by an attempt to avoid abstractions and unhistorical analyses.

The book raises interesting questions about the limits posed for education by capitalist schooling;[8] about spaces for progressive activity in schools;[9] and about the distance between 'the radical, pro-education elements within the working class', and 'the sceptical pragmatic majorities' within it.[10] But to answer these questions we must address the relationship between the political and economic; references to subterranean determinations are not sufficient.

Towards a Materialist Theory of Political Development

In a materialist analysis the mode of production is a serious context with implications for the study of the political; the relationship between the political and the economic must be addressed. Drawing a clear distinction between production and reproduction leads to 'economism' on the one hand, whereby the political is seen as a reflection of the economic, or 'politicism', an emphasis on 'relative autonomy' and domination 'in the last instance', as for example in the work of Althusser[11] and Poulantzas.[12] Problems of the concept of re-production are linked to difficulties caused by the distinction between economic and political levels as separate and autonomous in analyses which then focus on the political as a distinct object of study; articulations between the two levels remain unexplored.

Holloway and Picciotto

The advantages of the materialist theory developed within the CSE and elsewhere[13] are:

(i)   the analysis of the distinction and the relation between the economic and the political, as particularizations of the capital relation;
(ii) the distinction between state form and state apparatus;
(iii) the conception of 'crisis' as a restructuring of the capital relation;
(iv) the conception of the 'crisis' of education as a process of reimposition of 'bourgeois' social relations and state form upon the state apparatus — in this case the formal education system.

On this basis we will be able to see schooling as a condensation of patterns of the whole 'socio-economic conjuncture' as Donald states the task (p. 6 above), and therefore we can consider relatively complex mediations between levels rather than losing sight of them when emphasizing the simplistic distinction between political and economic and relative autonomy of the former.

The analysis below emphasizes capital-labour relations; it is assumed that people are classed subjects. Though the emphasis is on the general manner in which relations of production and state practices affect citizens, no account is given of the differential effects of state practices on men and women, un-covered by feminist research; people are not considered as gendered subjects. An awareness of gender-specificity of state practices exists. However, a feminist theory of the state remains largely undeveloped; focus is mainly on policies.[14] In the absence of such theorization questions of sex and gender are taken up and explored analytically in chapter 11, where particular focus is accorded to them, though sex-gender is an empirical concern throughout. Thus a dual analysis has been adopted, not merely because of practical problems, but also because of theoretical considerations — analytical independence of capitalism and patriarchy is assumed.

Holloway and Picciotto critically analyze the state derivation debate, based on 'capital logic'. The state is one aspect of the social relations of capital; it is a particular surface form of these relations and is stamped by their contradictions. The concept of class struggle as an essential aspect of the surplus value production is integral to the analysis. Relations of production assume separate economic and political forms though both are instances of the relation between labour and capital. This 'fetishization' of social relations is crucial, as the distinction is both real and illusory; it is real as long as struggles assume either political or economic forms; it is illusory in concealing the relationship of both to the capital relation.

Holloway and Picciotto, having established the state as a form of capital relation, and having affirmed the necessity of conceiving of the state as such a logical category, stress the need for historical analysis in order to understand the content of class struggle. They consider crises of accumulation, resulting from contradictions embodied in the capital relation; thus a restructuring of that relation is necessary. Capital becomes less able to reproduce[15] its own existence; counter-tendencies are mobilized, increasingly through the state. The very form of the state as a social instance raised above the production process poses limitations on the effectiveness of state intervention. The state, outside and alongside production (equipped with force), ensures the general prerequisites of production. The period of restructuring involves a 'legitimation crisis'; profound ongoing changes are accompanied by uncertainties and the form and content of social relations are vulnerable; their maintenance/imposition is increasingly difficult. This is manifested either in the individual refusal to accept 'bourgeois' norms of conduct within the state (absenteeism, indiscipline etc.), or in increasingly conscious political action.

A distinction between the state form and state apparatus is made. It is important in allowing us to consider education within the state sector in all its complexities as *state* schooling, which cannot be analyzed in isolation from its context. At the same time this context is not seen to *determine* what happens in schools, but rather, schooling has that context 'condensed' within it. A further advantage of this distinction is that we do not need to abandon all notions of 'autonomy' of education, but will be better able to understand such autonomy, and locate its basis in the changing relation between the state form and state apparatus. Thus we can try to formulate genuinely dynamic analyses of education, and move some way towards considering the 'historical conditions of 1970s' and locating the analysis therein.

The state form is an abstraction embodying the capital relation; the state apparatus is the machinery of the state. The *theoretical* implication of this distinction is that though there is a *relationship* between state form and state apparatus, this is not necessarily tight and constant, but dynamic, full of contradictions and complexities, and variable in significance, effectivity and strength over time. During periods of rapid capital accumulation disjunctures can develop between form and apparatus, particularly when class struggle is of low intensity. However, when accumulation reaches barriers, tackled through restructuring, the relationship between form and apparatus tightens up — instability incumbent with social change necessitates increasing control of institutions and people within the state apparatus, with the concomitant control of citizens. Thus the distinction is a theoretical device allowing us to consider relations within the state, and their implications for the relation between state and civil society, which is also dynamic. The *practical* implication of the distinction is that it is possible for radical individuals/groups to work within the state in the 'oppositional spaces'[16] located in the disjunctures; this is crucial in order to avoid a 'cog-in-the-wheel' conception when analyzing teachers and their work.[17]

A slowing down of the rate of accumulation in the immediate process of production leads to a pressure to reduce the amount of the surplus value transferred to the state through taxation. This leads to a pressure to decrease the expenditure of the state, whilst increased demands are likely to be made on it, such as tighter control of employees and increased efficiency in administration. This entails the restructuring of the relation between the state apparatus and 'citizens'.[18] The crisis of the state form, then, implies a crisis in the relationship between the state form and state apparatus. The possibility of individual refusal or rebellion and conscious political collective action signifies this. Not all work within the state apparatus is in detail determined by the state form, though the general framework is moulded by it.

The state apparatus as a sphere of operation for radical groups and individuals is a dynamic shifting balance of possibilities and limitations, which can be considered in empirical and historical analyses. People are integrated into social relations of capitalist, patriarchal society through the way in which the framework of their lives is structured by state activities into fragmented and atomised units on the basis of surface characteristics (for example constituents, owner-occupiers etc.); this will enable us to consider conformity as well as resistance and allows us to see these as active responses.[19]

Conclusion

In order to analyze schooling, consideration of the state is necessary. Questions of determination are addressed by developing a general theory which divorces state from production, but also notes the relationship between them, focussing on the capital-labour relation. This analysis remains neutral vis-à-vis gender, which must be considered through the concept of patriarchy, cutting across different modes of production, though assuming specific capitalist content (and form.)

To understand institutions within and of the state, such as schooling in this instance, a distinction between state form and state apparatus is made. Thus we can note both the relations of determination, and the disjunctures developed historically. It is a crucial argument here that in those disjunctures reside structures of opportunity, 'spaces', within which relatively autonomous practices are possible. Development of education and its expansion in the 1960s can be considered against the background of a formulation of the possibility of those developments. We can address the problems of expansionist policies and the 'crisis' of education that these led to in the 1970s through the concept of restructuring, affecting the capital–labour relations, and the relationship between the state form and apparatus. This is a task undertaken in the following chapter.

Notes

1 The work of Simon and Johnson has been particularly useful; sources listed in the bibliography.
2 The terms 'schooling' and 'education' are both used; however, in order to distinguish between what goes on in schools, and education as a broader concept, the word 'formal' is used wherever possible.
3 DONALD (1979) p. 40.
4 *C.f.* YOUNG (1981).
5 CARNOY (1975), GUMBERT and SPRING (1974), KARIER *et. al.* (1973), SPRING (1972).
6 Education Group (1981) p. 242.
7 *Ibid.* p. 173.
8 *Ibid.* p. 260
9 *Ibid.* p. 93
10 *Ibid.* p. 35
11 For example ALTHUSSER (1971).
12 For example POULANTZAS (1973).
13 HOLLOWAY and PICCIOTTO (1977 and 1978), CSE State Group (1979), London Edinburgh Weekend Return Group (1980), PICCIOTTO (1977), GERSTENBERGER (1977) and GERSTENBERGER, HIRSCH and BRAUNMUHL in HOLLOWAY and PICCIOTTO (1978).
14 For example DAVID (1980).
15 This refers to 'simple reproduction', MARX (1974).
16 The term is adopted from DONALD (1978).
17 ALTHUSSER (1971) refers to teachers 'trapped' in 'dreadful conditions'.
18 For example the rise of corporatism.
19 *C.f.* in particular WILLIS (1977) where the 'ear'oles' remain shadowy figures — cultural production, for Willis, resides in the lads.

Chapter 2

Restructuring, Resistance and Development of Schooling

During the 1960s formal education was characterized by quantitative and qualitative expansion. Schooling as a state apparatus enjoyed a considerable degree of autonomy; there was a disjuncture between the state form and state apparatus, within which 'oppositional spaces' were located. The theoretical attention to 'spaces' lends significance to a historical consideration of resistance and the extent to which it articulates with such spaces. Progressive education was located within the educational expansion and the associated autonomy. Hence, I shall argue, it became a casualty of restructuring, not in the least because of the links assumed between it and resistance.

Restructuring

Restructuring refers to a process of removing barriers to capital accumulation, which have developed because of the rise in relative surplus value production, the falling rate of profit and the rise in the organic compositon of capital. Such a process begins in the sphere of production, but, as the economic and political levels are both particularizations of the capital–labour relation, influences social relations outside that sphere. The mediations occur importantly through the state and find their impact *within* the state, necessitating a renewed closeness between state form and state apparatus, as the latter has, during a period of expansion, developed in a relatively autonomous direction.

The following historical account is based on various analyses of post-war developments in Britain, their focus ranging from finance capital to civil liberties. Two broad features of Britain must be noted first, though. The significance of *imperialism* has been that colonies, overseas investment and earnings allowed decline whilst preventing upheavals — Britain was able to maintain an obsolete structure compared to other advanced industrial capitalist societies. Further, *the defensive strength* of the working class has made a smoother course of restructuring unattainable.

Post-war years, leading up to the late fifties and the 1959 election, when

Macmillan told the electorate 'You Never Had It So Good', had contained a rapid expansion of world capital accumulation, and, in Britain, Keynesian techniques which postponed the resolution of structural problems. There was a social-democratic commitment to full employment and the integration of the working class. Gradually low rates of growth and production, and a fairly low wage economy undercut the brief period of affluence. The problems were a strong labour movement, lagging production, stagnant export markets, political dominance of colonial and financial interests, capital export, dwindling profits and a surge of foreign competition (Overbeek, 1978). The 1960s onwards were characterized by the institutionalization and displacement of class conflict, expansion and fragmentation of state apparatus, and the development of management techniques in the state apparatus.[1]

The 1964 Labour government was committed to the 'white heat of technological revolution'. There was an indirect support of profits, a direct redistribution of income, and understanding of the strength of the working class.

The second half of the 1960s began with the balance of payments crisis in 1965–66. An aggressive assault on the working class began, involving incomes policy, devaluation, rationalization, abandonment of the policy of full employment culminating in new proposals for the containment of unofficial strikes (In Place of Strife), which were abandoned. The 'structural collision path with the working class'[2] had begun, leading to the breaking of incomes policies, wages explosion and a wave of militant strikes at the turn of the decade: an 'oppositional milieu'.[3]

The 1970s began with a direct attack on the working class by the Conservative Heath government; the planning apparatus of the state was dismantled, voluntary restraint in controlling the working class was replaced by law — the Industrial Relations Act (1971) was an attempt to erode the power of the organized working class. In 1972 Heath's confrontation strategy was defeated. In a year beginning with Bloody Sunday the action of the miners brought about the government U-turn. Capital was reassembling forces, grant aid was given to industry,[4] and an incomes policy was adopted — thus Keynesian measures were used to restore profitability.

During this period Labour moved towards the left. After the elections in 1974, made necessary by the defeat of the Conservatives after the second wave of militant action by the miners, the Labour government was committed to 'getting Britain back to work'. This involved the 'setting of social passivity' (CSE State Group, 1979) and a 'reassertion of normal bourgeois relations' (Edinburgh CSE Cuts Group, 1978), after the 'foundation had moved' (Hall *et. al.,* 1978). With the 'stick-and-carrot' approach of Labour the working class was contained. Meanwhile a more aggressive strategy had been adopted with a higher level of structural unemployment and a restructuring of state expenditure and apparatuses linked to incomes policy. The Social Contract aimed to integrate the trade unions in a corporatist strategy.

Corporatist strategy characterized local government reorganization into fewer and larger units in 1974; this entailed centralization and bureaucratization.[5] At the same time public expenditure cuts and reorganization of fiscal control with the introduction of cash limits[6] indicated that social democracy had abandoned its aim to enlarge the public sector, the defence of which was left to workers in threatened services.

The period culminated in the 'winter of discontent' and the May 1979 election won by Thatcherist Conservatives. The debates during the election period included threats about continuing decline and exhortations that if common sense does not prevail and organized labour does not yield its 'negative' strength, the decline of Britain is going to be continuous and inexorable. It is to this 'negative' power of the working class that I now wish to turn, though such power is better defined as 'defensive'. Len Murray, former General Secretary of the TUC, said in 1976; 'We have always been very good at stopping anything we don't like, but not at starting something'.[7]

Gamble and Walton (1976) emphasize the defensive power of workers and the left to resist restructuring; this results in immobility. The tackling of declining profitability through reorganization of the process of production is rendered more difficult (McDonnell, 1978). Overbeek (1978) notes the workers' ability in the 1960s to fight against redundancies, and its significance in contributing to the productivity gap between Britain and the rest of the capitalist world. Cockshott (1978) argues that the low rate of production of the industrial sector is an effect of workers' power at the point of production. Panitch (1978a) puts forward similar arguments, and explains how the backbone of the industrial strength of the working class was formulated during a period of high labour demand creating favourable conditions for local bargaining led by militant shop stewards[8] close to the rank-and-file. Restructuring was not possible without the tackling of this industrial strength. It is difficult to assess precisely the pervasiveness of the influence of such stewards on plant level. But their significance is not a numerical one; what matters more is the existence of a trade union structure where the emergence of such activists is possible. Groups prepared to agitate and organize round militant issues and actions are disproportionately significant during restructuring. Corporate strategies depending on all parties being 'sensible' are not realistic, as oppositional spaces are occupied by groups determined to utilize them.

The monetarist policies adopted by the new Tory government have aimed to achieve a more productive industrial sector through the operation of market forces; both the owners and controllers of firms, and workers in them, are squeezed to be restructured. Through redundancies and massive unemployment a 'more realistic attitude on the shop floor' was achieved, and in November 1979 *The Observer* reported that in the CBI conference a 'smile on the managers' faces' was detected.[9] The Thatcherist Conservatives have been determined to accomplish what other governments have failed to do — to achieve a drastic restructuring of British society: breaking union power, rationalizing production and tackling resistance through development of law and order; there is a preparedness to take risks that are entailed in such a course of action: 'industrial revolutions are painful'.[10] Populist terms are used to justify grim necessities. Reform of the trade unions was a significant part of the Tory manifesto, including proposals on secondary picketing, closed shop, postal ballots etc., aimed to curb the power of extremists. Thatcherite restructuring is still in a flux; the degree to which the outcome will be successful is not yet clear. It is clear that populist demagogery is not solely relied upon — the existence of resistance is assumed and tackled. Behind the populist rhetoric repressive machinery is tightening[11] to aid restructuring in the face of the possibility of stagnation (Grahl, 1983).

Resistance

A period of restructuring entails changes in the capital-labour relation, and social relations between the state and citizens, as well as within the state. The outcomes of restructuring are negotiated and/or struggled over. In this situation militant opposition to changes is possible, and rendered potentially effective in influencing the direction of social change. State practices individualize and atomize people; they discount the significance of class, gender and race, and regroup people on the basis of surface characterization (chapter 8). Gerstenberger (1977) questions the usefulness of concepts of 'integration' and 'repression' in analyzing the containment of class struggle; the concept of 'control' is more useful. The significance of her argument is that there are no clear indices by which 'consent' can be measured[12]; absence of observable struggles does not tell us enough about resistance, nor does it tell much about what is condoned in the lack of action.

Thus resistance outside organized political action is significant. Miliband (1978) has applied the concept of 'desubordination' to the phenomenon; the term captures well what is argued here. I am focussing not simply on clear, observable class struggles and trade union action with identifiable aims and objectives, but on a kind of resistance which finds little expression in bourgeois political forms (such as parliamentary democracy, council politics at the local level, pressure groups and so on); nor does it find expression in organized radical struggles — though that it could potentially do so is its very significance, and has led to this discussion of resistance and restructuring side by side. Miliband argues that people in subordinate positions 'do what they can to mitigate, resist and transform the conditions of their subordination'.[13] This process may occur at the point of production in the work place, but is broad enough, argues Miliband, to refer to subordination wherever it occurs, and can be used for example to consider the position of women within the family. This desubordination finds no coherent political expression.[14] However the extent of it increased in the 1970s, signified by a pull from below within trade unions for instance.

Over-estimation of the significance of resistance outside organized working-class action did occur — this is understood in the context of restructuring and potential instability, when modernization 'of the industrial section was at the time fiercely fought against. A spectre of possibilities of interlocking struggles was perceived by Lord Chancellor Hailsham, quoted by Hall *et al.* (1978)

> the war in Bangladesh, Cyprus, the Middle East, Black September, Black Power, the Angry Brigade, the Kennedy murders, Northern Ireland, bombs in Whitehall and the Old Bailey, the Welsh Language Society, the massacre in the Sudan, the mugging in the tube, gas strikes, hospital strikes, go-slows, sit-in's, the Icelandic cod war, were all standing or seeking to stand on different paths of the same slippery slope.[15]

In the context of restructuring any pockets of militant struggle are seen to potentially unite sections of subordinate groups in a shared sense of discontent. Such a crystallization was never more than a possibility, but one not ignored by dominant groups in society; newspaper headlines such as 'Time bomb on Merseyside',[16] 'Young jobless look to violence',[17] and 'Give them a shovel or they'll pick up a brick'[18] express the perceived volatility of the situation.

The 'crisis' of education must be seen in the context of the crisis of social relations, caused by the mobilization of tendencies to overcome barriers to accumulation of capital. The rise of structural youth unemployment coincided with the development of aggressive youth cultures and counter-cultures; 'youth' was defined as a problem, which was seen to culminate in 1981 riots.

Formal Education in the Sixties and Seventies

The aim in this construction of education developments is to formulate an understanding of the 'crisis' of education in the latter half of the 1970s, and the 'crisis' of progressivism more specifically. Progressivism and the limitations and possibilities for radical educational practices contained within it provide the focus and frame for the overview.

The 1960s were characterized by an increasing school population, increasing expenditure, expansion of teacher training, and the spread of comprehensive reorganization. Against this material background occurred developments affecting teaching, learning and organization in schools, and future commitments seemed clear. In the spirit of optimism an education system appropriate for a technological society was being forged; advancement and steady growth were assumed; traditional education seemed inappropriate. The children and youth of the 'nation' were looked at in eager anticipation of this future. Children's potential was emphasized; poverty and deprivation had not yet been 'rediscovered'. New CSE examinations with greater teacher control and curriculum-determined examinations were welcomed. In 1963 the

Robbins and Newsom reports advocating expansion were published. Comprehensive reorganization gathered momentum through Circular 10/65.

In 1967 the Plowden Report 'endorsed'[19] the development of progressive practices within primary schools such as mixed ability teaching, individual learning, discovery learning, and compensation for 'deprivation' by expansion of nursery education and the setting up of Educational Priority Areas. The language of Plowden was still expansionist, the importance of resources was emphasized and the Report was associated with the equation more money means better quality. Progressivism at this stage did not seem esoteric, but something that could be firmly grasped, and that could co-exist with the 'demand' for 'objective assessment' of schools.

Towards the end of the 1960s, however, the heady days were beginning to draw to an end. The rate of growth of the education service was slowed down; resources were diverted to industrial investment; raising of the school leaving age (ROSLA) was postponed; Schools Council projects were deferred. The decade ended with teacher action. The 1969 DES annual report commented that the year was 'marked by widespread militancy among teachers'.[20] The new decade came in 'with a flourish' according to Rank and File, a left group with the NUT, 'on the crest of a strike wave the like of which was not experienced before or since'.[21] There were also school-based pupil strikes in the early seventies, hitting the headlines. The National Union of School Students came into being in 1971. The first Black Papers were published in 1969.

During the 1970s education could not longer be an area of experimentation and expansion, as the days of 'you never had it so good' were passing. Financial savings were regarded as necessary, and started with the Barber cuts in 1972/ 3; along with these cuts qualitative changes within the education system were forged. The myth of apolitical progressivism was blown — any unrest among teachers and pupils provoked strong reactions in the media. The extent of such unrest is difficult to ascertain, but that is not a crucial question — more important is the significance attached to resistance in the context of the fragility of social relations during a period of restructuring. Thus for example the *Evening News* wrote about Marxist teachers 'battling for the hearts and minds of our children' under the headline 'Marxist mind-benders in the classrooms'.[22] More frequently, however, the worries were expressed in terms of declining standards, and the equation between educational and economic expansion was replaced by the equation between progressivism and the 'crisis'. Thus wrote *The Daily Mail*:

> We've been told often enough that we are becoming the new poor of Europe. Now comes another even more disturbing charge: that we have become the dunces of Europe, too. What has gone wrong? Have we cheated our children by allowing them to be used as guinea-pigs for 'progressive' educational theories? Has not levelling out inevitably meant levelling down?[23]

The populist, Black Paperite terrain from which the more lurid charges emerged, was taken over by the Labour Prime Minister in his Ruskin speech in 1976, and the Great Debate and the Green Paper thereafter.

I shall now consider some developments focussing on teachers, pupils, curriculum and cuts, attempting to capture symptomatic changes. Formal schooling is becoming standardized and centralized — the aim is to consider how far-reaching the often quiet moves have been. If they did not always produce immediate or long-term results, this is because restructuring cannot be a straightforward process as it involves the possibility of intensified class struggle and militancy — outcomes are therefore negotiated and/or fought for.

Teachers

The decline of the school population began in the latter half of the sixties prompting amalgamation and closure of teacher training colleges. The questions were not simply quantitative — qualitative concerns were clearly voiced. Standards of entry to teacher training were raised; an all-graduate profession was aimed at. The professionality of teaching was emphasized — in 1975 the Houghton Committee on teachers' pay increased differentials; this was likely to undermine moves to collective work patterns and decision making.[24] In 1974 there had been a series of unofficial and official strikes and disruptions in London schools in a fight for London allowances. Post-Houghton the teachers in Newham who refused to teach classes over thirty were told 'this should not happen now'.[25] Militancy was to be curtailed through encouragement of professionalism.

Houghton was soon followed by calls for teacher accountability and monitoring, expressed through a concern for standards. Behind this shift lies the change in the staffing position, which began in the second half of the 1970s, as the growth of school population fell and declined for the first time in 1977. An overall teaching shortage turned into a teacher surplus. Staff turnover fell, and staff resignations dropped by as much as 40 per cent in some areas.[26] Indeed, the teacher shortage that had existed through the 1960s and early 1970s played an important role in the construction of schools as partly autonomous, with considerable degree of teacher control over the curriculum and examinations etc. As the expansion of the sixties continued, more teachers were needed year by year — quickly. Attention was paid to the recruitment of married women back into teaching, through part-time work and expansion of nursery provision. But the recruitment drive was directed also to graduates and boys in the sixth form. A survey of the attitudes of university students was commissioned by the DES; it concluded that teaching should be presented as a career which could offer rewards that these students were expecting; pay, status, intrinsic interest and the stimulation of the work. Teaching, however, tended to be regarded as dull, with restricted scope and prospects, and low status and pay. The department then launched an advertising campaign, aimed at married women on the one hand, and male school and university students on the other hand (it was assumed that the number of women graduates entering teaching would remain high); thus the advertisements with their focus on men drew attention to the salary scales of graduate teachers, and to the importance of education 'in a time of rapid change'. The emphasis was on career opportunities in teaching, and on 'the scope for new ideas and for managerial skills'.[27]

Autonomy of education in the 1960s is, therefore, partly explained because of the need to represent teaching as stimulating, offering opportunities for change and experimentation in an effort to find quick remedies to the teacher shortage. I also argue that this autonomy amounted to a disjuncture between state form and education as a state apparatus. Concerns of the 1970s certainly focussed on teacher radicalism and the need to control it. Such concerns could be voiced after the teacher shortage was over. Progressivism, with its emphasis on teacher control, had been important in reducing the limits set to the work of classroom teachers.

Some had taken seriously, and interpreted in a novel way the suggestion that schools were not just 'sub-assembly lines' for industry.[28] For example Chris Searle, whose book *Classrooms of Resistance* (1975) provoked a huge reaction, talked about his work as a teacher:

> The contradiction is that I'm working in an impure situation in order
> to transform it, and within a continuing power structure of which I
> disapprove, but which I am determined to subvert and transform.[29]

Though such teachers were in a minority, they were not insignificant. Whilst their work was often isolated and fragmented, a list of radical and libertarian organizations and publications in radical education[30] attests to the fact that such teachers and their work operated within rudiments of a framework, and reached a proportion of other teachers.[31]

Whatever the impact of teacher militancy, its perceived potential was assumed to be considerable. The militant sentiments quoted above, and the echoes of the Callaghan speech prompted the *Socialist Worker* on the one hand to announce that 'Callaghan calls for order in class (working class, that is)',[32] and an education correspondent in *The Guardian* on the other hand to talk about a 'battle plan' with the Secretary of State for Education, Shirley Williams, as a general 'brought in to win the campaign'.[33]

Pupils

Violence, indiscipline and truancy in schools emerged as a constant concern in the DES, Black Papers, media etc. In 1973 a survey into violence and indiscipline was conducted. Two truancy surveys took place. A joint circular by the DHSS, Welsh Office and DES concentrated on ways of 'extending help' to children with 'emotional' and 'behavioural' or 'learning' difficulties (and their families). Series of meetings of 'interested bodies' were called. HMI reports on 'Behavioural units' and 'Truancy and behavioural problems in some urban schools' were published. A conference on vandalism was organized jointly between the DES and the Home Office. ILEA started its Disruptive Pupils Scheme in 1978, diverting extra resources to setting up of special units. Urban programme funds were devoted to a range of projects, including provision for pupils with 'behavioural' difficulties.

Pupil resistance included school-based strikes and protests. For example a number of ROSLA pupils in Kidbrooke School walked out from the school in protest, marched to other schools to get more people involved and then planned to march to Westminster. Though they did not go to Westminster, their action (not using the school council, not writing to MPs etc.) signified the rejection of 'normal' channels and an attempt to forge new ones. Tapper and Salter (1978) discuss the NUSS, and its predecessor Students Action Union. They note the considerable difficulties a union of pupils is faced with; indeed the Union has not experienced great expansion (though its membership was nevertheless about 15,000 in 1975–76). The Union, in 1980, was argued to be 'in state of collapse'. Despite this, a Conservative and a Labour MP considered it sufficiently significant to merit a call for the Union to be banned from schools; largely because of the degree of control that Red Rebel, the Socialist Workers Party youth organization, exercised within it.[34]

The concern with the resistance of pupils in schools is to be seen in the wider context of the problem of youth discussed for example by Cohen (1973) and Hall *et al.* (1977), and the growing rate of structural youth unemployment. Frith[35] argues that the learning and training trends, the Green Paper, the Great Debate, the Manpower Services Commission reflect 'changes in the labour process, crises of accumulation and the high rate of youth unemployment'.[36] Concern is directed not simply at unemployability, but at unwillingness to work[37]; nor to any specific skills, but to 'general skills', a general set of attitudes. Within this context the significance of the growth of training is crucial. Changes in schools were not considered sufficient — the MSC was to accomplish vocational education with tight control. Its projects have been closely monitored, with little room for rhetoric or reality of autonomy. The rise of the MSC is discussed by the CCCS Education Group (1980) and Frith.

Curriculum

The concern for curriculum became prominent. The basis for a discussion on core curriculum was laid by a review of LEA curricular arrangements (1977), enquiring whether 'local practices meet national needs'. The question of core curriculum was raised by Callaghan in the Ruskin speech, and in the Green Paper which referred to 'over-crowded curriculum'. HMI undertook major surveys of primary and secondary schools. The Waddell Report on a single examination at 16+ was published in 1978. The shifts, changes and uncertainties of the discussions on 16+ are interesting, but what is of most significance here is that the proposals were linked to a definite process of centralization, with a central coordinating body outside the Schools Council. Such a central body would lay down criteria for each subject, possibly as much as three quarters of the syllabus might be prescribed. The exam boards would be rationalized and new administrative structures established.

The case of the Schools Council is illuminating — it opened up as a body controlled by teachers, concerned with curriculum development. It underwent several stages of reorganization; the significance of teachers' unions was reduced, and in 1978 the organization was firmly centralized with one new Secretary in charge. The Secretary of State for Education, Sir Keith Joseph, announced the closure of the Council in 1982. It was replaced by two new bodies, with members appointed by the Minister, one responsible for examinations, the other for curriculum. Plaskow (1985) notes that with the death of a representative forum, power shifted to the centre.

A further trend in the centralization process was the setting up of the Assessment of Performance Unit (APU) in 1975 to monitor aspects of attainment. The first survey took place in 1978. The APU was set up quietly, without much consultation and discussion about its constitution. The Bullock Report of 1975 made a number of recommendations related to literacy and language development, but only the concern for monitoring and screening of standards was firmly taken up. Thus, by the time Callaghan asked in his Ruskin speech what a proper way of monitoring would be, the question was merely rhetoric, as the procedure had already been established. Nor was the APU ever considered a political question, but 'a technical matter for the experts'.[38] When a headteacher criticized the language tests used in his school as not relevant to the preoccupations of the children etc., his response was dimissed by the APU as 'hysterical'.[39]

Central government has shown increasing interest in the general direction of the curriculum.[40] The corporatist approach to curriculum emphasizing the needs of industry, was reflected in the attitudes of the CBI and the TUC: the former referred to 'learning how the country earns its living'; the latter to 'a positive attitude to disciplines of work'. An education reporter fears that 'the secret garden of curriculum' is 'in danger of being ploughed up for the sort of prairie farming which produces dull uniformity'[41]. Curriculum developments are still in a flux, and carried out, partly, through cuts in expenditure.

Cuts in Expenditure

Cuts in expenditure had already begun before the Great Debate. The Green Paper emphasized that many of its proposals and recommendations could be achieved without additional resources. Often the onus was placed on the teachers — the DES annual report of 1978 stressed that 'The quality of education is inseparable from the quality of teaching'.[42] Already in 1968 the rate of growth of education was slowed down; the overall aim was to maintain standards. More considerable savings began in 1973. The decline of the school population has meant that if the numbers of teachers are based on pupil-teacher ratios, the curriculum will necessarily be affected in terms of the range of subjects, type of pupils to whom these subjects are available, and number of specialist teachers to teach them.

The cuts have particularly had an effect on progressive teaching, as it is based on the use of resources and small teacher-pupil ratios. Comprehensive evidence for this is difficult to obtain; some of the ways in which progressive schools are specifically affected is discussed in the empirical study (chapter 5). It is useful to cite here a survey of capitation cuts in one LEA in 1978, which concluded that the effects of these cuts led to a switch to more formal 'chalk, talk and writing' lessons, because of the rising cost of equipment and materials whilst financial resources are diminishing.[43]

It is important, therefore, to emphasize the *qualitative* effects of the cuts. The question is not simply whether cuts erode standards, and to what extent they do so, but to what extent the cuts impose a need to rethink and redefine education on the LEAs, the schools and the teachers. 'Realistic' schooling, giving thought to 'after life',[44] preparing pupils for the labour market and unemployment is mediated to schools through diminishing teacher numbers, diminishing resources, amalgamations, school closures, redeployment, monitoring and, in the eighties, publication of examination results and parental choice of schools.

The 1970s culminated in the advent of Thatcherism in 1979, concerned in the sphere of formal education to 'improve quality and promote higher standards'.[45] The promotion of standards as a priority became less significant, and by 1980 it was stated that 'the government's policy of maintaining and improving the quality of education must be viewed against the background of its declared prime concern with the national economy'.[46] The reduced expenditure on education was all that the 'nation' could 'afford'. It was also evident that financial resources were being withheld as there was no conviction that they would be properly used. Thus Mark Carlisle, the Secretary of State for Education, told an NUT conference in 1979 that 'even if additional resources were available, I believe it would be irresponsible for me simply to seek to pump them into the system and to assume that better education would inevitably result'.[47] Carlisle's response to HMI report on ILEA was to argue that it had shown that financial provision did not ensure good standards of educational achievement. His successor, Sir Keith Joseph, has laid the onus on schools — problems can be coped with by getting rid of ineffective teachers and heads, not by additional resources. Rhodes Boyson, a junior education minister, emphasized the need to tackle progressivism:

> In schools we have had child-centred education which led to deprived children, lower standards, disorderly classrooms, and defenceless and disillusioned teachers. Our present ills are the ripened and bitter crop of these seeds of the 1960s.[48]

The concern for core curriculum continues; the compulsion to introduce comprehensive reorganization has been lifted; the Assisted Places Scheme was initiated; there is a continued attempt to link teachers' pay to conditions of service (professionalism is used as a mode of control — the teachers unions emphasize professional autonomy, not just responsibility); in entrance to teacher training preference should be given to candidates from certain (non-social scientific) backgrounds; the Schools Council was closed; and the accusations that the principle of free education established in the 1944 Education Act is seriously eroded have been met with a response that the 'public purse is not limitless', and the principle of parental contributions is acceptable.[49] By now HMI is expressing concern that permanent damage to state education seems inevitable.[50]

The restructuring of the state education service has not been occurring without resistance. Difficulties have been caused in forging a new balance between central and local control, institutional realities of schools etc. Teachers' unions have been taking action; there have been a number of local disputes against school closures and redundancies; there was a long-running dispute about the dismissal of Eileen Crosbie for refusing to teach a large nursery class without proper ancillary help; action groups were formed to prevent the break-up of ILEA; in a number of LEAs parents have argued that the provision has been illegal on the basis of the 1944 Education Act — their complaints, however, have been received with equanimity by the Education Secretary, and attempts to use normal official channels have failed. A great deal of the resistance has been of a defensive nature, because of the aggressive and extensive nature of the accelerated developments within schooling since the Conservatives gained office. Though the Labour Party is committed to improve (if not restore) expenditure, it is not fundamentally opposed to the principle of centralization.

Conclusions

The expansion of formal education in the 1960s was located within a framework of a relatively thriving economy, stable social relations, expanding school population etc. In the 1970s the economic and social situation altered. Cooperative modernization of society had not been sufficiently far-reaching. A process of restructuring of relations of production and of social relations was considered a necessity, which had to be imposed, if not otherwise conceded to. This context had implications for schooling. Developments within formal education itself also sparked off restructuring therein — for example the end of teacher shortage, trade union militancy among teachers, criticisms of progressive education by the political right, coupled with the political left stating that progressivism did not go far enough in developing education.

Restructuring of formal education has been characterized by striving towards accountability, monitoring, standardization, centralization, growth of training under the Manpower Services Commission, and attempts to develop links between schools and industry. These processes are not straightforward and unilinear; the aims have been altered, halted or postponed in negotiations about them and/or struggles against them. Progressivism has been a particular casualty of restructuring; I shall consider reasons for this in chapter 3.

Notes

1 *C.f.* Cockburn (1977); her study of Lambeth Council gives an interesting account of these trends.
2 Hall *et. al.* (1978).
3 *Ibid.*
4 For example Rolls Royce and Upper Clyde Shipbuilders; the conflict on UCS provides an interesting microcosm of the determination of the organised working class; when workers began their sit-in, money came 'pouring in' as other trade unionists supported the action.
5 Cockburn (1977).
6 Cash limits and their broad impact is discussed by the CSE State Group (1979).
7 Quoted in *The Guardian*, 7 February 1979.
8 Panitch (1978a), pp. 22–3.
9 *Observer*, 11 November 1979
10 *Sunday Times* 20 July 1980, in a speech to Welsh Conservatives.
11 Hewitt (1982) p. xiv.
12 Integration itself may be best considered in passive and active levels.
13 Miliband (1978) p. 402.
14 *C.f.* Walton and Taylor's article on industrial sabotage in Cohen, S. (1971).
15 Hailsham, quoted in Hall *et. al.* (1978) — original in Griffith, J. (1974) 'Hailsham — Judge or politician', *New Statesman* 1 February
16 *The Guardian*, 24 January 1981
17 *Sunday Times*, 6 September 1981
18 *The Guardian*, 14 May 1981
19 Sharp and Green (1975), Dale (1979).
20 DES, *Education and Science in 1969*, p. 9.
21 Rosenberg, in *Rank and File Teacher*, February 1980, 70.
22 *Evening News*, 20 September 1977 — the teachers are linked in the article to social workers and probation officers — Hall's 'oppositional milieu' is reflected here.
23 *Daily Mail*, 1 November 1976
24 Teaching London Kids, No. 5 — also it can be noted that the NUT annual conference 1970–1975 debated teacher participation in decision-making in schools.
25 Prentice, quoted, in TLK No. 5.
26 Fairhall, J. (1976) 'Maths of Contradictions', *The Guardian*, 4 November
27 DES, *Education and Science in 1966*, p. 36.
28 DES, *Education in 1962*, p. 2.
29 *TLK* No. 7.
30 *Radical Education* No. 1 (1974) contains the following list of radical publications and organizations: Liberation Education, Teachers' Action Collective, Resources Programme in Education, Rank and File, Teachers' Action Against Racism, TLK, Campaign on Racism, IQ in the Class Society, Humpty Dumpty, Hard Cheese, NUSS, The A.S. Neill Trust, the Bootstrap Union, Further Left, STOPP, Schools Without Walls, Children's Rights Workshop.

31 JONES (1983) also considers the work of radical teachers. He notes that features of society were challenged (p. 32) and that obstacles for a closed relationship between education and 'needs of capitalist society' were created (p. 12). But his political aim at providing a socialist critique of progressivism, and his polemical contribution to future strategies leads him to emphasize the integration of liberal progressivism, and the 'deradicalization' of its concepts, and the progressives' overemphasis on the benevolence of the state, autonomy of schools, and the durability of their gains (p. 49).

32 *Socialist Worker*, 23 October 1976

33 *The Guardian*, 2 November 1976

34 *Times Educational Supplement*, 14 March 1980

35 FRITH (1978).

36 *Ibid.* p. 1.

37 FRITH, S. (1981) 'Dancing in the streets', *Time Out*, 20–6 March

38 Lady Young in a speech at the Institute of Education.

39 *Times Educational Supplement*, 6 June 1980

40 *C.f.* LAWTON (1984).

41 O'CONNOR, M (1985) 'A stab in the dark', *The Guardian*, 19 March

42 DES, *Education and Science in 1978*, p. xi.

43 *Times Educational Supplement*, 20 October 1978

44 Prime Minister Callaghan in his Ruskin Speech 1976.

45 DES, *Education and Science in 1979*, p. 62.

46 DES, *Education and Science in 1980*, p. ix.

47 Reported in *The Guardian*, 23 October 1979

48 Reported in *The Guardian*, 20 March 1982

49 CARLISLE, reported in *The Sunday Times*, 8 September 1980

50 Reports have covered both national and regional concerns.

Chapter 3

Progressive Education

The process of restructuring of formal education addressed progressivism, constituting the context for its 'crisis'. Why was this the case, and why was progressive education vulnerable to centralization and standardization processes? The range of meanings and practices associated with progressivism are discussed here, to aid the consideration of these issues.

An elusive concept of 'progressive' emerges when studying the relevant literature; one is confronted with an intricate web of philosophies, theories, methods and practices. 'Progress' is defined as 'forward movement, advance, improvement, increase'.[1] Therefore the concept implies value judgments: improvement from what, where to; advancement from what, where to; how does the movement forward occur; how does one distinguish between movements in different directions? Progress is a relative concept, comprehensible only within a framework. This is particularly obvious when progressive education is discussed — the term is used in different perspectives in different ways, and widely different aspects are subsumed under it often in a contradictory way.

Here I shall briefly consider the development of progressivism in America and Britain as discussed by a range of authors, and then note the difficulty of disentangling the existence of progressivism in educational debate and in schools. Different ways of viewing progressivism are introduced by contrasting the Black Paperite critique and Sharp and Green's analysis of a progressive school. The existence of separate strands of progressivism focusses the discussion of differing perceptions of it. These strands — the libertarian, the liberal and the socialist — are then illuminated.

Development of Progressivism

America

Carnoy, Spring, Karier, Violas, Gumbert[2] and Bowles and Gintis (1976) discuss the emergence of progressive education in state schools during a period of restructuring of capitalism, as an appropriate mode of control promoting stability, integrating new workers and tackling dislocations created by urbanization and the rise of modern technology; traditional education was failing to do so. The progressives were labour leaders, educators, political philosophers, corporation heads, financiers, politicians etc. Their goal was an organized corporate structure.

Bowles and Gintis argue that the progressives developed a new concept of discipline. Spring notes that 'freedom' was frequently used to describe educational activity in the strongest period of progressivism in the early half of the twentieth century; children were taught to feel free through child-centred education. In fact the aim was internalization of control, when compliance was no longer the appropriate response in a hierarchical, bureaucratic society. Group-work and cooperation in this context became an effective means for the achievement of conformity which is not merely outward.[3] Group-work could also ensure that alienation and isolation experienced in modern, technological capitalist production would be counteracted. The encouragement of creativity was seen to serve the same purpose.

Progressives were also concerned with the intelligent use of science and technology. The 'good' society was to be an efficient society, where professional expertise had an important role to play. Thus meritocracy and specialization characterized thinking about school organization. Intelligence tests, curricular differentiation and streaming were prevalent in the device of 'tracking'.

Many of the educational thinkers sought justification from the work of John Dewey, who argued that teaching and learning ought to engage the whole child, and should adjust to its growth, needs, background etc. 'Real' problems should be introduced to children, in the context of cooperative group activity. This would prepare for intelligent participation in a democratic society. From Dewey's work developed a strand of progressivism in America which emphasized child-centredness and diversity in educational practice. But a strand emphasizing the need to direct children, the imposition of unity on them, the choice of appropriate activities by teachers, the use of group activities as disciplinary measures, the differentiation, specialization, and selection drew from the work of Dewey as well. This strand is called, by the authors under consideration, 'society-centred' rather than 'child-centred', and 'meritocratic' rather than democratic.

The otherwise thorough work of these authors gives us little information on what was actually happening in schools. Where some evidence is given, connections between such evidence and other aspects of analysis are not always made. This problem stems partly from the fact that progressivism is not sufficiently defined. The widely different thinking and prescriptions of educational activities do not become sufficiently differentiated, when the practice in schools is considered. Thus, for example, Violas can emphasize the 1930s as a time of wide-ranging debate, whilst in schools one could find activities such as loyalty oaths, whereby teachers pledged that they were not teaching anything related to Communism.[4] It is, then, also difficult to understand the 'retrenchment' that developed later, and particularly to see what structural trends this retrenchment corresponds to or represents, and to what extent it consists of one form of rhetoric answering another. The authors see no scope for action, or 'spaces' within schooling; there is a sense of determinism in their analysis.

Britain

Selleck (1968) analyzes the emergence of the 'new education' against the background of the changes round the turn of the century; successful industrial development in America and Germany, loss of some European markets, slower development of British industry, coupled however by the opportunities provided by the colonies. Imperialism co-existed with the rise of trade unionism and organized political action. Selleck divides new education into several strands. The 'practical educationists' did not think that formal education was relevant to the 'industrial needs' of society; schools should be brought closer to 'real life'. The 'social reformers', particularly the Fabians, wanted a 'managed democracy', whereby the effective training of the young was seen as an important investment in the future 'progress'. 'Complete' and 'all-round' development was emphasized. The 'naturalists' wanted to provide for the 'natural growth' and 'budding' of the child, whereby the teacher would be passive and the pupil active, in order to allow the child to realize all its potential. The 'Herbartians' on the other hand emphasized the teaching and moulding of the child. For them the child was made, and a clear method based on formal steps was offered. The influence on educational practices by the 'new educationists' was uneven, but it did serve to shatter the domination of the 'old education' shaped by payment-by-results.

Stewart (1979) traces progressive education back to the eighteenth century, and argues that there were progressives both in working class and middle class schools. After this period progressive innovation in elementary and in secondary schools was halted, and was, for a long period, identified with independent middle-class schools. Selleck (1972) has studied their development in the early decades of this century. New schools were founded, for example the Little Commonwealth by Homer Lane in 1913. The theories of progressives were diverse, and so were their practices. A new concept of the teacher's role emerged — s/he was to be a 'sensitive observer'. There were differences in the amount of power invested in the teacher, but at least his/her overt authority was reduced. Linked to this, self-government by pupils was practiced — again the extent of it, and the scope of issues within its orbit, varied greatly. Formal timetable was often dissolved. Subject-curriculum was changed to informal activities. There was concern for 'self-expression', 'self-realization' and 'inner growth'. Uniqueness of each individual was emphasized. Learning was to be directed by the children's 'needs', 'interests' and 'activities'.

There was less emphasis on academic development, and more concern for emotional and social development.

Gradually progressive ideas widened their appeal. Selleck cites the Board of Education official guide *Suggestions*, which, between the wars, expressed some sympathy to progressive theory. The Hadow Report (1931) encouraged thinking about the curriculum in terms of activities to be fostered and interests to be widened rather than merely compartmentalized knowledge. During this period adoption of progressive practices could by no means be argued to have been widespread, but, Selleck points out, progressive ideas became dominant in training institutions, and became the established educational theory. Jones (1983) discusses progressive education in the 1960s, and notes differences to, and continuities with, progressivism in the 1920s and 1930s.

Progressivism in Schools

In order to grasp what progressivism consists of, it is helpful to formulate a kind of 'ideal type' of progressive education — in it I shall include what I take to be the main descriptive features of the practices at school level which are subsumed under the blanket term. In a progressive school:

(i)   mixed ability, flexible, vertical groupings work together and/or individually in an open plan classroom under a team of teachers;

(ii)   the day is 'integrated', the curriculum is problem- or concept-based;

(iii)   a wide range of resources is drawn upon (audio-visual equipment etc., but also the local community in various ways);

(iv)   the teaching-learning is child-centred, based on the pupils' interests, needs and skills;

(v)   the teacher is a guide and supporter in the child's pursuit of learning;

(vi)   academic learning is balanced by social and emotional learning, emphasizing creativity and self-expression;

(vii)   decisions in the school are made by all those involved in it.

Some schools may combine many of these features, but when we talk about the 'crisis' and retreat of progressivism notable since the seventies, it is important to remember that many schools deemed 'traditional' contain features from this list of ideal-typical progressive characteristics,[5] and, further, many individual departments within schools may contain features not prevalent in the rest of the school.[6]

That progressivism is diffused and not merely concentrated in schools deemed 'progressive' is important; because of this diffuseness it is difficult to estimate the spread of progressivism. Indeed it has been argued that in practice the number of progressive schools, even in the sixties, may have been considerably smaller than has been assumed.[7] However, as the significance of progressivism has not simply been school-based, the influence of the features outlined above may have been more significant than has been assumed on the basis of a lack of a large number of clearly identifiable schools with progressive profiles. This seems to be supported by the Leicester School of Education ORACLE research. Galton and Simon (1980) argue that the labels 'progressive' and 'traditional' are inadequate guides when researching schools — they identified six different teaching styles. On this basis the authors criticize the research of Bennett (1976) as making simplified distinctions which weaken the overall conclusions.

The Bennett research *Teaching Styles and Pupil Progress* has been particularly influential — it was unusually received, as seldom has a smallish research report attracted so much mass media attention. Bennett concluded that teachers using formal methods were more successful in teaching basic skills than those using informal methods, and that creativity and self-expression of pupils did not suffer under formal methods. Criticisms have been made of Bennett's statistical methods[8] and his research design.[9] For example Bennett gathers information on the basis of three different styles — formal, mixed and informal. When outlining the findings, mixed and formal categories are often collapsed into one, to form a dichotomy with informal methods — it is not clear why such affinity should exist between formal and mixed methods, and not between mixed and informal methods.

To reiterate, it must be noted that though the impact of progressivism is not clear, its ideal typical features are found in schools deemed 'traditional' as well as 'progressive'; the significance of progressivism has been widely, if thinly spread. Progressivism has been criticized in terms of falling standards, but there is no conclusive proof for this argument. Hence I shall probe further into the assumptions of critiques. From the Conservative side, I shall consider the Black Papers; from the neo-Marxist side the work of Sharp and Green.

The Black Papers

The Black Papers criticize schools for falling standards, which are attributed to progressivism and liberal reforms with egalitarian aims.

> The pendulum has already swung too far. It is necessary now to get very tough with the egalitarians, who would abolish or lower standards out of 'sympathy' with those who fail to measure up to them. We must reject the chimera of equality and proclaim the ideal of quality.[10]

I shall not address the claim about falling standards — I argued above that evidence for such a claim has been inconclusive. Wright (1977) has systematically analyzed the Black Papers and noted inaccuracies. I shall try to capture the flavour of the Black Papers, and to consider selective underlying themes, which illustrate that the roots of the criticisms of progressive education lie in broad political and social questions. In the discussion of strands we can consider whether such criticisms address the reality of progressivism.

The Black Papers link progressive education to anarchy, and note that parents are rightly suspicious of it. A 'realistic' approach to education is advocated. Comprehensive schools lower standards; thus the aim is a system where 5 to 8 per cent of children go to direct grant and grammar schools while the rest go to what are still called comprehensives. The importance of the schools for able and motivated children lies in maintaining overall standards by showing examples of excellence. Independent schools must exist because 'private education is going to be an essential feature of any society that wishes to maintain its liberties'.[11] Expansion of higher education is favoured — the authors indicate what is realistic: 'a hierarchical system, in which many students read for some kind of general degree in a variety of institutions, and only a few study specialist Honours courses'.[12] Views on examinations are guided by similar notions of reality: without examinations the education system would 'fail to prepare children and students for the realities of adult life'.[13] Streaming is essential as preparation for future realities:

> Society is inevitably hierarchical. Streaming teaches children this fact of life and that if they wish to do well in the hierarchy they must use their intelligence and work hard.[14]

Black Paper realism, then, implies a hierarchical, competitive, and disciplined society based on private property. Such a society is considered natural and inevitable. The organization of schooling must reflect that society.

Concern is expressed, however, for the disadvantaged position of working class children. Comprehensive education is criticized because it 'will inevitably lead to far greater social inequality than exists at present'.[15] The authors argue that an able working class child cannot thrive in a comprehensive school; it can do so in a grammar school. This is the case particularly if the former employs child-centred, informal methods.

> the notion of informality and that of school do not ... mix. It is precisely the purpose in setting up such separate and expensive institutions to enable learning to take place that they shall introduce coherence and order where none previously existed.[16]

Indeed, 'the world is a noisy, chaotic and restless place',[17] where

> There are few restrictions and adolescents are nearly all to some extent rebellious, but they find there are no brick walls available against which they can bang their heads, so they vent their pent-up feelings on railway carriages and on rival youth groups. How much better it is for them to find an outlet for their feelings by breaking some school rule which will not do much harm to anyone.[18]

The concern for anarchy indicated worries about counter cultures. The concern for vandalism and aggressive youth cultures indicates worries about working class adolescents.

The conservative sentiments and Conservative politics of Black Paperites are more important in guiding their critique of comprehensive schools and child-centred methods than a concern for standards. Their writings echo the nineteenth century exponents of education for 'lower orders' which bemoaned the lack of discipline and orderliness in the lives of working class children as noted by Johnson (1976a and 1976b).

The focus of Black Papers, then, is not a question of academic standards. The Papers do include less impassioned discussion of discovery methods[19] than the quotations above indicate, but this debate has the conservative 'back to basics' thinking as an underlying theme. Thus the Papers provide a political critique of progressivism and its methods and theories, cloaked in populist rhetoric of contrasting anarchy and realism; in professional expertise emphasizing the objectivity of assessment; individualistic stress on achievement devoid of social context, dependent on individual efforts and aptitudes; and a naturalistic conception of society.

Sharp and Green

Sharp and Green (1975) conducted a study of the infant department of a progressive primary school in the early 1970s within a sociological, neo-Marxist framework. They provided a critique of progressivism, located within an analysis of capitalist social structures and processes which reproduce dominant social relations, and conclude that there is a gap between progressive intentions and outcomes. The results of progressive methods are in fact similar to those of traditional methods. This is partly explained through ambiguities in the 'child-centred' rhetoric, but these ambiguities are reinforced by the way in which the realities of a stratified, inegalitarian industrial society penetrate the classroom.

Mapledene School had an atmosphere of 'relaxed informality'. The classes were vertically grouped, the school buildings reflected the methods used, the range of resources was wide, the teachers aimed to develop the 'whole child', and valued social and emotional learning etc. The authors observed and interviewed teachers, and then related the 'teacher perspectives' to the 'social structuring of pupil identities', 'staff relationships' and 'parent/teacher involvement'. Contradictory aspects in teachers' approaches, and in their classroom practices were considered through asking what problems they were related to.

The school was situated in a working class area. The teachers linked their notion of progressivism to the idea of compensation; the pupils were seen as deprived. This called forth the need for the teachers' 'expert knowledge'. All the children were to be treated as individuals according to the school ethos, but nevertheless early labelling and categorization occurred. The pedagogical practice of encouraging children to engage in various activities independently and according to their own interests, or 'busyness', released the teacher to 'handle the situation'. The children were expected to engage in activities they chose, but certain choices were more acceptable and valuable in the teachers' terms than others. By making choices the pupils were unknowingly contributing to their own labelling. Success and failure of pupils is invested in themselves.

In the classrooms there was an impression of an environment with minimal control, but the 'deep structure' showed considerable direction. The hierarchical differentiation is a solution to the problem of order inside the classroom, and to the meeting of expectations outside the classroom. These observations lead Sharp and Green to conclude that 'the radicalism of the "progressive educator" may well be a modern form of conservatism'.[20] They suggest that

> the rise of progressivism and the institutional support it receives are a function of its greater effectiveness for social control and structuring aspirations compared with more traditional educational ideologies whose legitimacy was already being questioned.[21]

Progressivism provides a new mode of social control.

The critique of Sharp and Green attempts to clarify what actually happens in a 'progressive' school, and suggests that the imperatives of selection etc. give a significance to child-centred practices which is unseen by its advocates and practitioners in the school studied. In the absence of a clear conception of the stratified nature of society they are operating within, the progressives remain utopians, and 'unwilling victims' of wider structures till they develop a conception of their own location, and of what is feasible within it. For Sharp and Green progressivism is something of the emperor's clothes, and its significance may lie in it constituting a more effective mode of control than traditional practices.

Sharp and Green conducted their study during a period when progressivism was still officially endorsed. Hence there is no discussion of factors leading to the Great Debate and the 'crisis in education' in the latter half of the 1970s. Their work thus leaves us with our question addressing the reasons of the 'backlash' against progressivism, and has complicated it somewhat — if progressivism constitutes a more effective mode of control than traditional practices, why did the decline of progressivism begin, amidst loud 'noise'[22] of the clarion call of the Black Papers followed by the Ruskin initiated orchestration of the Great Debate?

It is necessary to consider the development of social relations over time, and the process of restructuring marked by uncertainties and instabilities. Restructuring has affected education as a state apparatus, which has gradually been centralized, standardized and brought in line with the state form after a relative distancing during the expansion of the sixties (chapter 2). Progressivism requires a degree of teacher autonomy and resources, neither of which were consistent with the aim of centralization and cuts in expenditure; the latter has been the major device through which restructuring has been achieved in the state apparatus (in housing, health and social services etc. as well as education). Jones (1983) notes the opportunistic strategies used to advance progressive education — this led to over-emphasizing the autonomy of schools and the benevolence of the state. Progressive concepts were open to deradicalization and integration through selective acceptance.

But we are still left with a partial picture. We still have to resolve the co-existence of Sharp and Green's analysis and the Black Paper claims. It would be too easy to dismiss the latter as mere rhetoric. Further, we have not yet solved the problem with which we began this discussion — the elusiveness of progressivism. It is to illuminate these issues that I turn to a consideration of differentiation within progressivism.

Strands of Progressivism

The ideal type of progressive practices (above) is not sufficient to clarify the elusiveness of progressivism, nor its contradictory character. A discussion of the main broad strands within it deepens the understanding of what is contained under the rubric of progressivism. These strands are identified on the basis of the theoretical and political thinking and ethos rather than practices. They emerge from the debate and analysis focussing on progressivism in the seventies and find their significance in the discussion on the decline of progressivism. Restructuring formulates the context against which the developments towards centralization and standardization, eroding the basis of child-centred schooling, must be seen.

The strands discussed are broad. They are not exhaustive nor mutually exclusive. It is precisely the flow between them, the blurred edges, and the coexistence of strands in the debate, in the thinking of educationists and in the ethos and practices of schools that colours progressivism as a whole. In reality distinctions are difficult to make.

Dale (1979) addresses a similar question; he emphasizes the need to disentangle the loose interwoven net of progressive education; he is aware of the complexity of progressivism and tries to account for it; and he is aware of the added depth provided by contextualization. But there are problems. Dale notes that his analysis has been extracted from 'the broader social and political context' and adds that it could be embedded in an account of the state and the role of education in contemporary capitalism; thus the 'unchanged demands of the education system' and the 'unchanged distribution of power' could be considered. But, Dale concludes, educational processes are complex, and cannot be 'read off' from other structures and processes. The relationship between 'society, state and schooling'[23] is seen as complex; nevertheless references to 'unchanged' 'demands on education' and 'distribution of power' are made. The assertion of the independence of the education system and its analysis leads to crude characterizations of a static framework the effect of which remains unclear in terms of outcomes and mediations. Here I shall attempt to consider determinations *and* disjunctures within a framework which allows for the complexity and dynamism of the capital relations, state form, state apparatus, formal education and relations between these.

The three strands later identified are the libertarian, the socialist and the liberal. The distinctions compartmentalize progressivism in a way which allows us to disentangle the significance of differences between libertarians and socialists in terms of their analysis of the relationship between state and schooling, their characterization of the individual versus the collective, their strategies of action etc. The differentiation also enables us to consider points of fusion between the two, in militancy, in teaching practices, in conceptualization of progressivism etc. Though libertarianism can be characterized as utopian romanticism (Sharp and Green), oppositional potential must also be considered; libertarian teachers, when exposed to the limitations in realization of their educational ideology and theory in schools, may shift towards the socialist position in a search for an explanation of these limitations. The liberal strand is most clearly characterized by the kind of conservatism that Sharp and Green refer to. However, in the context of restructuring, unemployment, the 'problem' of youth etc., even liberal progressivism constitutes a potential location, if not a source, of instability through its emphasis on the individual and his/her potential, its requirement of resources, its emphasis on a broad range of interests and objects of study etc.[24] I shall now consider each of the strands separately, in order to develop the suggestions made here.

The Libertarian Strand

Humanitarian libertarianism developed in independent schools, stemming from disillusionment with society, emphasizing potential of children, to be realised in a free, individualized environment. Anarchist libertarianism developed in state schools, emphasizing equality, critical analysis of society, anti-authoritarianism and individualization combined with a class perspective.

A. S. Neill, founder of Summerhill, was an influential advocate of education in freedom. Children should not be moulded in any way, but should be allowed to develop in their 'own way', in their 'own time'. These children are free from hate and aggression, able to 'live' and 'let others live'. They are happy, balanced, sincere and free from repression. The belief in the potential of children was coupled with a disillusioned conception of society. Adults cannot, therefore, teach children, but must help them to become 'self-regulated'. Children are helped to become free in an approving environment where no-one tells the child how to live; the good side comes out 'automatically'. Methods are not particularly important, but children must be interested in what they are doing. Emotional learning is emphasized, but emotions must not be moulded. Self-government was seen by Neill as an important aspect of this kind of environment: 'Free children don't like leaders.'[25]

How were schools like Summerhill able to flourish? Why did they remain in the independent sector? Neill indicates the preparedness to compromise: 'You can imagine that you are one step ahead of the Establishment but if you take two steps you may meet with disaster'.[26] The analysis of external constraints was located with a vague definition of societal framework. The 'establishment' consisted of 'those who support the status quo . . . It was once a class affair, but is not any more; snobbery is not as strong as it was'.[27] Constraining influences could not easily be comprehended. Thus Neill states, puzzled, in 1971: 'No man is evil, he only becomes evil when made so by others, but why break and mould children is a mystery'.[28] Neill emphasizes the need to act 'instinctively', 'without knowing'. Yet he believed that reasons could be found, and by 1977 he referred to Reich's work:

> 'he says that the powers in the state are determined to keep their power and the only danger to that power is the revolution among the masses.' This is why they 'get hold of young people and they castrate them symbolically by making them a bit fearful, punishing them, sex guilt and religious guilt; so that when they grow up you get a society of people who haven't the guts to rebel'.[29]

Humanitarian libertarianism did not confront the society it was disillusioned with. The libertarians may aim for fundamental, large-scale change, but the means through which these are sought for are often not developed, and individualistic solutions are resorted to.

What is the impact on children? Neill discusses free children, who are not 'propagandizing rebels'.[30] The main emphasis is on inner qualities of individuals, rather than on their circumstances. Neill explains why ex-pupils do not get involved in political activities:

> 'I'll give you one or two examples. Two are professors, two are university lecturers, one's a heart specialist, one's a surgeon, one or two are lawyers — they've got jobs to do, so what can they do for a sick humanity? . . . What can they do practically? . . . As one of them, a professor of mathematics, said to me, he said the only thing I can do is to bring up my kids freely, as happily as possible and hope that I influence my neighbours, which is about the only way I think you can do it.[31]

The main emphasis is on day-to-day life rather than action to change social structures. Neill's example also indicates the position of ex-pupils in the class structure, with high status and material rewards.

The self-government in Summerhill reflects daily preoccupations; children make decisions about matters related to 'their communal life', and are not asked to decide on matters 'beyond their ability to grasp'.[32] Therefore it provides a limited framework. The fundamental decisions about structures in the school are already made, and the pupils are left to define their lives and those of their peers in that context.

Punch (1977) in his analysis of Dartington Hall adopts a similar interpretation. The school, he argues, responded to the needs of alienated intellectuals. Children are believed to be capable of self-determination. Punch suggests that the main focus of self-government is the legitimization of authority through application of group pressures to conform, development of cohesiveness, possibility of debate with all points of view, and through pupils being complicit in the formalization of rules of interaction. Ex-students found it difficult to conceive of themselves in terms of social classes. A large proportion considered themselves 'left-wing', but few were engaged in political action. Privatization is emphasized by Punch; the ex-students indulged in 'symbolic progressive rituals' stressing their distance from the conventional middle-class.[33] Punch notes that the ex-students were ill-prepared for political action, because of their tolerance, attempt to avoid prejudices etc.

Spring (1975) refers to the search for the 'ownership of self', free from internalized authority and ideological domination. The individualized perspective of the libertarians is linked to the faith in the human potential when allowed freedom to develop it. Value judgments may be made, but the aim is not to operationalize them. Friedenberg notes that 'even if I thought students largely fools and knaves I would still want them to have real power to influence the course of their lives'.[34] The contradictory sense of such power without an analysis of its limitations and possibilities can, however, lead to a political vacuum. Thus a group of American students call for the dissolution of constraints without any sense of structured obstacles: 'The forces which presently destroy a student's self-concept and feeling of control over his own fate must be eliminated immediately'.[35] What is required is a change of attitudes. Such conceptions do indeed leave the students ill-prepared for political action and dealing with structures and organizations. The students are unable to explain *why* schools are authoritarian, inflexible etc.

Humanitarian libertarianism, developed in independent schools, remained safely at the fringes not so much because it was pushed there, but because it propped itself there in the beginning, and made no great efforts to shift. While the libertarians in private schools in Britain were not shifting to the state sector, there were others who were influenced by their ideas, and interested in introducing them selectively into the state system, transforming the ideas in the process of doing so; these are the anarchist libertarians. They express concern for fundamental social transformation. An editorial in the magazine *Lib Ed* explains:

The Anarchist view is that education must be a cooperative, voluntarist process. Our critique of state schooling rests upon our perception of it as authoritarian, divisive and therefore profoundly anti-educational, serving excellently the needs of static society. It pursues its own narrowly defined concept of excellence, thus

> condemning most students to failure; it reproduces the class divisions of an unequal society; it views itself as the means whereby the commodity 'knowledge' is transferred from those possessing it to those lacking it; the price it exacts from the students for this transaction being their solidarity and autonomy.[36]

The editorial argues that such an analysis of state schooling is not fundamentally different from a Marxist conception; however, the differences lie in a stronger emphasis given to the relationship between the teacher and pupils, and the libertarian emphasis on the need to erode the authoritarian aspects of that relationship, whilst acknowledging the process of schooling as negating this attempt, through the limitations posed by its structure. Thus it is argued that the libertarian aim could not be 'oppositional ways of teaching' that socialists are interested in, but 'revolutionary ways of learning'.

Independent progressive schools are seen by the anarchists to have made a valuable contribution, but they are criticised for remaining 'ghettoes for the trendy, privileged few'. A concern for egalitarianism is integrated with the concern for the development of children's potential in anti-authoritarian settings. The contradictions within the state system are noted, and a distinction between libertarian and liberal conceptions of education are made. Libertarians believe that fundamental changes are needed — the humanitarians seek for these on the level of individual children; the anarchists on the level of societal structures. Realization of their thinking has involved compromises, but both disassociate themselves from liberal reformism to which I now turn.

The Liberal Strand

There are two tendencies within this strand: the child-centred and the society-centred (p. 27 above). The former emphasizes the needs of children, and genuine learning for intrinsic rewards. The latter also contains assumptions about the needs of society and ways of meeting them. A common thread is that in an industrial, complex, technological society traditional methods are no longer appropriate. Schools need to introduce skills of research and retrieval of information, and promote flexibility and an ability to cope with rapid social change. The needs of society provide the starting point, but lead to child-centred approaches.

Maria Montessori, the founder of Montessori schools and methods, believed, like Neill, that children ought not to be moulded; they ought to exist within a supportive environment. Adults cannot impose on children. When teachers observe, guide and make available, they can watch the unfolding of the complexity of human beings.

> It is the creative forces which must develop, and we must not make ourselves substitutes, in an arbitrary manner, for the divine work which is accomplished in every living being. Indeed we cannot be

more than cooperators in educational work with creation; we cannot, therefore, force the child to follow our promptings, but we must provide the means best adapted to help the child in his voluntary work.[37]

Development is a process of unfolding, and education must not interfere with it, but facilitate it.

Montessori's work began in Italy in 'Children's Houses' of redeveloped slum tenements, in 1906; the houses were to allow women to work, confident about the care of their children. Montessori did not concentrate her efforts with the privileged. She wanted to consider the needs of the poor people realistically, and fit the schools to these. But parents had to cooperate, meet the teachers weekly and accept advice given to them regarding their child. The teachers were to lead by showing example; indeed the 'directress' had to live in the tenement, as 'a moral queen among the people'.[38] The aim was to change the tenement houses from 'places of vice and peril, into centres of education, refinement, of comfort'.[39] Child-centred practices based on the needs of children as they are revealed in the progressive classroom have a fit with the needs and values of a society developing along liberal, humanitarian lines (Montessori also emphasizes the commercial viability of rehabilitation of tenements). Montessori methods are based on an idea of progress and social amelioration.

An appropriate example of child-centred liberal progressivism is Mapledene School analyzed by Sharp and Green. The authors argued that the educational thinking and practices of the teachers in the school existed in a political vacuum, whereby the structural constraints characterizing schooling occurred completely unchecked, reinforcing inegalitarian stratification, through informal selection processes, though the teachers professed to be concerned for the needs of each child as a 'whole' child. The end result was the promotion of social control in an effective way with apparently minimal amount of imposition.

Evidence of the use of child-centred methods for social control in practice and in rhetoric can indeed by found. The Norwood Report (1943) used the notion of child-centred education to justify the tripartite system which was realized in the 1944 Education Act. The psychological arguments about different types of children with different types of needs were condensed in the recommendation for three broad types of school, and the psychological testing that had been linked with progressive learning theories rationalized the selection procedures. This interesting link between the psychological learning theories and testing procedures under the rubric of progressivism is made by Finn *et al.* (1977).[40]

That within the tripartite system the secondary modern schools were to cater for the needs of the less able children in an appropriate way is still reflected in comprehensive schools which commonly, either through explicit streaming or processes of option choices, offer the more academic pupils a selection of traditional subjects, while, as Sheila Browne, Senior Chief Inspector for HMI, notes that for 'the less able' there is 'a strong chance of more "personal development", i.e. careers guidance, health education, community service, and so on'.[41] Thus, partial adoption of progressivism has often meant its use with children deemed unsuitable for the traditional academic curriculum.

Progressivism has not remained in the domain of 'progressive' schools, but schools labelled traditional have adopted features of it. It is such piecemeal adoption which is a response to day-to-day realities in the classroom — problems of control in teachers' struggle for survival when met by resistance, rebellion and desubordination. Willis (1977) emphasizes that progressivism does not constitute a new pedagogic practice in a real sense, but offers practical solutions to practical problems. Corrigan (1979) locates progressive education in the 'liberal soft centre', and argues that it is unable to pose alternatives, as questioning is encouraged only 'within the bounds of the existing system of things'.[42] Tapper and Salter (1978) note the diversity of progressivism, but argue that child-centred approach and opposition to traditional education are shared by all: the progressives also share a faith that a concern for the development of the whole child is going to lead to a more humane and democratic education and society. These authors are not primarily interested in analyzing progressivism, and refer to it almost in passing. Nevertheless, as the elusive nature of the concept of progressivism as a short-hand reference for a wide variety of practices has tended to confuse the debate, it is important to point out that such generalizations, whilst not inaccurate, are incomplete, as they refer to selective aspects or approaches.

Entwistle (1970) explores the child-centred approach as a 'useful instrument' in schooling, and wishes to transfer it from its image as a 'play thing of a lunatic fringe' into the mainstream. He shifts through the 'narrative' and 'technical educational prescriptions' entailed in child-centred education to arrive at a kind of schooling in which 'individual integrity' is not threatened by 'insistence upon social obligation', but both are harmonious within 'the plural character of the democratic society'. Here we find a trend of progressive thinking which promotes understanding of how to live in society, the structure of which is not questioned and critically analyzed, but taken for granted. Ball (1981) discusses the introduction of mixed ability teaching in Beachside Comprehensive and concludes that both its adoption and assessment occurred primarily as a function of its greater effectiveness as social control. Hunter (1980) considers participation in schools. In a case study he indicates how such participation is tokenist and patronizing, again legitimating social control. He refers to a school council meeting where the headteacher initiates discussion on how to combat vandalism.

Within the liberal strand several facets are contained. To recapitulate on them:

    (i)   the child-centred trend concerned with the rights/needs of children,

and learning theories without explicit theories of society or schooling;
(ii)   society-centred progressivism, which starts from the basis of the
present society, and perhaps its evolution through technological
change, and emphasizes the need for new methods in education
which in their flexibility and informality are better suited to
equipping individuals to changing circumstances;
(iii) the trend connecting child-centred individualized education to
equality of opportunity, where each child is able to fulfil its
potential — this is linked to the Plowden approach with its emphasis
on compensation and resources;
(iv)   the adoption of aspects of progressivism in a traditional, formal
framework, either as a response to difficult situations in terms of
day-to-day control of pupils, as a solution to the provision for
pupils with low achievement within an institution geared to examinations, or through the work of individual teachers or departments on the basis of an educational ethos different from the
majority ethos in the school.

Bernstein (1975) makes a distinction between visible and invisible
pedagogy. The former is dependent on strong classification and frames, the
latter on weak classification and frames.[43] Invisible pedagogy, argues
Bernstein, is used by the new middle class in its desire to differentiate itself
from the old middle class. The invisible pedagogy is used mainly in early
socialization, and therefore contains a 'hidden curriculum' of strong classification and framing. It is also based on class assumptions with specific
concepts of time, space and social control. Its educational consequences are
therefore dependent on the social class of the child. Yet

> inasmuch as the move to weak classification and frames has the
> *potential* of reducing insulations in mental structures and social
> structures, has the potential of making explicit the implicit and so
> creating *greater* ambiguity but less disguise, such a code has the
> potential of making visible fundamental contradictions.[44]

Liberal progressivism may not simply lead to adaptation and adjustment,
therefore.

Though the outcome of liberal progressivism may not challenge the
structures of society, and inegalitarian stratification may indeed be reinforced
as well as reproduced, when the context of restructuring is introduced, it is not
possible to assume that the child-centred practices simply encourage conformity. Frith (1980) argues that the learning trends in schools in the 1960s,
which were based on humanization of formal practices, even at this low level
of innovation and change militated against trends in industry emphasizing
control and a need for a workforce with 'generalized skills'[45] consisting of a set
of appropriate work-related attitudes.

The Socialist Strand

This strand of progressivism adopts aspects of child-centred approach, curriculum innovation, non-authoritarian teacher-pupil relations and informal teaching methods. This adoption occurs within a socialist framework. There is a distinction to be made between those socialist teachers concerned with trade union action and wider political struggles who consider innovative work in schools as misguided because of limited results[46] and those emphasizing the need to develop ways of teaching and relating to pupils in their own schools, or through forging links with other teachers in other schools, or with the trade union movement. Many of the latter teachers, as well as the former, are critical of what they consider 'bourgeois progressivism'.

Whilst espousing progressive ethos and methods, the second group of socialist teachers reject much of what they interpret as progressivism:

> Progressivism is a petty-bourgeois ideology of utopian reformism, and its perspective has to be rejected. We have to identify those practices within progressivism that represent gains for working class interests in education, and incorporate them within a socialist perspective.[46]

Similarly, a collective of teachers, Big Flame, explain that

> As socialist teachers we often use progressive methods. ... But, unlike the progressives, we have a clear picture of the relationship between education and society, and we know that, unless there are fundamental changes on the nature of that society, 'the crisis in education' will go on wreaking havoc in the lives of teachers, pupils and parents.[48]

The emphasis is on the adoption of progressive methods within a framework of a critical analysis of society.

An early example of the relationship between progressive and socialist perspectives is found in post-revolutionary Soviet Union in the work of Krupskaya, discussed by Castles and Wustenberg.[49] Krupskaya adopted what she considered to be the best ideas of bourgeois progressives, and combined them with the principles of polytechnic education. She was interested in theories about the needs of children and how they learn, but combined these with an analysis of their location in schools. In a revolutionary society adults should not dictate to children what they ought to learn; traditional subject divisions were not appropriate; theoretical study divorced from its context would not be desirable. Thus education should co-exist with productive work, which would provide a context for skills.

Radical socialist educators have aimed to develop education that fosters critical intelligence. They have made a distinction between schooling and education: the former is conservative, the latter inherently revolutionary. Education transforms the learner's thinking. Freire's method of teaching literacy, developed in Latin America, embodies this kind of approach. Freire (1972) criticizes the 'banking method of education' and argues that true revolutionary education is based on the learner as an active subject of the process of learning, not its object. The teacher and learner are trying to understand the life and circumstances of the learner; this process of 'decodification' provides tools for dismantling internalized images of the dominant classes (among Latin American peasants the 'culture of silence'). Freire calls this 'cultural action for freedom', which leads to genuine liberation and critical thinking, rather than domestication, which is the end result of the 'banking method of education'. Education challenges reality. Freire's thought has been influential in this country as well, for example in the emphasis on 'critical literacy' among radical teachers; there have been attempts to develop Freire's methods and apply them to western circumstances.

Donald[50] discusses a CSE Mode III media studies course, which is based on 'oppositional pedagogy'. The oppositional elements are a stress on practice, an attempt to forge a new relationship between pupils and the media — a shift from passive consumption to active, critical production is encouraged. Donald writes that the course 'is designed to reveal and analyze the repressive, and to find ways of putting the emancipatory into practice'.[51] He emphasizes that there is nothing innately radical about the course. The emphasis on oppositional potential co-exists with an awareness of limitations stemming from an analysis of the relationship between schools and society. The balance of limitations and possibilities is also discussed by a group of social studies teachers discussing resources they have produced. Their aim has been to make their politics explicit in the materials, hoping that pupils come to perceive their own lives as political.

> We are in no sense claiming that materials such as these can bring about the kinds of changes to which we are committed, but we do see them as having a contribution to make . . . towards making possible other ways for pupils (and teachers) to act upon the world.[52]

Socialist progressives do not share the optimism of libertarians, but emphasize the framework within which possibilities exist.

It is difficult to assess how widespread the kind of work described above has been, and what its effects have been. It is clear, however, from the network of various publications, organizations and conferences that this trend was significant.[53] Publications such as *Teaching London Kids* have combined libertarian and socialist progressive perspectives and content focussing both on debates and analyses, and on examples of work carried out in schools, and discussion of available resources, combined with an emphasis on anti-sexist and anti-racist struggles within schooling.

Awareness of limitation co-exists with a belief in potential for resistance. Chris Searle compiled English work of pupils in an East London school; in the introduction to the book *Classrooms of Resistance* he notes:

> As to the children whose work is presented in this book, the more
> I teach here, the more I am convinced of their strength and.
> magnificence, and the closer the bankruptcy of the present system
> comes, the brighter the future approaches.[54]

The book provoked widespread reaction in the media — significance was
accorded to the potential of 'Teaching revolution in the classroom' etc. Searle
emphasizes the distinction between socialist education and progressive education 'degenerating into aimless projects'.

The events at the William Tyndale School in the mid-seventies illuminate
issues discussed here, and link the consideration of progressivism, restructuring
and the question of 'spaces'. The school operated a radical progressive
perspective — the teachers considered their activities within an oppositional
framework, and combined their teaching work with militant trade unionism
in an area of London containing relatively strong radical elements within the
NUT. The events occurred when the centralization and standardization
processes were gaining momentum, and contained a complex constellation of
political forces, provoked national controversy, and culminated in the Auld
enquiry and the dismissal of the teachers involved.

The Tyndale teachers were critical of liberal progressivism:

> The contradictions have been papered over with triple-mounted
> pictures and production line creative writing. This moribund prettiness,
> devoid of all motive except the transference of middle class values
> to working class children, has been embraced by many schools,
> especially those with a strong middle class parental element.[55]

They wanted to develop a progressive school with socialist aspirations.
However, the teachers argued that their practices were not unusual, and could
be found in other London schools. The specificity of Tyndale lay in the
combination of radical educational philosophy and practice and a militant trade
union stance. They practiced positive discrimination, prioritizing 'deprived'
children explicitly, for example by diverting resources to them. They dissolved some of the 'correspondence principle' (chapter 1) by the head not
assuming all his traditional responsibilities, but devolving them onto the staff;
this aspect is critically noted in the Auld Report. Ellis argued[56] that the teachers
were attacked for what they 'might do'; they were the 'wrong kind of people'.

The potential of the situation was significant in a wider sense. The
Tyndale teachers were linked to militant London teachers. Gretton and
Jackson (1976) suggest the ILEA was worried about dealing with the school
resolutely in the early stages (its failure to do so was criticized in the Auld
Report) as London schools were seen to be 'hotbeds of left-wing political
activism'[57] and an 'explosion' of the 'politically volatile' Islington teachers was
feared, which might have spread through neighbouring Hackney to other
areas in London. In the event even the militant branches of NUT were unable

or unwilling to fully take up the teachers' case which was not defended by the union executive.

Nor were the teachers able to generate significant organized support among the parents and the local community. They were not seeking to cooperate with parents, and in many ways their attitude resembled that discussed in connection with Montessori schools, and Mapledene School above; the teachers relied on professional ideology in order to justify their educational practice; they as teacher-experts knew what to do with children, on the basis of their knowledge and training.

The involvement of Black Paperite rhetoric can be noted. Dorothy Walker, a teacher in the school and critical of its practices, wrote that 'all that happened at the school reflects a highly successful policy *if the aim is to* provide *material for future revolution*'.[58] Of interest is also the involvement of the local Labour Party, which wanted to disassociate itself from progressivism, certainly in the form it assumed in Tyndale. The Labour managers claimed that their concern with the school was educational; it was ineffective in achieving what it set out to do; yet political channels were utilized in tackling the school. The stance adopted by the Labour Party illuminates the social democratic reorientation towards education in the seventies as noted by the CCCS Education Group (chapter 1) and the contradictory aspects of the Labour Party resulting from different orientations within it, from trade unionist socialism to middle class parliamentarism. The constitution of the Islington Labour Party itself is specific, and highlights Labour Party contradictions in a relatively extreme way — this cannot be explored here, but must be noted in order to avoid simplified generalizations.

The events indicated the disorganization of radical socialist teachers, despite the existing networks. When confronted with a situation where large-scale action was required, the challenge proved insurmountable. The Defence Committee could not agree on the best line of defence in terms of practice or principles.[59] Without the official support of their union, and with the crumbling of the defence the Tyndale teachers were left isolated facing an enquiry. Two teachers wrote their reflections on the enquiry, referring to it as a 'piece of state magic':

> to take part in an enquiry, militants have to 'behave', act in what the state would deem to 'responsible' manner, that is, they have to suspend their militancy ... The militants themselves are now operating in total contradiction with their own previous actions. The Tyndale group having illegally obstructed an inspection, opened a 'rebel' school, demonstrated outside ILEA's offices, attempted to raise the banner of revolt all over London and indulged in violent polemics against their many opponents, put themselves in the ludicrous position of convincing Auld that they were really quite a decent bunch of ordinary, submissive teachers. This they did in the illusory hope of winning in the state's own arena.[60]

Through the enquiry the activities of the teachers were channelled into formal categories of bourgeois democracy; the basis and impact of the activities were simultaneously eroded. The oppositional spaces were closed.

In the discussion of restructuring and specifically of the restructuring of the relationship between the state form and state apparatus (chapter 2) I suggested that the process is directed to the disjuncture that has developed between the two during a period of expansion, within which 'oppositional spaces' are constituted and potentially exploited by radical groups such as Tyndale teachers. However, once the action is channelled into conventional, legal, administrative forms, it can at the same time be stifled, as happened in the case of Tyndale. This is not to exaggerate the actual significance of such episodes; the response of the left in education was weak and disorganized. But in a society undergoing restructuring, disruptions assume a new significance in the context of instability and the fragile nature of social relations due to the contradictory changes being forged through struggle. The centralization and standardization trends in the sphere of schooling indicate that the school did not simply provide a rhetorical target — real, long-term changes in state education were occurring alongside the redefinitional activities.

Fletcher *et al.* (1985) discuss four case studies of innovative comprehensives which faced considerable opposition — they were 'schools on trial'. The dates of the trials, and the underlying issues leading to them, the authors argue, indicate boundaries set for innovations. But, they add, these four schools were merely 'the tip of the iceberg'; this was indicated by other schools contacting them, offering sympathy and recounting their own stories. Hewitt (1982) refers to civil liberties existing in 'a gap between prohibitions' and that 'prohibitions are closing that gap'.[61] Thus progressives overemphasized spaces, as Jones (1983) argues, but, as he notes, for a short time the problems encountered by reform were spurs to further radicalization. This 'testing', in the context of the political and economic situation in the seventies contributed to the perceived necessity of restructuring or eroding the spaces, of 'closing the gap'.

Conclusion

In the next section the discussion moves on to an analysis of the empirical materials gathered in an in-depth case study of a progressive school. It is appropriate now to summarize what has been suggested thus far as a way of formulating an understanding of the crisis of progressive education.

During a situation of relative prosperity in the post-war years, in the context of an expanding education system, partly because of the expanding school population, partly because of the increased significance placed on education in liberal/social democratic ideology, new ethos and practices developed in schools which entailed a development of a new mode of control, as suggested by Sharp and Green, and Bernstein. The development of these practices can be linked to teacher quest for professionalism and increased autonomy, and the state accommodation to these, because of the severe teacher shortage, which remained a problem through the sixties. To attract new teachers (especially males), teaching was presented as having a high status and a great deal of scope for satisfaction; this was consistent with the emphasis on teacher professionalism and autonomy.

At the turn of the decade a new situation was evolving. Expansion was drawing to an end, as the school population reached its peak, and as economic stringencies were seen as necessary. Restructuring, beginning in the sphere of production, affected all sectors of society, and caused relative instability. This was responded to by periodic trade union militancy. Among young people the growth of aggressive youth cultures such as punk rock coincided with the increase in structural youth unemployment. Teachers adopted a more aggressive trade union profile than before, and pockets of organized pupil resistance developed, whilst individual rebellion and 'desubordination' was discovered as expressed in the concern for vandalism and lack of discipline. Progressivism had developed in the context of teacher autonomy and expanding resources. It was seen to provide spaces within which the actions of even small groups of teachers and pupils could assume significance out of proportion to their size and scope. Socialist progressivism was seen to incite pupils into revolution; libertarian progressivism was seen to ignore the need for discipline, order and basic skills; liberal progressivism was seen as misguided and unrealistic, ignoring the realities of adult society that pupils were to enter into. The combinations of the various aspects of progressivism, with the ensuing consequences, could be observed in the case of the William Tyndale School.

Thus occurred what has been termed the 'attack' on progressivism, which coincided with the process towards the centralization and standardization of schooling. This was achieved largely through cuts, which eroded the basis of progressive education, with its dependence on diverse resources. With the simultaneous advent of monitoring teacher autonomy was narrowed (the cuts in teacher training, and the contemporary reorganization of that sphere must be remembered as well). The flexibility and teacher control necessary in child-centred education were less and less possible. Progressivism lacked a solid power base, as Dale and the Education Group, CCCS, point out; therefore any defence was difficult to organize. The progressives had isolated themselves within a professional ideology which placed them on the defensive, and isolated them from parents, local community and the rest of the trade union movement. The collapsing social democratic alliance was unable to support progressive education. In this kind of situation the mass media rhetoric played an important role. As the Education Group of CCCS argues, conservative populism found itself 'knocking at an open door'.[62]

Notes

1 The Pocket Oxford Dictonary.
2 Carnoy, M. (Ed.) (1975), Spring, J. (1972), Karier, C.J. *et. al.* (Eds.) (1973), Gumbert, E. and Spring, J. (1974).
3 Kilpatrick, quoted in Spring (1972) p. 60.
4 There were loyalty oaths in twenty states — Violas in Karier *et. al.* (1973).
5 Notably mixed-ability teaching and resource-based learning.
6 For example English and social studies departments.
7 *C.f.* Bennett (1976).
8 For sample Sterne, M. A. (1976) in *Education Gurdian*, 4 May
9 For example Galton and Simon (1980)
10 Maude, A. (1971) 'The egalitarian threat' in Cox and Dyson (Eds) p. 40.
11 *Ibid.* p. 32
12 *Ibid.* p. 33.
13 Cox in *ibid.* p. 77
14 Lynn in *ibid.* p. 82
15 Szamuely *ibid.* p. 131
16 Bantock in *ibid.* p. 112
17 Johnson in *ibid.* p. 99
18 Johnson in *ibid.* p. 100
19 Bantock in *ibid.*
20 Sharp and Green (1975) p. viii.
21 *Ibid.* p. 224
22 Donald (1979).
23 The term is adopted from Young and Whitty (1977).
24 A shifting of emphasis from DES to MSC, and from education to training reflects the significance attached to liberal progressivism.
25 Neill (1971) p. 104
26 *Ibid.* p. 105.
27 *Ibid.* p. 105.
28 *Ibid.* p. 115,
29 *Lib. Ed.* No. 21, 1977.
30 Neill (1971) p. 12
31 In *Lib. Ed.* (1977)
32 Neill (1971) p. 66.
33 *Punch* (1977) p. 143.
34 Friedenberg, in Gross B. and R. (1971) p. 146.
35 In Gross, B. and R. (1971) p. 156.
36 *Lib. Ed.* No. 29 autumn 1980; it is interesting to note that the teachers involved in *Lib. Ed.* tend to work in state schools. Punch (1977) refers to a conference in 1965, where 'old' progressives from the independent sector, and the 'new' progressives within the state sector could not find much agreement.
37 Montessori (1962) p. viii.
38 *Ibid.* p. 53
39 *Ibid.* p. 53
40 They note that Susan Isaacs who ran a progressive school, and Cyril Burt, advocate of testing emphasizing hereditary aspects of intelligence as measured by IQ, wrote a joint appendix to the Hadow Report.
41 In *Trends in Education* (1977) No. 3.
42 Corrigan (1979) p. 148.
43 'Classification' '*refers to the degree of boundary maintenance between contents*' — Bernstein (1975) p. 88. 'Frame' '*refers to the degree of control teacher and pupil possess*

over the selection, organisation, pacing and timing of knowledge transmitted and received in the pedagogical relationship' — BERNSTEIN (1975) p. 89
44 *Ibid.* p. 146.
45 Frith (1978), a paper presented to the conference of the Socialist Teacher Alliance.
46 For example the Rank and File Group within the NUT.
47 HATCHER, R. (1979) 'Beyond progressivism: Teaching in a transitional perspective, socialist perspective', *Socialist Teacher*, 7, spring.
48 Big Flame, *The Crisis in Education*, p. 9 April 1977.
49 CASTLES and WUSTENBERG (1979b and 1979c)
50 DONALD, J. (1978) *Media Studies: Possibilities and Limitations*, CSE Conference Paper.
51 *Ibid.*
52 INMAN, S. 'Whose values' *Teaching London Kids*, No. 7
53 Education Group CCCS (1981) briefly discusses the existence of such teachers, and networks between them.
54 SEARLE (1975) p. 12
55 ELLIS *et. al.* (1976) p. 44
56 Open University television programme on the school.
57 GRETTON and JACKSON (1876) p. 104
58 WALKER, D. (1977) p. 40
59 For example the *Newham Socialist Teacher* No. 2 June 1977 criticized an open letter that the Defence Committee sent to the *Times Educational Supplement*.
60 ELLIS, T. and HADDOW, B., *Tyndale 78*, p. 4, circulated pamphlet.
61 HEWITT (1982) p. xiii.
62 CCCS Education Group (1981) p. 177

Part Two: The Case Study

Chapter 4

The Paradox — Progressive Education in a Conservative Local Authority

Greenfield College, 'the most progressive school in Europe'[1] is located in a Conservative local authority, Leicestershire. This authority achieved early comprehensive reorganization, is widely renowned for progressivism, and in it we find a school which is considered particularly radical. I aim to convey the flavour of Leicestershire, and to illustrate the possibilities of relatively autonomous directions at the local and the school level, and limitations posed on them — these will become increasingly evident in the discussion on Greenfield College in chapters 5–7.

Central and Local State

The central state, during the seventies, has been characterized by a shift towards greater bureaucratic and fiscal control of state apparatus, of services and employees; this has, indirectly, led to a greater control of citizens. During the fifties and sixties there was a greater degree of local autonomy. Thus, rapid development of education in Leicestershire was possible, because there were fewer statutory controls set at the central level (Holmes, 1973). Progressivism became significant as a reality rather than rhetoric.

Relationships between Leicestershire and central level have not been characterized by conflict. Educational developments in the sixties were of the 'endorsed' kind. Moreover, distinction at the local level between the elected members of the county council and the officers must be made. The educational changes were initiated and planned by the officers under the approval of the members; the achievement of this approval is discussed below. The re-organization of local authorities, public expenditure cuts, fiscal control and the context of recession led to a stronger emphasis on Conservative policies and greater restrictions on what is approved by councillors. Liberal conservatism has been gradually eroded, also because the ascendancy of the Labour Party and the Alliance has led to Conservative loss of overall majority, struggles over community college cuts and closures, and radicalism of groups of teachers and schools; a more conflictual stance has developed.

Restructuring

To understand the context for the emergence of progressive education in Leicestershire, it is important to draw attention to the relatively smooth restructuring processes occurring at various crucial moments of historical development; both in the economic and political spheres, in industry and in government, the county has been characterized by liberal moderation. Relative stability and prosperity have provided the basis for such liberal conservatism. The gradual decline in prosperity has not been characterized by aggressive restructuring as much as with stagnation to be understood in the context of national and global trends.

The industrial and political background of Leicestershire is relatively smooth.[2] The contraction of industries such as hosiery has coincided with the growth of others such as engineering. In the context of industrial stability, and control invested in the traditionally ruling group,[3] political opposition has not been characterized by a great deal of militancy, nor have responses to oppositional activities been particularly repressive. Evans notes that in their politics and in their geographical location Leicester and Leicestershire 'belong to the centre'.[4]

Development of Education in Leicestershire

Innovation has occurred within a context characterized by efficiency, clear organizational principles and structures, and an administration assuming its influence largely through detailed and extensive knowledge of developments. Against such a background the political control of the administration by the Conservative Council has not been characterized by imposition, but by detached approval in the face of low financial demands, and efficient deployment of resources, and, because of consultation and information directed to parents, little opposition from the local community. Control, administration and development of education have been relatively trouble-free.

Comprehensive reorganization, the Leicestershire Experiment and Plan[5] was presented to the Education Committee in very practical terms. Emphasis was on the possibility of reorganization without a large rebuilding programme, by modifying the functions of existing schools.[6] Secondary modern schools became high schools and grammar schools became upper schools, to which pupils move at the age of 14. The DES formally approved the plan in 1967.

Leicestershire schools, then, have enjoyed a relatively great degree of autonomy within the framework of a close advisory relationship between schools and the LEA, and within the context of an authority well informed about its schools. The administrative ease of the county has been a contributing factor (from the centre the distance is about 15–20 miles to most places). The autonomy of schools has limits as well, within the confines of the national education system as a part of the central state apparatus; locally the autonomy is restricted by limits of acceptability, the definitions of which are varied and flexible, linked to the context. A retired head explains that:

> The basic element in the relationship with the officers at the County Hall is that they're happiest when things are going without any kind of trouble — by trouble I mean response from either parents, employers or county councillors or the press. And to put that more positively, they genuinely do leave the head and the school to run itself, if it doesn't run into any difficulty, or any known difficulty.[7]

Autonomy has real significance as long as developments engendered do not attract opposition. The local authority officers, who, on the whole, have adopted a relatively progressive outlook, have to handle queries and objections from the elected members of the Council, from parents and from employers. These filter back to the schools if they are sustained, and if they attract publicity.

Progressivism in Leicestershire

Innovation has started in primary schools, where experimentation and spread of progressive practices were facilitated by the removal if the 11+. New methods were made possible, encouraged and supported, but stemmed from the 'grassroots' (Holmes, 1973). Thus there is a great deal of diversity among the schools — but central threads can be discerned.

The first is an emphasis on the '*individual*': 'each child is considered as an individual and all his instincts for discovery and creativeness are encouraged and given scope'.[8] The second is the concept of the '*whole child*', stressing all the child's potential. The role of the teacher changes; in the individualized framework s/he gets to know each child, respects its individuality, and gives it scope for expression. The teachers become 'learners' and are seen so by the children.[9] The third is the *autonomy* of the individual whole child, who must be allowed to develop its potential unhindered. A conception of the world as changing rapidly means that adults cannot dictate to children as in periods of greater certainties. The pupil who is an individual and autonomous must be treated as an adult; relationships between pupils and adults must change.

This framework entails increased teacher responsibility. Heads are encouraged to participate in all the school's affairs; this can filter down to the pupils. The granting of greater responsibility to groups hitherto with few opportunities in decision-making occurs within a definite framework of hierarchy.

> Our experience has been that teachers given responsibility . . . grow in stature and no serious conflict has arisen, perhaps because a clear policy framework exists and senior members of staff have been party to it.[10]

That pupil autonomy is backed by a hierarchical authority is indicated in the comment:

> Discipline needs to become self-discipline as the pupil grows up, so that appeals to authority (always likely to be necessary from time to time, goodness knows) must not be allowed to remain too frequent or too automatic.[11]

Integration is emphasized in the educational debate in Leicestershire. Schools should not be expected to 'produce appropriate work forces for industry and commerce',[12] but well rounded, informed, responsible people who consequently do have the required attitudes to the labour market. Though the historical and social locations of pupils are not ignored, it is stressed that it is more important 'to think in terms of the individual rather than of pre-selected groups'.[13]

Integration is a concept useful in considering Leicestershire's pioneering community colleges, as is evident in the following discussion:

> Every society needs common institutions that are capable of bringing together people of diverse interests and positions to share experiences ranging beyond and above the immediate claims of self-interest. . . . The Community Colleges can fulfil, in a wide sense, a social as well as an educational and cultural role by providing places not only for company and gossip — but centres in which the social conscience of the community can be expressed and enlarged.[14]

The colleges were inspired by Cambridgeshire village colleges, based on the work of Henry Morris. The principles of the colleges were outlined in the 'Leicestershire Scheme for Further Education and Plan for County Colleges', which was accepted by the Ministry of Education in 1951. The control of the community colleges was to rest, as much as possible, with the local community, who would be involved in the government and control of finances. The aim was to move away from old paternalistic thinking behind evening classes. The emphasis has been on democracy, and the management of the colleges has been left to those using them; however, Mason envisaged the Education Committee standing in the background 'like a wise friend'.

An important aspect of the concept of community colleges has been the new emphasis that is given to questions about the nature of schooling and education. This has been done in a liberal democratic framework, where it is hoped that the co-existence of adults and young people in integrated provision leads to the notion of education as a life-long activity, to cooperation, to broadening of the concept of education, to overcoming some of the aspects of schools which are inconsistent with the desire for harmonious, adult-like communities, through the inter-relationships between young and old, staff and voluntary workers, formal classes and informal groupings etc. Overall, the community colleges have been a success story.[15] They were considered an

economic and practical way to provide adult education. This was called into
question in extensive cutbacks, discussed below.

One Liberal Progressive School

The assumptions contained in progressive developments in Leicestershire
locate it in the strand of liberal progressivism. To illustrate this I shall consider
one progressive community college to illuminate these principles and to
provide a background against which developments at Greenfield College can
be viewed in their continuities and discontinuities with the Leicestershire
tradition.

The book *School for Community*[16] discusses one community college which
began its life in new open plan, flexible premises. The ethos and the organization of the school are based on principles of individualization, attention to the
whole child, consultation and democracy, and an informal concept of staff-
pupil relationships. The planning of the new school took place among the staff
through committees with voluntary membership. The head participated in all
the committees, and remained responsible for the school organization; because
of his final responsibility for decisions, he reserved a right to reject or modify
them.[17] The concept of democracy meant consultation, where the head retains
influence without being authoritarian. The scope of consultation is broad, but
based on the assumption of a shared framework, and a degree of consensus
about parameters of possibilities. For example the school Council, comprised
of student representatives, could decide on matters with the approval of the
head. Hannan (1975) in his study of the school reports that in a Council
meeting the head used his veto against the majority opinion to change the
constitution.

The school does, however, aim to treat students as adults, and to provide
'individual tailor-made time-tables'. The prime concern is for 'each student's
self-discovery', based on individualized principles. The concept of integration
can be discerned in the head's wish to 'break down barriers' of 'class, money,
neighbourhood, intelligence, sex', and to create 'a caring community'.[18] Thus
the head considers the school not really to be 'like a school'. Along with
tolerance, understanding and a flexible framework based on an attempted
dissolution of social groupings, those who do not conform are either seen to be
at fault individually, or considered unable to cope because of their difficult
background; they 'have not learnt to adjust to our ways, (and) bring with them
frustrations and deep personal problems which make them a burden to
themselves and a liability to others'.[19] This is comparable to Sharp and Green's
(1975) discussion of attitudes of teachers to 'deprived students' and their
background.

Liberal Progressivism: Stability and Crisis

In practical terms, integration means that of an individual to the community without social barriers. The concept of integration can be translated into a concept of control within a framework of a liberal-democratic consensus. This is significant in a consideration of the apparent paradox of a progressive Conservative authority. Because progressivism in the area has been based on liberal democratic values, providing scope for day-to-day solutions to teachers' problems, increase in autonomy, control of one's working situation, professional status, and an emphasis on the need for small classes and generous resources, it has been attractive to teachers. It is also significant that innovations at the school level are located within a reasonably clearly delimited framework, and a local authority well informed about developments in schools, due to efficient administration based on consultation and considerable contact. The autonomy of schools has existed within a context where there have been possibilities to predict the direction of changes through careful building programmes, appointment of heads etc.

The early seventies was a period when, nationally, attempts at restructuring were met by militant responses from large sections of workers. In Leicestershire such problems were not broadly prevalent; restructuring took place gradually Continued progressivism in the county throughout most of the seventies[20] can be understood within this context, whilst its disintegration, nationally, began at the turn of the decade and early seventies. But with the advent of the Conservative government in May 1979 the situation changed, and indeed the cuts in education in Leicestershire in 1979/80 exceeded the government guidelines. In October 1980 Leicestershire was included in a list of authorities with the lowest capitation in the primary sector. After the Conservatives lost their overall majority in 1981 some of the cuts have been restored.

The cutbacks in community colleges provide an interesting set of questions about educational autonomy. It was suggested above that community colleges provided an economical way of providing adult education, youth work etc. and that they consisted of an integrated provision, and were widely used by the local community which exercises a considerable degree of autonomy in government and the control of finance. Despite this success, the community side of the colleges was singled out for cuts which the Principal Adviser for Community Education considered 'savage', amounting to the 'dismantling' of thirty years of work.[21] In 1980 the colleges were required to raise a 'levy' of £100,000 — which already eroded the notion of local autonomy the colleges were based upon, and imposed great financial burden on them.[22] Further imposition followed, and the employment of adult/community tutors paid for by the authority ceased. It was expected that ten out of the twenty-seven colleges might have to close. However, the local reaction was so huge and critical, that the worst predicted cuts did not materialize.

The interesting questions raised are several. First, it has been suggested that considering how economic the colleges have been argued to be, the local autonomy was the reason for the extent of the cuts. The Principal Adviser argued that the colleges 'belonged to the people' in a very real sense, and not to the Education Committee, and asks whether the reason for the cuts is that 'these are too powerful community settings away from the direct control of the few'.[23] Those involved in community education argue that the concept of community colleges developing under local control did not satisfy the authority. Thus, secondly, the cuts can be interpreted to be significant in terms of their qualitative effects on the colleges, as well as in terms of quantitative financial savings for the authority. One development pointing in this direction was the insistence that all those teaching in community education had to be part of a panel of teachers controlled by the authority; this has limited chances of fast and flexible organization of classes on minority topics of limited interest. Thirdly, the local control of community colleges has not always been perceived to proceed along the principles of integration and responsibilities based on consensus and shared assumptions. This is indicated in a response by one member of the Education Committee to what she calls a 'hysterical reaction' to cuts, and an 'orchestrated' and 'planned offensive' against them.[24] Qualitative concerns are expressed in her critique of 'ludicrous', 'luxurious' and 'extravagant' notions of community outside committee control. She concludes that community education 'has caused more trouble for officers and county councillors than any other form of education'.[25]

The cuts in community colleges, and the local elections coincided with the recession, with increasing unemployment, and increasing signs of unrest in the county — such as an Anti-Nazi League counter march developing into a violent battle between demonstrators and the police, and a riot in 1981 in Leicester. The face of liberal conservatism within this situation is more difficult to maintain. Though it is not yet possible to analyze the real significance of the changes in the stability of social relations in the area, some shifts are indicated by the Conservative loss of overall majority in local elections.

Conclusion

I have addressed the paradox of a Conservative progressive authority by noting the smooth restructuring in the context of a relatively stable industrial and political background; the liberal democratic assumptions of progressivism; and the pragmatism with which innovations have been realized. I have noted the hardening of authoritarian conservatism in the county, with the advent of a Thatcherist national administration, a certain degree of unrest and evidence of differential interpretations of the consensual framework on educational developments.

I shall now begin an in-depth consideration of one progressive community college, Greenfield College, indicating continuities and discontinuities of the liberal progressive tradition, the existence of different strands of progressivism in the school, the scope for autonomy, the limited framework within which it exists, and the contradictions and tensions in the school because of the uneasy balance of limitations and possibilities. The school organization and ethos, the way in which teachers and students are located in these and perceive these are discussed. A sufficiently complex and differentiated picture of progressivism is sought for the understanding of both left and right critiques, and the tension between social control and oppositional spaces.

Notes

1 Editorial, *The Times Educational Supplement*, 4 September 1970.
2 EVANS, KINLEY, FOGG, HURD and MOONfiELD in PYE (Ed.) (1972).
3 EVANS in PYE (1972), p. 30 writes: 'The list of members of the first County Council reads like a roll-call of the important county families ... and the six chairmen who held office for the first fifty years were all drawn from their ranks'.
4 *Ibid*. p. 13.
5 MASON (1957, 1960 and 1963).
6 Leicestershire Education Committee minutes, May 1957–February 1958, p. 26
7 In an interview.
8 MASON (1963) p. 5.
9 KALLETT in MASON (1970), p. 41.
10 RUFFLE in FAIRBAIRN (1980)
11 FINCH in FAIRBAIRN (1980) p. 225.
12 FAIRBAIRN (1980) p. 7.
13 DODGE in FAIRBAIRN (1980) p. 93.
14 FAIRBAIRN (1980) p. 40.
15 A study by the University of Leicester, established that the community colleges are used by 20 per cent of the members of the local community — the national average for the attendance at adult education establishments is 4 per cent. Reported in the *Times Educational Supplement*, 10 October 1980
16 ROGERS (1971).
17 *Ibid*. p. 34.
18 *Ibid*. p. 149.
19 *Ibid*. p. 150
20 Several new schools opened, particularly in the early seventies.
21 HARVEY, B. in the *Times Educational Supplement*, 17 October 1980.
22 Discussed in the *Times Educational Supplement* 21 October 1980 and 20 March 1981.
23 HARVEY *op. cit*.
24 Monica Lawrence, reported in *Leicester Mercury*, November 1980.
25 *Ibid*.

Chapter 5

The School

To explore and illustrate general considerations raised in Part One, one school was chosen for an in-depth case study. I argued that the disintegration of progressivism as an official, endorsed 'creed' was linked to the process of restructuring and its impact on social relations and on schools as state apparatus. I suggested that the analysis will be incomplete without considering the specificity of progressivism. The questions centred on the paradox of progressivism as an efficient mode of control on the one hand, and as a framework with oppositional potential on the other hand. The elusiveness and contradictory character of progressivism was noted, and related to the existence of different, if interlocking strands within it, based on divergent political thinking and a variety of conceptions of what schools ought to be doing. An acquaintance and analysis of one school enables us to consider these issues more thoroughly.

A Leicestershire community college, Greenfield College, provided an appropriate location for the exploration for several reasons: it

- (i) is a state school, and a neighbourhood comprehensive;
- (ii) is situated in a Conservative local authority renowned for its progressivism;
- (iii) is a relatively 'pure' progressive school, in that it opened in new buildings with new staff;
- (iv) has a strong early history as a centre of controversy, but had survived for nearly ten years;
- (v) operated on the lines of participatory democracy;
- (vi) contains teacher-pupil interaction characterized by informality and apparent non-authoritarianism;
- (vii) is concerned with curriculum development;
- (viii) is a secondary school of upper tier, having to concern itself with public examinations;
- (ix) is a community college.

The intense research period took place from autumn 1978 for two years, there was a follow-up period of two years, and then intermittent contact till spring

1985, when an updating took place to pursue the effects of ongoing external pressures, indicated in the debate on democracy which culminated in the suspension of democratic structures in February 1985. The aim is to present a picture whereby tensions and contradictions ongoing in the history of the college illuminate the crisis that has been reached. Greenfield College has negotiated with what progressive education can or cannot, should or should not, be. It provides rich material for illuminating and clarifying issues about progressivism.

In this chapter categories of curriculum, democracy and relationships are used to introduce the ethos and structure of Greenfield College; its history is considered selectively in order to illustrate the pressures and dilemmas of a progressive school during a period of restructuring. In chapters 6 and 7 we return to the same categories and introduce new levels of complexity to the description.

The Local Area and the Opening of the School

The school is situated on the outskirts of Leicestershire. Local and adjoining industries consist of knitwear, hosiery and engineering. The social composition of the catchment area was analyzed by Evans[1] in 1976/77, using the Registrar General's social class categories:

I	II	III Non-manual	III Manual	IV	V
%	%	%	%	%	%
5.3	18.1	24.1	33.1	10.8	—

The predominance of category III is evident. The rate of unemployment has been relatively low until recently. A new upper school, Greenfield College, opened in the area in 1970. The Director of Education, Stewart Mason, was closely involved in the work of the architects, designing a school based on principles of learning developed in primary and high schools, and with integrated community provision. The school was to be a landmark of resource-based, child-centred, individualized learning. It was received as such — *The Times Educational Supplement* called it 'the most advanced working model in Europe' — 'a school we'll love to hate'.[2] The local paper, *Leicester Mercury*, considered it 'a monstrosity'.[3]

Initial Organization

The staff who gathered for workshops to plan the new school had, it was stressed, a chance to 'rethink the total processes of learning with the school'.[4]

The curriculum consisted of broad study areas. Mode III syllabi were used where possible. Scope for individual variation was to be allowed. Rules against anti-social behaviour were to be approved by everyone, and enforced through 'constant insistence' rather than punishments. The teachers should be concerned, interested adults, providing stimulus and guidance. No formal guidelines for democratic structures were made, but emphasis was on policy-making by participatory groups.

Concern was for the development of a flexible system, capable of evolving and changing. Indeed the situation in the school has been fluid. Change has been both in the direction of consolidation and tightening up, altering some of the initial zest of the College, and in the direction of further innovation. Each new innovation is preceded by a great deal of discussion about repercussions vis-à-vis students and the external world, mediated through the governors, parents, local employers, local newspaper, education officers and councillors. I shall now try to outline the shape the school began to assume, and the direction of movement over the years.

Curriculum

Major changes in the organization of the curriculum occurred in the beginning of the third year of the school, sparked off by dissatisfaction of the teachers and disenchantment of the students. During the second year ways of improving the situation were discussed; after lengthy debates '*teams*' were introduced.

The teams were to develop the fundamental principle of respecting individual students' *autonomy*, which could only flourish within a non-authoritarian framework. Education should be a *collaborative exercise* between the teachers and the learner, based on a dialogue between them. The curriculum working party noted that

> for many of us *the* fundamental principle underlying our aims at Greenfield is that of the individual student's autonomy — that is to say that each individual student should be as far as possible responsible for directing his own course of study with all the help and guidance his teachers can give him. The job of the school, its teachers and its curriculum pattern, is to create the conditions in which autonomy can thrive ... we must try to match the education to the pupil rather than blame the pupil for failing to correspond to the kind of education which is on offer.[5]

A new organization based on the integration of the academic and pastoral organizations was considered necessary — a move in the direction of 'mini-schools'. The educational principles and the ethos of the school did not change, but the conception of teachers on how to put these into practice developed. The alternative that emerged was the team-system.

A team consists of five to six teachers and 120–150 students. The central core of education takes place in teams, where students spend about half their timetable; the other half is spent in specialist subject areas. The teachers, as tutors, are responsible for the overall progress of students in their own group. In 'team-time' students are engaged in self-directed work in humanities,[6] mathematics, art and science,[7] with the aid of the tutor.[8] The teams are expected to provide a flexible, informal framework within which the students can pose problems and explore issues in a variety of ways, together with the teacher. The relationship between a student and a teacher is ideally that of mutual respect, tending to be close, relaxed and personal.

The teams have evolved to a central structure of Greenfield College. They provide the hub of a student's experience in the school — they are the homebase, where informal contacts enable negotiation to take place, substituting many of the rules and regulations defining acceptable behaviour commonly found in secondary schools. But because the structures of democracy, curriculum and relationships are considered interconnected by many Greenfield teachers, the present crisis of democracy and the suggested new management structures are seen as inimical to the ethos of teams, which are becoming, according to some teachers, administrative shells. But before considering present day developments, let us outline the structures of participatory democracy as they were.

Democracy

The formal democratic structures which evolved during the first year, were seen as integral to the College by the teachers:

> Our system of internal government, in which every member of staff and the student body has a part that can be taken, derives from the system of learning. The more a student takes responsibility for studying, the more a student will need a voice in determining the conditions of study; the more teachers are expected to coordinate their implementation of curriculum, the more they will need to determine the organization of the available resources and distribution of responsibilities.

Until recently the outlines of participatory democracy have remained the same, with variations over time in the vigour of activities across the school. In this chapter the formal structure is described, and the operation of democracy is illustrated. Chapter 6 and 7 introduce differentiated teacher and student perceptions on democracy.

The supreme policy-making body is the moot, open to all in the school, including non-teaching staff and students; all attending have one vote each; anyone is eligible to call a moot. The moot sets up various committees. The

Standing Committee meets every fortnight, and is responsible for decision-making not involving changes in policy.[9] The membership of staff is by rota, and all staff are on the Committee in the course of one academic year; their participation is well-structured. Membership is open to students, and two from each team can be registered as having voting rights (anyone can attend meetings); student participation is dependent on their initiative. Other important committees have elected membership, but attendance is open to all — allowances, finance and staffing committees. Appointment committees are elected whenever appropriate.

Ad hoc committees are constituted by the moot on specific issues when deemed necessary; for example when it cannot arrive at a decision. A crucial principle is that a moot should operate by *consensus*, not by simple majority. Those disagreeing with moot decisions can challenge them by calling a new moot, or not abide by them, as the moot cannot enforce its decisions; the rule of thumb is that at least two-thirds majority is needed before decisions are implemented. Discussions can be prolonged in order to arrive at a formula which is acceptable to all. The moot is dependent on its ability to interpret the body of opinion in the school and to arrive at a compromise on this basis. This conception of the role of the moot has developed over the years; it has been questioned and challenged, as indicated by conflicts between moot and the trade union, the NUT — the discussion is introduced here and developed in chapter 9.

The Union

An attempt was made to use the moot as a body of control, when a section of NUT members went on strike for half a day in 1976, as part of their campaign against the introduction of Houghton relativities.[10] It was argued that the trade unionists could not take action without first consulting the rest of the school through the moot.[11] One teacher opposed to the strike reflected later in an open letter:

> For the first time in the life of this school, a group of teachers chose to commit themselves to a course of action, on a matter of vital concern to everyone who works here, without finding it necessary or desirable to consult the moot, or to inform the standing committee, or to seek to achieve a broader consensus among the members of the school community as a whole. That is to say they acted in defiance of the principles of government to which we subscribe.

Particularly militant trade unionists have resisted such interpretations and have questioned the value of the moot, if it attempts to control the teachers in an authoritarian manner.[12]

The Students

The students, in principle, can participate in moots and in the Standing Committee, and outvote the staff; there is a safeguard against this: sectional vote is not considered acceptable, as it is unable to interpret consensus reached through compromise.[13] However, in general student participation is minimal, and often confined to a small number of sixth-form students. Yet at times students have participated in moots en masse, when they have felt that the issues have directly concerned them, and when the moots have been publicized and have taken place during school-time rather than after school. On occasions moots have been called by students. However, student participation is not formally structured in the same way as staff participation;[14] reasons for attendance and non-attendance are further discussed below, especially in chapter 7.

The Head

Traditionally a headteacher in conjunction with his/her deputies controls curriculum, organization and finances. By this definition Corbett[15] concluded that the Principal of Greenfield College was not a headteacher in 1971. He participates in decision-making with other members of the school, and is expected to play an active, experienced part in it, but, excluding charismatic influence and wider range of information available to him, has no more formal influence than the rest of the school. Neither did the first two heads reserve a right of veto,[16] though they noted that they would be forced to resign if they were expected to carry out policies they strongly disagreed with. The head and the deputies form the executive of the school and share the responsibility for the overall running of the school.

The moot has existed within the confines of the power of the head, as conventionally viewed. The local authority has dealt with the principals as if they were responsible for decisions. This relationship between the heads and the LEA has implications for the school. Some of the information communicated to the head by the authority is confidential, and he is not able to divulge it to the rest of the school, even though it may be important for internal decisions; the principals have also been able to influence decisions by withholding information or by having to select what information should be communicated. All this has had an effect on democratic processes. The teachers have been reluctant to place the principals in situations which they would find difficult to defend.[17] Due to increased pressures and to his background in the liberal progressive Leicestershire context the present Principal has perceived his role differently; I shall return to this below.

The Parents

The role of the parents is unresolved in any clear-cut way. The first head emphasized the participation of parents, and the importance of their influence on the school. The need to keep them well-informed about events in the school was stressed. But no clear decision has been made whether parents should participate in formal structures.[18] However, when the moot in 1973 made a controversial decision criticized by the governors, a further moot ws called to which parents were invited. In the Standing Committee a proposal was passed that at this moot anyway the parents ought to be able to vote. The school's problematic relations to parents are discussed below.

The Governors

The role of the governors in the running of the school is not very clearly defined: they are to oversee the general direction of curriculum and conduct in a school. They stand somewhere between the local authority, the local community and the school. Their work is largely concerned with the maintenance of the fabric of the school, and making representations to the local authority about the needs of the school. The governing body consists of representatives of the education authority, political appointments, representatives of parents, a teacher governor, and the head.

A specific aspect of the governing body of Greenfield College is that though it is entitled to be involved in making appointments, this has been left to the teachers, except in the case of senior posts when teachers are represented in the appointing panel, but do not control the outcome. Because of this voluntary delegation the maintenance of good relations with the governing body is considered essential by the teachers. If the governors lost their confidence in the staff they could exercise significant influence by assuming control over appointments. Therefore the moot has been reluctant to make decisions the governors may disapprove of; the role of the principal is crucial again, in interpreting the opinion of the governing body to the staff. The strategies advocated by teachers have been differentiated; in debates both acquiescent and aggressive stances have been suggested.

I have outlined the formal structures of the participatory democracy in Greenfield College, and considered the position of relevant groupings. The complexity of the operations of democracy will be further elucidated in the discussion of events and features of the school, culminating in chapter 12. Here we can note that the democratic structures privilege the teachers, but pose them in tense relationships with the executive and the governors as mediators of external pressures.

Relationships

The concept of autonomy has implications for the relationships in Greenfield College, as well as its curriculum and democratic organization. According to the school ethos, the relations between teachers and students are guided by a search for non-authoritarian relationships, democratic in spirit, providing a foundation for the development of autonomous learning. The teachers must know the students as 'whole children', in order to develop their strengths. This is particularly important with unmotivated students, with whom teachers engage in communication aiming towards 'conversation', approached equally by both parties, so that an interest which can be built upon is found. Faced with cuts and external pressures in 1980, Susan emphasizes this process:

> (We must not) deny one of the fundamental aims which teams were established to facilitate: that of encouraging students to take charge of their own learning, to pursue their own interests in whatever direction, with the guidance of a teacher who knows them well and can identify their needs and interests. To such an aim there is no easy answer. It takes time and effort ...[19]

The relationships in the school are characterized by informality and friendliness, without impinging trappings and mediators familiar from secondary schools; there are no staffrooms, no uniforms, no register call, no formal deference, no separate dining areas, and the communications between teachers and students are relaxed and warm.[20]

The first name terms have been one significant and symbolic aspect of the relationships between students and teachers. This mode of address was adopted without a great deal of planning; it evolved in the first days of the school, and now involves all teachers.[21] Outside the school it has been a focus of criticism[22] whilst inside the school it is accorded considerable importance. Despite the importance attached to it, this gesture in itself does not affect the relationships between teachers and students fundamentally. The institutionalized roles of each cannot be dissolved through such a symbolic device. The significance of first name terms, however, lies in *what* it symbolizes; a willingness on the part of the staff and the students to review these institutionalized roles critically, and (ritualistically anyway) to overcome them.

The respect for the students and the 'space' surrounding them is countered by an emphasis on achievement of acceptable standards of behaviour through constant insistence on the part of the staff. The balance is not always straightforward. Attitudes to control on the part of the staff are diverse. The problematic questions surrounding the issue of control — the shifts and ambiguities, the differentiations — are addressed in chapters 6 and 7 considering teacher and student perceptions and tensions between individualized, personalized interaction, and institutionalized roles of each.

History of the School

Selected events and processes are considered in order to discuss the dynamics of tensions and contradictions characterizing the development of an innovative school. I shall begin by discussing the campaign against the school and HMI inspection and rallying of parental support; it was not forgotten though, and a renewed attack on the school has been triggered by the introduction of parental choice of schools; the precariousness of Greenfield College has yet again been underlined.

The Conflict

Despite an apparent paradox, Greenfield College contains trends in education in Leicestershire. But such trends were developed further than had been intended;[23] the limits of educational principles based on liberal values and teachers were tested. This was clear in a dispute between the Director and the first head before the school even opened; the former impressed upon the latter that democracy implied consultation, but the head made ultimate decisions and bore responsibility for them.[24]

The first head left during the second year because of ill-health. When the LEA appointed his successor, there were a few worrying but not alarming considerations; the College had been overspending and some dissatisfaction was expressed by parents. On the whole the authority was supportive and did not wish to antagonize the strong and enthusiastic staff firmly committed to its principles. But care was exercised in the appointment of the new head. His interview followed a conventional course, but he was called for a supplementary question concerning the relationship between the Principal and the moot. Without denying the democratic principles of the school he managed to allay the worries of the Director and others that he would be capable of asserting his authority if the situation so demanded.

The teachers were on the whole satisfied with the progress of the school in the first two years. Problems, such as the high school students in the same premises, the fairly conventional feeder schools, and disinterested students, some of whom were bussed from a council estate in the city of Leicester, and thus detached from the school[25], were tackled by the third year — high school students moved to their own premises; the team structure was introduced. The atmosphere of the school was positive and confident, if somewhat chaotic,[26] and difficult for many students (introverted, quiet, those used to more discipline at home and at school) to handle. But it was also, for many teachers and students, 'electrifying', as an ex-student recalls:

> ... we were all sort of on cloud nine, really, ... under this impression that we were the chosen few; they were euphoric days when the sky was the limit. I was being educated in the broadest sense of the term. The teachers kept saying 'you can do it, you can do it'.[27]

But the campaign[28] against the school gained momentum and culminated in an inspection in the fourth year. This led to an exoneration[29] of the school, even if not wholehearted and shared by all. The pressure begun to build up in 1982, when an enquiry was called for again;[30] the school has steered a difficult course since, which has resulted in an impasse in 1985, as described below.

The conflict surrounding Greenfield College was linked to Black Paperite debates. A parent sent to Rhodes Boyson a copy of an open letter she had written. The Black Paperite concern for the disadvantage of working class children in comprehensive schools was repeated. The issue of 'parent power' was raised,[31] and greater restraints on experimentation were called for 'because of present unrest' and because, locally, of the reorganization of local government.[32]

A further interesting facet was the parent support and opposition. Parents due to send their children to Greenfield were often critical, but those with children already there tended to be more supportive. This can be connected to teacher strategies. When the school opened there were no consistent efforts to inform and involve parents. The local community was considered too conservative to accommodate the aims and practices of the college. The teachers relied on notions of professionalism whereby they were the experts who could decide on schooling/education appropriate for their students. The new school also had a large number of lengthy meetings, and teachers were already using a great deal of their time outside school hours. When the teachers considered it necessary to tackle parent worries and dissatisfaction, they adopted a strategy of visiting a majority of the homes. Though this contributed to the parent support for the school, it did not reach prospective parents. This choice of individualized, personalized method was characteristic of Greenfield. Minchin[33] refers to the contradictory stance of the staff, which largely adopted an authoritarian attitude towards parents whilst encouraging participation and practices tending towards non-authoritarianism within the space that they had defensively created for themselves through the notion of professionalism (further explored in chapter 9).

The conflict lost its momentum but did not subside; it has found expression throughout the life of the school and has gathered new strength. The external pressures on the school indicated the limited framework within which possibilities for radical development exist. The accelerated restructuring of Thatcherism is influential, but it is evident that throughout the 1970s the potential opposition was at the forefront in the discussion on directions in the school, and found expression in many contradictions.

'Democracy in One School'[34]

The questions about progressive innovation in Greenfield must be seen against the background of active local questioning of the school, at times crystallizing into a campaign against it, waged normally through a combination of the local media, prospective parents and Conservative politicians. The dominant concerns about education during the seventies, sparked off by conservative populism as expressed in the Black Papers, have found direct routes of mediation into Greenfield through an active critique of the school on the one hand, and through the cuts in expenditure on the other hand. The critique of the school is not directed at its democratic processes, but tangible aspects such as discipline, standards of behaviour and trade union action.[35] However, these are connected to the democracy. The school ethos links the tenets of participation to educational philosophy, theories of learning and the aims of the school. It is considered impossible to encourage students towards the goal of autonomy through self-directed learning whilst assuming the regulatory functions traditionally found in secondary schools. If regulation is not precluded successfully in Greenfield (for example, there are problems of control), some of its concrete manifestations are (uniforms, detentions and so on).

I shall now consider historical incidents to illuminate the conflicts, expressed in differentiation between teachers who feel that in order to safeguard the important achievements of the school it must not incite strong opposition, and those who believe that the achievements are of insufficient value if they cannot be spread wider within the state system.

The contradictions found expression in the academic year following the inspection. The high school sharing the campus with Greenfield was experiencing problems. The teachers were intent on preserving and developing a self-government similar to the upper school. When the head refused to accept staff involvement in the allocation of points, an open breach followed, whereby his authority was disputed by the teachers on the basis of principles of democratic participation. The staff of Greenfield took no action to support the high school teachers, though they were sympathetic to their fight. It was considered that the College could not survive if a militant stance supporting colleagues was adopted.

The concern for survival did not only mean that the teachers decided not to undertake such controversial action. When the high school suffered accommodation problems with overcrowding, it was suggested that the College, at the time containing a smaller number of students than it was designed for, should share some of its space with the high school. In a moot a group of teachers emphasized that the upper school which was experiencing stability for the first time could not be expected to accommodate children younger than the age range for which it was intended. If the high school children were admitted, the advance of innovation would be held up in the College. A representative of the high school asked what the College was offering to other educational institutions 'if it had to be nurtured and cosseted and cocooned to such an extent that no other school in the country could emulate it'.[36] A second group of teachers within the upper school argued that it was not possible to ignore the plight of the high school; anyway, the existence of one third year team in the College could not retard educational development. It was concluded that as the meeting was characterized by 'an atmosphere of ill-feeling', and as only about half the staff supported the high school proposal, it could not work; the importance attached to consensus and compromise is indicated.[37]

These two episodes express the conflict experienced by the teachers in Greenfield College in their attempts to safeguard its achievements, whilst trying to avoid insularity and stagnant consolidation. The existence of different approaches indicates the significance of various strands within the school — the liberals tend to stress survival; socialists and libertarians argue for a need for solidarity contained in trade unionism. The next example illustrates issues related to trade unionism during a period of intensified restructuring of state education.

Contradictions and the difficult situation of a staff of an innovatory school were expressed in an episode of a non-appointed science teacher that took place after the education cuts began to have considerable impact in Leicestershire after the 1979 election. In 1978/79 the student figures for 1979 were forecast to rise in Greenfield, and the staffing allocation was increased. On the basis of this allocation the teachers organized the staffing for the following academic year. Meanwhile, however, the increase in the roll of the school did not match expectations, and, further, the county introduced new staffing ratios (see below). The College, then, opened in autumn 1979 one science teacher short on the basis of the initial allocation to the school which had been used internally to finalize the curriculum arrangements.

The teachers decided to consider the non-appointed science teacher as an absent teacher for the purposes of the 'totting-up' process used by the NUT to operate its no-cover policy. This resulted in 300 fifth-year students being advised not to come to school one day, with wide coverage in the *Leicester Mercury*.[38] The totting-up process was to continue, and more students would be excluded again. The response of the Director of Education and the chair of the governors was negative; if the College attracted hostile publicity, they could not guarantee their capacity to support it when faced with questioning from the Education Committee and the rest of the Council. The Principal was also opposed to the action for these reasons, whilst an overwhelming majority of the staff had agreed on it. In a Standing Committee meeting[39] the executive position was outlined, and the staff were appealed to to give up their action. The Vice-Principal suggested that the governors, because of their strong disapproval, might take over appointments, now made by the staff. Militant teachers responded that the democratic processes in the school should not be used as a 'stop-gap'. One teacher expressed the worries of the staff in considering the implications of their action — how far could they go — where did they stand — where would they stop? The battle that would ensue would entail a confrontation with the local state.

The teachers discussed whether the school had a strong case on which to fight, whilst all agreed that in terms of the curriculum requirements they needed the extra science teacher. Thus it was a crucial deliberation about a response to staffing determined by criteria other than curriculum. With shrinking rolls in the majority of schools, staffing without due consideration of curriculum needs has caused problems.[40] The stance of Greenfield teachers, if widely adopted, had important implications for action against expenditure cuts. The framework of restructuring would be questioned.

The issue was resolved by postponing the action, which was not taken up again. The whole episode indicated that the teachers were able to take some united action; that the repercussions were considerable; and that, faced by this, the staff would split into those prepared to carry on against odds, those who were prepared to compromise their stance on national issues as they considered the survival of Greenfield important for themselves and for safeguarding alternatives in secondary education, and those who would question what the best tactics would be. The episode also indicates that there is a connection between the democratic processes and militant trade union action in Greenfield College (this is developed in chapter 9); this connection was seen by those involved with the school: the governors and the local education authority. Union action in Greenfield was not interpreted in the same way as union action elsewhere; it was seen to indicate the collective radical will of the teachers, crystallized through the democratic processes, and realized through the union.

The isolationist dilemma of the Greenfield College is expressed in the debates about appropriate tactics; by not campaigning against the cuts the school would reinforce its position as a relic of the past era of progressivism, unable to adapt to changed circumstances, and forced onto the defensive, surviving by adopting a quiet profile publicly; by taking trade union action the school could set into motion a process with consequences affecting the internal organisation of the school, and its aims and objectives.

The solution adopted tends to be accommodation through inertia when faced with the magnitude of the task, whilst simultaneously attempting to develop forward initiatives within the school; such efforts require increasing staff energy, and imply further pressures on teachers faced with the consequences of expenditure cuts in maintaining child-centred teaching and learning. Frustrations are expressed by Trevor:

> We have such a progressive system that it prevents me from taking union action not approved by Conservatives. If this is the spirit of progressivism then is it survival? What does survival mean? — buildings and shells not worth it. We can do anything as long as we don't upset anyone.[41]

Students and Democracy

Student views on democracy are discussed in chapter 7; here I shall recount selected events in order to illustrate and elaborate the operation of formal democracy vis-à-vis the students. The events indicating student activity must be seen against the following background:

(i)   in general student participation is low (chapter 7);

(ii)   student participation (unlike teacher participation) is not built into the structures and processes of formal democracy;

(iii)   the teachers tend to consider the majority of students as conservative and suspicious of innovation and change (chapter 12);

(iv)   informal democracy is considered more important by teachers than formal democracy (chapter 6).

The student strike

The teachers participated in union action which involved an operation of sanctions whereby they would not engage in any voluntary activities. When the majority of teachers as NUT members were going to leave the school premises during lunch breaks, the Principal wrote to all homes to inform parents and students that the school would be closed during these breaks. A group of students organized a strike, whereby a number of them walked out to the school gates to picket, stopping cars entering the College car park, and talking to them about their action. The motivations of those involved were mixed: some felt that their action was directed against the teachers who were taking authoritarian measures against the students by excluding them from their school and their team areas, or who were only interested in their own salaries and not sufficiently concerned about their teaching; others felt that their action was taken in order to support the teachers and to draw attention to the issues in the local area; some did not have motives beyond wishing to be involved in something exciting, different from ordinary school activites. The teachers took no steps to prevent the student action, but a couple of them were always found with the students at the gates, on the one hand seen by the students to express solidarity with them, on the other hand concerned to make sure that everything ran smoothly, and that there would be no trouble. Thus the striking students were amiably supervised by friendly teachers. The sixth-form students threatened to organize a sit-in, as they were not prepared to cooperate with a decision made without consultation. Therefore, though several teachers did leave the premises, the school did not close, as a sufficient number of them stayed behind to enable it to remain open; this was largely a consequence of the student action.[42]

The minibus moot

The school had at its disposal a minibus, financed through the school fund; it was proposed that the minibus contract be terminated; a moot was called to discuss this. A sixth-form student,[43] attending with a few other sixth-formers, argued that the moot had not been sufficiently publicized, and should therefore be postponed; a new moot should take place in school-time. All those present readily agreed to postpone the moot, but there was considerable debate as to whether it should take place at school-time; an affirmative decision was made (though several teachers opposed it). The school-time moot was attended by over 200 students. Though some of them attended 'for a laugh' and did not participate in the proceedings, many spoke and made suggestions dealing with broader questions about the control of the school fund as well as the minibus. The attendance of large numbers, and the student initiated advertising and timing of the moot indicate that simple notions of 'apathy' are not applicable.[44] Other moots attended by large numbers of students have concentrated on issues such as smoking, the structure of the school day, music in the college, teacher-student ratio, vertical teams (chapter 12) etc.

The-hole-in-the-wall

This incident occurred in a team, and assumed the role of mythical evocations within the College. As the school expanded, a new team area was set up, comprising of two separate rooms effectively splitting the team. The teachers considered this unsatisfactory, and wanted an opening made into the wall adjoining the two rooms. In a team meeting the students decided against 'a hole in the wall'. Thus the matter rested for the remainder of the academic year. The following year two teachers left and were replaced by probationers; a new meeting was called and the students were informed that it was not possible for two probationary teachers to work in one area, whilst the experienced teachers were concentrated in the other — thus either an opening should be made between the two areas, or tutor groups would need to shift so that the balance of teachers could be maintained. The students, faced with these alternatives, now opted for a 'hole in the wall'. The teachers were either delighted that the students were prepared to take a stand against the teachers, or drew the conclusion that if a hole-in-the-wall was wanted in the school, the students could not be consulted, as they did not like change, found it threatening for their security, and did not have sufficient understanding of the way in which teams operate to make an informed decision. Subsequently, the mention of the hole-in-the-wall would evoke shared meanings amongst the staff, even though there were some differences in the way that the implications of this were interpreted.

The National Union of School Students

The history of the NUSS within the school indicates that the tensions in the above incident do not imply an existence of strong oppositional elements within the school. The NUSS is allowed to operate openly in Greenfield College. Its membership varies from year to year[45] and its activities are not consistently organized. The members who have been involved in recruitment frequently experience problems. Some students are opposed to the idea of a union for school students in principle, others have not heard about it; some feel that though NUSS may be important in other schools, in Greenfield College it has no role to play, as all important reforms in the school have already taken place.[46] Students involved in the NUSS did not come across hostile teacher attitudes; whilst some were not enthusiastic, others were positively encouraging.

The balance between actual and potential student participation is further discussed in chapter 7; their views on democratic structures are explored; the existence of possibilities and limitations for radical action within formal structures is considered. Here I have illustrated that despite the overall low participation by students, the openness of the democracy in the school goes beyond mere rhetoric towards significant activities.

Allowances

The operation of the allowances policy in the school indicates the problems and dilemmas the teachers have to tackle, and the differentiated approaches they adopt, thus illustrating the democratic structures further, anticipating the existence of different strands among teachers (chapter 9), and the importance of professionalism in understanding processes in the school (chapter 9).

The school operates its allowances policy within an externally determined framework which imposes a hierarchical salaries structure with scales and incremental points. Within this framework the teachers determine the allocation of points according to their own criteria. The operation of the policies has been problematic, and principles they draw upon have been subjects of controversy. The policy is committed to the lowering of differentials, and the 1976 criteria state that this priority commits the school to pay 'particular attention' to those on lower scales. The overall experience, years of teaching and the careers expectations of teachers should be considered. The operation of criteria has proved difficult, when periodically several teachers were eligible for movement between scales, but the school has insufficient points for all.

The problem of how the decisions should then be made has been a long-lasting one. The school has refused to allocate points for responsibility or efficiency; this has implied that 'random' selection of those moving upwards has been a solution. The criteria include a negative one, whereby a teacher not seen to fulfil his/her role should not be eligible for movement. In 1981 the criteria were changed and now 'consideration' is given to the lowest paid. A new criterion stated that where there are insufficient points, candidate's contribution to the school will be considered. However, the problems were not solved; there was disagreement about the evaluation of teachers' contribution, and the effects of such evaluation. The Allowances Committee changed its status to an Executive Committee. The debate has continued. After a series of moots in 1982 the criterion calling for consideration of the candidate's contribution was deleted.

The operation of allowances poses tensions and contradictions, and the teachers must consider their attitude to aspects of professionalism which the salary structure determines. Those emphasizing the development of criteria to discriminate between teachers in order to promote the deserving ones do not argue their case in terms of supporting hierarchy and competition, nor consider their suggestions as affirmation of the Burnham Committee principles, but see themselves as pragmatists whose thinking is guided by 'market principles': to keep experienced teachers within the school chances of promotion must be available; to attract skilled experienced teachers the school must offer them scale points. Others feel that the school must not be too defensive when dealing with external impositions, and must not allow developments inimical to the cooperative, democratic structures; they ask how many 'career teachers' the school can 'afford'.[47] These controversies go to the heart of what an innovatory school can and wishes to accomplish; what is realistic; what is an unacceptable compromise. The controversies were not resolved, and gradually the new principal disregarded the internal policy in a build-up leading to the crisis of democracy in 1985.

Divisions

In chapter 6 the existence of different strands among the teaching staff is considered. Here I shall anticipate that discussion by indicating the surface divisions among them, evident in the daily life of the school, and noted by the teachers themselves. These divisions have significance both for formal and informal structures within the school.

The staff are less differentiated in Greenfield College than in many schools; the almost non-existent representation of the Conservative right, and the widespread membership of the NUT are indications of this; divisions, however, do exist; the following categories are used within the school.
— The 'plodders' and the 'inspirationalists'. The former are pragmatists who emphasize professionalism; teachers must carry out duties towards students even if these compromise radical ideals. Schools may be seen as capable of only limited changes, whilst on the level of individual students meaningful results can be achieved. The inspirationalists attempt to derive their practices from their educational and political thinking. They are more likely to emphasize innovation, and give more attention to interaction than administration. They are less likely to emphasize examinations, and more likely to relate to external demands aggressively.
— The child-centred and society-centred teachers. The former, often English teachers, emphasize interaction with individual students, conversational teaching and learning, and work related to the needs and interests of students; exploration of their identities and the role they play in society etc. The society-centred, often social studies teachers, emphasize the students' location in society and are likely to encourage factual, evaluative work,

whereas child-centred teachers use creative writing as a medium more extensively.

— Team and subject teachers. The divisions between these are such that the latter feel that teams have assumed such a significance that the realities of subject teaching are ignored and isolation is experienced. This is significant in decision-making, as isolated voices are less likely to be heard, or to carry an impact.

— Teachers in different teams. Teams have become largely self-sufficient entities. This assumes significance in decision-making: do teachers have their own team's interests in mind, as opposed to the interests of the whole school, the definition of which is difficult anyway because of differentiations?

A range of channels of communication and informal networks exists in the school. These precede and undercut democratic procedures, and influence making and carrying out of decisions. The networks are formulated on the basis of above divisions and others (such as male/female, old/new teachers, executive/others etc.) and also on the basis of friendship links evolving during the natural contact through work with colleagues, or outside the school. Such networks are important; in a complex situation retrieval of information is not straightforward. Lengthy conversations precede moots which have been described as rehearsals of arguments as a public exercise.

Thus the democratic structures combined with the team structures and the school ethos emphasizing individualization[48] have led to fragmentation which influences processes within the school. It is difficult to move beyond debate and to initiate action, and to ensure the carrying out of initiatives.[49] Teachers value flexibility implied by this; proposals can be adapted in the process of execution, so that they are better suited to their purposes. But this also underlies the frustration with the democratic structures; it can take a long time to reach decisions on problems. The fragmentation in the school reinforces itself — different opinions and practices may not be collectively tackled; the school develops in an uneven, differentiated way under the surface of unity and shared ethos. Fragmentation also gives further scope for the operation of informal processes, increasing the chances of manipulation by determined groups of teachers, and enhancing the relative importance of informal processes over the formal democratic structures.

Expenditure Cuts

I have argued that restructuring is mediated to schools through public expenditure cuts. The education cuts began in the first half of the 1970s, but the more extensive cuts after the advent of Conservative administration in May 1979 are of particular interest here. I shall consider some of the cuts and their impact on teachers and students.

The teacher pupil ratio (TPR) is important in a child-centred progressive school operating on principles of individualized learning, the axis of which is the relationship between a student and a tutor. The changes in the TPR in Leicestershire have been as follows:

(i)   in the first half of 1979 the ratios were 1:18 for the fourth and fifth years, and 1:10 for the sixth form;
(ii)   these deteriorated to 1:18.4 and 1:12 in 1979, 1:19 and 1:12.5 in 1980, and improved to 1:18.5 and 1:12 in January 1982.

In Greenfield the staffing ratio was also affected because of the loss of a teacher assigned to the school because of adult attendance in day classes. The roll in the school increased and thus no actual teachers were lost, but the number of teachers did not rise at the same level as the number of students; in effect the school lost several teachers over a period of two years. The impact of this was considerable: increased teaching loads, larger tutor group sizes and teaching group sizes in subject areas.

Cuts in capitation in real terms have also affected the school; a cut with even more impact was the 40 per cent cut in ancillary time. The audio-visual technician had to go, and through a reduction in technician hours science and design have been affected, as well as library and resources centre, offset printing etc. Audio-visual aids are used less, equipment is not maintained, there are restrictions in the work that can be done.

The school has attempted to reduce the impact of the cuts on students; therefore the staff feel under more pressure and there is a tendency towards stress and low morale. This combined with the larger teaching groups influences the interaction between teachers and students. The relatively smooth dealing with conflicts and control of the students is dependent on constant insistence rather than punishments and sanctions; such an approach requires a great deal of time, aiming as it does in student cooperation in defining anti-social behaviour. As such negotiations take place within individualized interaction, the amount of time teachers have with each student is reduced — thus quicker, more authoritarian measures are resorted to increasingly:[50]

> a girl in my tutor group is quite a difficult character . . . takes up a lot of time. If you had a smaller tutor group, that wouldn't become such a problem, but I mean at various times I've really exploded at her . . . I hate doing that, getting into a situation where you get so excited, so tied up with it, because you can't really cope with it because of lack of time and pressures so that you end up doing something like that which you think is very bad.[51]

The pressures on teachers are also divisive: in day-to-day situations colleagues become more frustrated with the stresses of, for example, not being up-to-date in marking. When the College is also trying to introduce innovations, the teachers are posed with the dilemma of increasing the amount of leisure time used in connection with school work, adapting their teaching, or not keeping up with preparation, marking and attendance at meetings.

The cuts also pose a dilemma on the teachers as trade unionists — what action should be taken, when, and how far. This was indicated in the above discussion of tensions surrounding action against the non-appointment of a science teacher. Some teachers express worry about militant action which would put the College in a delicate situation, because of its unusual features. Other teachers feel powerless, partly because they are critical of their union, which, they feel, has not taken an effective stand against the cuts, and has not been successful in developing forms of action likely to be effective. A further group is prepared to take action, but is frustrated because of the lack of interest colleagues and teachers in general are seen to show. The conflicts among the staff ensuing because of the pressures they are under serve to erode solidarity in the school.

The students have been affected with the changing atmosphere in the College; their opportunities have decreased in terms of the subject choices. Access to the library is reduced. Where the cost of materials in the 2D-3D work has increased, some students are less likely to afford them. Because of the lack of ancillary help, health and safety standards in the College, for example in science work, are in danger of deteriorating. More diffusely, the opportunities for learning are narrowed in terms of the range of activities available to each student. Even more difficult to substantiate is the change in the atmosphere of the school, and the changes in student teacher interaction, particularly as these still remain rather informal. Though such features remain, the quality of relationships is less relaxed, and there is less scope for the depth of relationships.

The increased pressure to produce good examination results, reflecting the overall concerns in the country, as expressed in the main themes in the education debate, is mediated to the school through the governors and the operation of parental choice whereby a progressive school on the defensive, must present itself in formal, traditional terms. The teachers become more concerned with learning oriented towards examination demands and with organizational features which facilitate this. Practices constituting internal streaming are more likely despite the school ethos and the educational and political perspectives of many teachers. Janet thinks 'there is a tendency to put more energy perhaps into kids who we think are going to do well'. Whilst teachers had to struggle for continued effective operation, there was concern for ongoing innovation and an active rather than a reactive stance. But the pressure intensified.

The 'Impasse'

Pressure from the LEA (with its new Director of Education appointed in 1984) and the governors, dissatisfaction among a section of teachers and the criticisms of the democracy by the executive, three of whom (including the Principal) arrived in the school in the eighties, led the Principal to suspend the formal democracy in Greenfield in February 1985. There had been growing concern about 'good practice', differentiation between teams, fragmentation, difficulty in implementing policies and disagreements about allowances. This occurred in the context of worries about parental choice and publication of examination results. The new members of the executive were located in the liberal Leicestershire tradition,[52] and wished to review the structure and organization of learning in Greenfield.

Considerable debates took place about democracy as a whole, allowances, appointment, curriculum and relationships in teams. In spring 1984 the executive's 'Green Paper' demanded discussion of changes. In autumn 1984 a series of moots took place, and a new democratic organization was developed by the end of term. The initiation of the changes was not successful — there was not sufficient support either from the executive or teachers critical of the change. Meanwhile a dispute had been triggered by a delegation of striking miners invited to speak in the school. The Principal opposed this, as did the LEA, who launched an enquiry which concluded that the management structures of the school were not adequate. There were also some disputes about allowances, where the Principal considered it necessary to disregard Staffing Committee recommendations about the scale on which two new appointments were to be advertised.

These events led the Principal to suspend the formal democratic structures which could not be reformed, he argued; they could not make 'hard' decisions required to meet the challenge of the eighties realistically. The Principal requested all teams and departments to choose coordinators to oversee the work in their areas and to participate in a central committee. The moot would be replaced by a six-weekly staff meeting. Alternative proposals were put forward by teachers, but these were not accepted by the Principal, though he made some changes in his proposals. Overall, negotiations were made more difficult by the withdrawal of goodwill by teachers who participated in national NUT action. The discussion of the impasse continues in chapter 13.

Conclusion

Several trends expressing continuities with schooling in Leicestershire are found in Greenfield:

(i)   innovation spreading from primary to high to upper schools;
(ii)   resource-based, child-centred, individualized learning;
(iii)   informal staff-student relationships based on notions of 'adult community' as preparation for citizenship;
(iv)   integrated community provision;
(v)   delegation and consultation within schools.

The continuity with Leicestershire tradition helps us to unravel the paradox of a 'most progressive school in Europe' within a Conservative authority. The discontinuities have emerged after the opening of the school. The directions of Greenfield indicate the possibilities contained within schooling based on rhetoric and structures of progressivism, which were developed further than had been expected within the state system, with a number of features sustained in a hostile educational climate tending to coordination, centralization and standardization. However, limitations posed by the framework within which the College operates are evident — many of the tendencies in the school are contradictory. The selective discussion of aspects and events portraying the structure and history of the school has aimed to illuminate the limitations and contradictions, and the tensions that these pose within the school. The increased precariousness of Greenfield practices has resulted not from a hostile atmosphere as much as from measures which have mediated this atmosphere of restructuring; most notable are the cuts, and the operation of parental choice. The impact of the cuts, both quantitative and qualitative, indicates that restructuring has made inroads into the school affecting practices, organization and atmosphere despite teacher attempts to resist the erosion of their principles, and some success in further innovations. The latest significant development in 1983 is the school's decision to participate in a Manpower Services Commission pilot scheme Technical and Vocational Education Initiative (TVEI), potentially increasing external control, linking education and training, eroding personalized individualization and the child-centred ethos (chapter 13). Considerable opposition to participation in the scheme was raised, but those favourable to it argued strongly that the benefits of increased resources and staffing associated with it could not be forfeited by a short short of both; pragmatists considered accommodation to restructuring unavoidable.

Notes

1 Evans, discusses the characteristics of the area in an uncompleted PhD thesis, University of Leicester.
2 *Times Educational Supplement*, 4 September, 1970
3 *Leicester Mercury*, n.d.
4 In an internal document entitled *The Main Aims*, preceding the opening of the school.
5 An internal paper by the curriculum working party in autumn 1971.
6 Leading to social studies and English CSE/GCE.
7 By now most teams cover science.
8 The pressures of deteriorated staff-student ratios have led, recently, to co-tutoring, whereby two teachers share one tutor group.
9 If interpretation is open to doubt, the Standing Committee or anyone wishing to challenge their decision, can call a moot.
10 In 1975 these increased differentials among teachers, and were strongly opposed by groups of teachers.

11 A proposal was put to the moot, and passed:

> whenever any one group within the school contemplates pursuing a course of action which is acknowledged to curtail the freedom of action of other groups within the school, it has an obligation to consult those whose freedom of action is threatened, and to seek ways of preserving, if possible, the freedom of all.

12 A teacher wrote in an internal paper:

> The moot is a meeting ground and can never be used to tell trade unionists how they should act in relation to their employers, their trade unions or any other groups they consider to be within the orbit of their interest ... We are not replacing the authoritarian regime of a headmaster with an unauthoritarian Moot. The final authority and ultimate power must remain with the individual.

13 This was not evoked in the case of vertical teams, chapter 12.
14 Teachers are expected to attend. For example those not attending a Standing Committee meeting when they are on rota send in their apologies.
15 *New Society* 15 April 1971, pp. 627–30.
16 This can be compared to the Leicestershire Head discussed in chapter 4.
17 When, in conjunction with the trade union action described later in the chapter, the Head explained he could not support the stance of the staff in meetings with governors, the teachers spent a great deal of time discussing the implications of this.
18 The participation of parents is problematic. The intention initially was that they should be able to attend moots, and indeed have done so, but their attendance has not been encouraged, and when they have attended, the teachers have been uncertain as to whether they should have voting rights.
19 A paper presented at an internal conference.
20 BERNBAUM (1973) argued that the majority of teachers were more concerned with 'expressive' rather than 'instrumental' ideals.
21 Only once I heard a student in a conversation refer to the Head as 'Mr.'.
22 For example: 'many staff are now called by nicknames to their faces' — a criticism quoted in the *Leicester Mercury*, 1 September 1952
23 A retired head suggests that the Conservative Council started to review Mason's work only after he retired, and may not have approved all developments.
24 An ex-teacher, close to the first head, recounts this:

> (The Director) thought that (the first Head) meant that there'd be a lot of consultation and a lot of sharing of things but in the end of course it would be the principal who made all the decisions.

> The Principal was told that his wife could not be appointed because of a Leicestershire rule, and that she must resign.

> And (the Head) wrote back saying I'm not prepared to say she must resign, this must be a decision for the staff to take, we're going to be a democratic school and it's not my decision, and (the Director) wrote back an extraordinary letter in which he said, of course it's your decision, by saying the school's democratic you mean that staff are to be consulted, not they're to make the decisions, you're the person who makes the decisions ... So I don't think there is the slightest doubt about what (the Director) thought — he didn't take that bit seriously and was very shocked when (the Head) proposed it.

25 The top achievement range had been creamed off to grammar schools in the City of Leicester.

26 An ex-student describes the school:

> the students were running around, coming and going quite freely, calling (the teachers) anything that happens to come to mind, walking in and out of the staffroom.

> In the beginning there was a staffroom, but this is no longer the case.

> Some of (the first students) were absolute thugs ... and of course the school gave expression to that ... as they could wear skinhead regalia. (There were) gangs of thugs walking round the school ... and all these do-gooder middle class educationalists running after them 'come now, wouldn't you like to do some sociology'. (in a recorded interview)

27 *Ibid.*

28 The worries of some parents had begun earlier, but found more consistent expression during the third year of the school. A parent wrote a critical open letter to the Principal; this was published in the *Leicester Mercury*. A Parents Action Committee was formed, outside the PTA. A petition opposing the College was organized with a greal deal of publicity. A Conservative MP visited the school — his criticisms were reported in the *Leicester Mercury*. The paper called for an enquiry into the College. This call was adopted by the leader of the Conservative group, days before the first local elections for the new reorganized local authority. After the elections the Education Committee recommended a full inspection instead. The MP tried to instigate an enquiry, but this was not authorized.

29 Nearly a thousand parents had signed a statement deploring the publicity that the College had attracted. In June 1974 a meeting of parents expressed overwhelming support for the Principal and the teachers.

30 *Leicester Mercury*, 1 September 1952

31 In CCCS Education Group (1981) there is a discussion of the Tory concept of parent power.

32 *Leicester Mercury*, 16 March 1973

33 Minchin (1975).

34 A team magazine contained this quote: 'Trotsky said "A single socialist state cannot survive indefinitely without outside support and extension of the revolution arising." Can a single democratic school?' This refers to the problems of Greenfield College posed by its nature within the state system in an increasingly hostile climate as far as progressive education is concerned.

35 This concern is strongly expressed by the Director and the officers of the LEA as well, and by the governors.

36 Moot minutes, 2 February 1976.

37 No allocation was made, it was decided that the high school and the authority were to solve the problem.

38 Under a heading 'Mothers hit out as action keeps pupils at home, 22 September 1979

39 I attended the meeting.

40 For example a number of recent HMI reports on the effects of the cuts in public expenditure in schools.

41 My minutes of the meeting.

42 Executive reluctance to enforce the decision was also relevant.

43 This student, Gregg Spencer, is referred to in chapter 12 as well.

44 For example Yeo (1974).

45 Thus NUSS membership has been floating — during the research period from about thirty to 100.

46 This information has been gained on the basis of a questionnaire, and informal discussions with students.

47 MINCHIN (1975) *op. cit.*
48 This individualization affects teachers as well as students.
49 This was observed on several occasions during the research.
50 Teachers made references to being 'rattier' with the students — the teachers have larger teaching/tutor groups to contend with and hence less time for negotiation and persuasion. The atmosphere of the school tightened up somewhat — for example more commands to the students.
51 Henceforth quotations are from recorded interviews unless otherwise specified.
52 They all had teaching experiences in the liberal progressive school described briefly in chapter 4.

Chapter 6

The Teachers

The aim in this chapter is to add further depth to the description of the school ethos and organization (chapter 5), and to emphasize diversity, contradictions and conflicts thus illuminating the complexity of the social formation under study. The categories of curriculum, democracy and relationships are used, illustrating teacher perceptions and practices in the important fields of innovation in Greenfield College. The categories of class, sex-gender and race focus on teacher views on the differentiation of the student body, and their implications for teaching, learning, achievement and the construction of student careers (further discussed in chapter 10). The public expenditure cuts are returned to, to reaffirm the context of restructuring (chapter 2) within which the teachers make their daily decisions. The range of such decisions is focussed on through a brief discussion of teacher profiles. This leads us to a consideration of the crystallization of the teachers as thinking subjects with educational and political frameworks into different strands, introduced in chapter 3, and developed here.

Curriculum

Curriculum in Greenfield is individualized and personalized; 'autonomous' learning (chapter 5, p. 62) is the aim. The teachers' role is to interpret the interests of students and to cooperate in the organization of their learning. Teachers tend to be flexible about how they equip students; Sarah: 'I think we modify our expectations in the light of what we know of our students. Therefore I would set different goals to different students to some extent'. Students are considered to need differing activities and experiences because of their ability, achievement, home background and own expectations.

Differentiation among teachers is illuminated in the debate about social studies teaching;[1] should areas of study be introduced to students systematically? Child-centred teachers stress the importance of students' interests, but acknowledge their influence on the directions of students' work. But particular study areas are not considered important in themselves; they reflect the interests of teachers, and are used as facilitators of learning in situations where students stand back. Secondly, teachers consider there to be important areas of study, but these are not systematically introduced to the students, but are developed in discussion sparked off by students. Thirdly, teachers do think there are important areas of study, and they do make these consistently available to students, but there is no firm organizational framework for this.

Such persuasion without compulsion has been typical of Greenfield. But some teachers are concerned that students may receive a narrow, superficial education.

> *Jill*: if they don't happen to light on doing one of those topics in their projects, or they don't happen to make a racist remark, or they don't happen to get into a fight with an Asian kid or a West-Indian kid, then whatever their prejudices might be, are just sitting there underneath the surface, and we haven't actually confronted that and neither brought out their prejudice and made them sort of think it through, or challenged it in any way.

Also there is concern that students will rely on common sense knowledge drawn from parents and mass media based, ·in Leicestershire, on conservative assumptions.

> *Angie*: The whole idea of autonomous learning is a bit peculiar ... I mean no-one's autonomous, and it's not as if the world is a kind of natural place, and that they can just pick from the world what they want to study. I mean obviously people pick from their own experience and that's ... necessarily limited, everyone's experience is limited. And I think some of the kind of learning that goes on here perhaps consolidates the limits on people's lives rather than extending the boundaries.

A fourth group of teachers is prepared to introduce topics to students across the team within a relatively firm structure, whilst also allowing for individualized, 'self-directed' work.

> *Edward*: ... I don't find any contradictions in introducing a topic of work, and the very attendance of school is a compulsory exposure to some sort of body of information ... and my job is to introduce topics ... which are interesting and which will pick up the students' imagination, and get them to consider their own position and their own viewpoints and develop (them).

Other teachers criticize such 'prescription' as a regressive step in a school which has attempted to move beyond authoritarianism and teacher imposition.

Behind the school ethos of dominant and/or shared understandings about curriculum, differentiated, even contradictory positions among teachers exist, reflected in thinking about practices. A mixture of educational, political and occupational thinking is reflected in teacher positions. Their approach is guided by varying emphases on the relationship between individual and society: some focus on the individual experience, some on the context which delineates that experience, and others shift focus towards the collective.[2] The practices of teachers are formulated on the basis of:

(i)   notions of professional responsibility — the way that the teachers perceive their role vis-à-vis parental and student expectations of qualifications and preparation for leaving school;

(ii) notions of effectivity — the strategies and tactics that are considered to be successful in the context of the day-to-day realities of teaching;

(iii) educational thinking — notions of learning, of teacher-student relationships and of adult-youth relationships;

(iv) political thinking — position on individuals vis-à-vis structures and frameworks of society, notions of personal choice and control versus external imposition and determination.

Whilst most teachers disassociate themselves from the main-stream educational thinking and practices of schooling, they are aware of some of the contradictions, tensions and problems which their position and practices within state school entail.

> *Edward:* I don't believe it's right to appear neutral when in fact you're not neutral, because I think there's a dishonesty involved there. I would like to think that I manage to express my views without overwhelming students with them, but I'm quite open to criticism that I don't — I don't know.

Though there are such differences, the hallmark of Greenfield College is still personalized, individualized learning. But internal critique of the effects of such learning has been developing and there have been shifts towards collaborative learning between students. Interest in group work stems from critique of practical, political and educational aspects of individualized learning. Group work is valued because it encourages solidarity and cooperation, introduces students to skills needed in adult life, adds a new dimension to learning, and influences interaction between teachers and students. Practically, introduction of group work has been suggested as a way of tackling the effects of restructuring; it can overcome obstacles posed by expenditure cuts and deterioration of teacher student ratio allowing less time for teaching individual students.

Difficulties have been countered when collective activities have been introduced to students. Shane, a science teacher, recounts problems:

> . . . the kids very rapidly when they come here get this idea that they really can choose work and it is very hard to deflect them . . . I think they feel autonomous as people . . . that they have as much right to do

> something as you have or anybody else, which is a thing we are
> encouraging them to do, and ... it is taken up so powerfully that
> when you then say to a group of kids, look this lesson I don't want
> you to work on the bit that you have been working on, I want you to
> do something together ... you have got to sit there for about half an
> hour discussing with them why you want to do this, and they say no,
> no, this is a sort of school ... I want to carry on with this, I don't have
> to do any sort of group thing, and what right have you got to tell us to
> do it ... (so you) end up with a great big discussion about it (and the)
> time has gone, and you haven't actually done the group thing.

Child-centred teachers think that cooperation should be developed in the context of discussion between friendship groups; systematic introduction of group work is seen to imply increased structuring and imposition.

Group work is difficult because of student expectations, formulated before arrival at Greenfield, and reinforced by the ethos of the school. Obstacles to systematic introduction of collaborative learning are many; increased demands on teacher time make concentration on particular aspects of their work difficult. Stronger emphasis on examinations hinders group-work — exams are undertaken by individuals. The fragmentation of structures and processes within the school (referred to in chapter 5) poses complications to the introduction of consistent changes. Therefore realization of groupwork is hindered by aspects internal to the school, *and* aspects related to the context of restructuring, imposing limitations and pressures which reduce the autonomy of the teachers, and narrow their scope of operation — 'spaces' are eroded (chapter 1).

Examinations

Through examinations constraints and requirements are posed on Greenfield College. Emphasis on certification has strengthened; greater importance is attached to qualifications during a period of youth unemployment; the publication of examination results required by Conservative legislation directs the simultaneously introduced parental choice to specific assessment of prospective schools. Centralization and standardization of schooling thus finds expression at school level.

Teachers in the College are, overall, critical of public examinations — they impose restrictions on teaching and learning, limit the students' expectations, mediate external pressures, and erode scope for aspects of development valued by teachers. The worries and dilemmas posed by certification are usually expressed in terms of a discussion focussed on individual students. The dilemmas are explored here through themes of contradictions, egalitarianism/ hierarchical differentiation, professionalism, individualization, all in the context of restructuring.

The central dilemma revolves round differentiation of practices vis-à-vis individual students. Flexible requirements are posed on students. Differentiation of expectations with regard to public examinations is related to the philosophy of respecting student interests, and also to an assumption that there is no direct connection between certification and location in the labour market.[3] But the dangers and problems of differing expectations are also noted, particularly vis-à-vis working class students. Conflicts are experienced by teachers who wish to have regard to egalitarian principles of the comprehensive movement *and* take into account individual needs, whilst not posing social mobility as a goal to be strived for regardless.

Solutions are sought at the level of individualized negotiations with students. Such solutions are partial, and teachers are faced with recurrent dilemmas, often involving a great deal of consideration.[4] Professionalism provides a less problematic solution. The examinations, paradoxically, solve the problems posed by examinations. One teacher describes the pragmatism of staff which leads them to channel majority of students towards examinations: 'you make everybody do exams, so it's a sort of egalitarian way ... exams help to motivate everybody'. In fact, then, only a small proportion of students leave the school without having attempted examinations.[5]

The discussion of problems and solutions (remaining partial) indicates contradictions and uncertainties experienced by teachers and the ways in which examinations pervade the daily reality of the school influencing student teacher interaction and teaching and learning. The importance of examinations is mediated through expectations of parents and students; governors; the local education authority; the central government (through its legislation for the publication of examination results in particular); and the teachers' perceptions about the value of qualifications in the labour market.

Decisions about examination orientation of teachers versus specific students, and the orientation of the students themselves are dependent on teachers' assessment of their ability and achievement orientation. This places particular onus on teachers who have to negotiate the career of each student on the basis of assessment.[6] The pursuit of egalitarian practices, and the differential handling of students are difficult to reconcile. Yet those teachers who reject the necessity of a hierarchical society with a differentiated division of labour, where the examination system is structured to encourage success for some and failure for others, can find themselves as direct intermediaries of that system. The teachers are aware that if they adopt egalitarian policies towards examination preparation they will nevertheless preside over a process whereby some achieve and some do not.

> *Janet:* I suspect that it's true that kids with working class background go to working class jobs and kids with middle class background go to middle class jobs — it's just the same as in any traditional school. I don't think we have any effect on that. I don't think we can change

the class nature of society through schools like this. Even if all schools were like this.'

Thus teacher solutions are dependent on political perspectives and on a degree of pragmatism adopted through occupational thinking based on a particular analysis of the work of a teacher, linked to notions of professionalism. Though there are differences between teachers' thinking and practices, the uniformity of the pressures and the tendency to adopt individualized solutions are significant. The school starts from individualized premises, and draws its philosophy from these, and turns to them in the search for rationalization of practices. If examinations pose a problem that they also help to solve, the strategy for coping is given through individualization as a practice as well as an ethos.

In conclusion David draws attention to the specific role of examinations in Greenfield College in ensuring parental approval, student motivation and local approval — should results 'slip badly', 'somebody will ring a bell and that's the playtime over'. One of the aspects of the 'playtime' is the democracy in the school; it is located within a precarious 'space'.

Democracy

The discussion here focusses on the differentiation of teacher positions, informal structures, marginalization of teachers, and views on student participation. The formal structures, and the contradictions imposed by the restricted scope of the democratic processes were considered in chapter 5 — the operation of democracy was illustrated through substantive areas such as allowances.

Differentiation of Teacher Positions

The teachers in Greenfield value the scope to formulate elements of their teaching, and the work experience they are gaining.

> *Thil:* I'd find it very difficult to work in a situation where I didn't have the ability to determine my way of working to some extent. The school offers me a variety of ways of (doing so).

But there is differentiation in the amount of value placed on democracy, depending on the scope perceived within it. Four positions are identified. First, democracy is seen as a valuable feature of the school and the possibilities it offers are considerable.

> *Danny:* the idea of having no hierarchy, the idea that your views are as important as anybody else's and likewise any other single

person's idea is as useful and as poignant as your own is incredibly important.

Similar sentiments are expressed by a probationer.

> *Angie:* I certainly feel that I'd be listened to a hell of a lot more here than anywhere else. I mean for example, if I wrote a paper, you know, me as a probationer, my thoughts, it would be taken fairly seriously, I think.

Second, there is concern with limitations in the operation of democracy, but it is valued because of its influence on the day-to-day work in school; Sharon used to think 'that participation was very important, because it meant self-determination in a sense', but she has 'swung round to the view that what happens is that you do get coopted'. The optimistic views on democracy have been tempered by experiences of teachers over the years. Janet emphasizes cooption:

> I don't think we're democratic at all. I think we are co-opted into making management decisions, and we think we are making them out of our own free will ... We go to committee and because we make collectively decisions which normally a head would make we think that's somehow democratic, but the forces that control them are outside the school, as they are for the kids ... What we have got is responsibility without any power. And that's the worst position you can be in. We are responsible for carrying out decisions which we didn't choose, we wouldn't choose if we had the choice, and yet we have the responsibility for operating them.

She continues, however:

> But that's not to say that what we get is worthless. I think ... what we have got is quite important because it makes life more pleasant in the day-to-day running of the things ...

Third, the futility of the democratic structures because of their time consuming aspects is noted; Shane would like to see more delegation:

> I think there's a general feeling that the democracy thing has ground to a bit of a halt, and that it's become diversified and it's now very difficult to get anything done, because there's so many different aspects to every major decision that has to be made.

Suggestions have ranged from giving more scope for the executive to formulating an executive committee of teachers, but changes were feared to erode participatory democracy and encourage divisions of activity and passivity. Fourth, the management function of democracy and the problems of participation for teachers as trade unionists are emphasized, and higher value is placed on union activities (conflicts between union and democracy were referred to in chapter 5).

Informal Structures

Attention was drawn to the informal structures in chapter 5. These structures, operating in conjunction with the formal structures, contain possibilities for the concentration of influence (on policy decisions) and power (to secure scarce resources). Such informal structures are based on individuals or groups of teachers with a shared work situation, or comparable educational and political outlook. Above Shane emphasized that everybody's views counted; others, for example Dora, are more cynical:

> ... you find constantly all the same people in the same jobs, which happens year after year, but with different labels on them, and the same as when it comes to appointing staff, you get the same people on the appointing committees, year after year after year ... it's a question of you nominate me and I will nominate you half the time.

The emphasis on the individual and on autonomy, the formation of teams, the importance of face-to-face interaction, the dissolution of the staff room, the pressure of time, the concern by teachers for the control of their work situation, their delight at having escaped some aspects of traditional schools (such as control by hierarchies) expressed in their predisposition to work alone in the daily teaching[7] have led to fragmentation within the school, giving scope for informal structures as powerful determinants.

Power, an ability to attain scarce resources in particular, is significant in securing a pleasant working situation wanted for a number of reasons: it makes the job more satisfying, allows the teachers to function more efficiently within the intense requirements of student teacher interaction based on a minimum of sanctions and a maximum of acquaintance and persuasion, and it frees them to focus on the students as much as possible.

> *Teacher:* ... all ... teams will do various kinds of manipulations about new teams, and who goes where, how many kids you have in your team and so on. There are people (who feel) that we've looked after ourselves very well, because we have a kind of core of experienced people, and some people are very resentful of that.
> *Interviewer:* How do you manage to do it ...?
> *Teacher:* Partly because we are a tightly knit ... team ... and when you got a team that's strong and united about something, it's very hard to break them down.

When the needs of a team or of a specialist subject are in conflict with the needs of the school as a whole (as perceived by the majority of the staff), teachers who are part of influential networks and channels of communication, who have the support of others, or who form a strong, cohesive group are able to manipulate the situation, and pursue their own ends.

The importance of channels of communication lies in the complexity of the issues in the school, and the wealth of information required to make and influence decisions, and to exercise power over the allocation of resources. Within informal and fragmented structures the acquisition of an understanding of a situation cannot be derived from formal structures.[8]

A further aspect within the school significant to democracy is the process of *marginalization* affecting individual teachers, who may then find it impossible to assume influence or power in the events of the school. They find it very difficult to become members of committees[9] and find few avenues except voting at moots. Those who are marginalized tend to reside outside the main channels of communication and major informal networks. Thus they tend to be subject, not team teachers, and they are often women. Such teachers are seen to have created their own isolation; they may not share the views of the majority ethos, and do not reside in any particular grouping with an alternative, critical ethos. Their marginalization is often confirmed through them being considered as bad teachers.

The democratic structures in the school, then, cannot be understood simply through a consideration of the formal structures, nor through a consideration of the variety of teacher positions and analyses of democracy; it is also important to consider the nature of relationships within the school. Many teachers feel that the democratic nature of the teacher-student interaction during the daily contacts is more important than student participation in the formal structures (chapter 5). Before we discuss the nature of the relationships, it will be useful to indicate the range of views on student participation, introducing ambivalence among the teachers, which found expression in the decision to implement the 'vertical teams' (chapter 12). Issues discussed briefly here will therefore be developed later.

Students and Democracy

In general students do not participate actively in democratic structures (chapter 5). The reasons for this, as interpreted by teachers, are varied. First, it is argued that the actual participation of students in formal structures is not crucial; what matters is that their consent is sought in the day-to-day teaching/learning situations, and students see this happening. Secondly, it is assumed that student participation is limited because they feel satisfied with the structure of the school and its running. Thirdly, a majority of students are considered apathetic and unconcerned about the framework within which they exist in the school. On the one hand this is seen as a reflection of the short period they spend in school; on the other hand it is seen as a reflection of student views on democratic processes, which are considered tedious, boring and complicated.

Shane draws attention to the potential problems if students did participate:

> I think the weakness of any kind of student involvement so far has been a unwillingness among the students to look really much beyond their own position ... I don't think you can run the school in that kind of factional way.

Thus student participation in democracy is seen as necessarily limited.

> *Jonathan:* I don't really believe in student democracy ... if the students really were to take charge, you'd find yourself (going through) the same things over and over again every two years. It's a learning process, democracy and ... it's good for them to learn, and that's as far as I feel student democracy should go.

Janet notes that granting participation in formal structures has been possible because, overall, students do not take advantage of it.

> ... it's easy to give formal democracy when the students don't actually operate it. I think if they did operate it, we wouldn't have it ... there's a lot of kidding of ourselves really.

The emphasis on informal structures has already been noted. But not all teachers think that in atmosphere and spirit the school is democratic vis-à-vis its students:

> *Janet:* They don't really know about the democratic structures; the way they ... ask you if they can do things ... shows that they really haven't got much of an awareness of the fact that this school is not supposed to be like that, and they're supposed to be able to make decisions collectively ... In the day-to-day running of the school they don't experience it as democratic at all I don't think.

But many teachers do also strongly favour student participation, both formal and informal. Attention is drawn to situations where students have been influential in decision making.

> *David:* If issues arise in which they (are interested) they don't seem at all reluctant to use what they've got and of course I'm giving them every encouragement to do so.

But the problems of giving it structured status and expression are such that few teachers, despite their concern, are prepared to make the effort necessary. A working party on democracy was constituted, but only a handful of members of staff participated[10] along with sixth-form students. Though teachers are under considerable pressure, allocation of teacher time is linked to prioritization of issues; other aspects in the school have received greater teacher attention. Student participation is considered, at best, transient, because of their short stay in the school. Concern is expressed about the conservatism of student positions; their participation is seen as potentially detrimental for radical innovation (chapter 12). Thus whilst student participation in democratic structures is viewed in different ways by teachers, overall such participation is not greatly encouraged, and the structures do not incorporate students in the same way as they incorporate teachers (chapter 5). It must be noted, also, that a small group of teachers, critical of democratic structures in the school in general, encourage students to participate within the NUSS rather than in what are interpreted as coopted management structures.

The 'Impasse'

Teachers were critical of the new structures proposed after the formal democracy was suspended (chapter 5), but again there were differentiations in their positions. The radical socialist, trade unionist, feminist and libertarian teachers argued that the changes eroded the ethos and structures of the school, and introduced new hierarchies which were detrimental and unnecessary. A second orientation was sympathetic to the Principal's concern about 'good practice', and thought that changes were necessary, but did not want to erode the democratic character of the school. A third orientation emphasized that the staff could not exonerate themselves from the difficult situation that had developed. It was now necessary to look at the Principal's suggestions and to develop a workable compromise. A fourth orientation accepted the Principal's right to make decisions, and the role of teachers to teach. This included teachers who had viewed democracy as cooption anyway, and some new teachers who considered themselves to be doing a job as teachers, whose view of schools was more apolitical than that of radical teachers and those radicalized during the dispute. Some teachers remained frustrated, demoralized and critical of the 'hard-liners' as well as the Principal who was considered unsympathetic to the school. The feminist teachers in the women's groups considered the new structures male-orientated and to the detriment of the women in the school. Many teachers were looking for other jobs. The impasse is further discussed in chapter 13.

Relationships

Autonomous learning implies, according to the school ethos, equality of relationships between teachers and students; both are to cooperate on a task which engages each of them intellectually in the search for, and recreation of, information and knowledge: 'we treat students as individuals, we're prepared to talk to them as individuals and relate to them as equals'. Experiences within the school, and the changing educational climate nationally and locally, have led many teachers to question the possibility of such equality — but they remain critical of authoritarianism; Janet:

'It's silly to pretend that you and (the students) are in an equal position in the school ... But I don't think that gives me the right to tell them to do something and expect them to jump, just because I told them to, or give me the right to belittle them or intimidate them or make them do just what I say, but I think there are certain areas where I think I should try and influence them to say the least.'

Thus, despite problems, informality and respect remain important aspects of interaction in Greenfield.

Relationships between teachers and students were observed in one team over a period of two years. Whilst there were differences among teachers in the approaches adopted, and in negotiations engaged in depending on their educational and political thinking, their conception of the occupational and professional aspects of teacher role, their sex and personality, there were also similarities in strategies adopted, goals worked towards and in the existence of shifts in interaction emphasizing at times the professional aspects. All teachers knew a great deal about their students, their interests, background etc. Others, however, were particularly interested in the homes of students, in terms of parental expectations or the nature of familial relationships and their impact on student career in school. The teachers ranged from relatively 'strict' to quietly consistent[11] to relatively volatile.

Control within the team related to a set of acceptable activities ('get on with your work') and acceptable behaviour ('stop walking about disrupting people'). Means of control range from insistence, persuasion, nagging, joking, shouting, separating students, and, occasionally referral to the Vice-Principal. The degree of teacher control and influence on students' work varied. The teachers differed in the amount of scope given to students in 'doing nothing',[12] in checking their whereabouts, in the amount of 'pushing' that was considered necessary, and in the amount of control they assumed over the work of students, through devices of routinization such as 'plans', and through resources made available. The teachers in general adjusted their methods and expectations and ways of communicating and interacting on the basis of their conceptions of individual students.

Punch (1977) emphasizes the function of student involvement in progressive boarding schools in providing a medium through which control, cohesion and legitimation are achieved. In Greenfield College the informality of teacher/student relations serves a similar role. In the absence of the sanctions commonly available in secondary schools, the teachers are dependent on constant insistence which can be successful only through a large degree of student consent. Thus the semi-symbolic access to the formal democratic structures, and the sense of consultation and self-determination in day-to-day issues are important. Similarly the close relationships between teachers and students, whilst facilitating the kind of learning that Greenfield has been developing, also make more of the student available for control; s/he is more vulnerable when more of his/her private self has been revealed. This delicate balance affecting students also has an impact on teachers.

The negotiated nature of interactions has been noted. Whilst such negotiations are individualistic and personalized, it is important to note that they take place within a definite framework of cultural and structural aspects pertaining both to the institution in question, and to the general societal constructions condensed within it, and to the range of cultural fields the teachers and students inhabit. Thus, each time a teacher meets a student and they negotiate, they do so within a framework of one set of socially organized positions and experiences meeting another set of socially organized positions and experiences, relating to features such as conceptions of the ethos of Greenfield College ('in "a school like this" one should/should not ...'), conceptions of the role and nature of schooling, teachers, students, adults, children, males, females etc. All of these articulate with social class, mediated through biographical[13] aspects.[14] Such negotiations can assume a variety of directions and reach a variety of outcomes, depending on the time available to participants, the perceived importance of issues, the existence of an audience, and its character and role. The range of significant aspects, and the weight of relative importance attached to these in differing circumstances lead to *shifts* in interaction, the importance of which is discussed in chapters 7, 10 and 11.

In the course of teacher/student interaction the teachers acquire information about the students, and on this basis make judgments about the kind of strategies to be used with each student, about the appropriate examination preparation, and also about the relative importance of cognitive and affective learning. Social learning may be considered particularly important for those students who are considered 'difficult';[15] and also it may be considered important for those students who are particularly concerned to achieve well in examinations, and whom teachers assess to be very instrumental in their attitudes towards learning, and who need to have their perspective broadened. Some students successfully resist such attempts, and nevertheless manage to complete their examination preparation without considerable problems; others find this more difficult, and do not know how to use the teachers in terms of their expertize, whilst warding off their attempts at personalization. The assessment of the need for social, personal learning interacts with the assessment of the students' ability, yet at the same time the teachers make a distinction between ability and capacity to achieve. Many teachers are aware of this dilemma; solutions are sought for vis-à-vis individual students.

Teacher Conceptions of Differentiation of the Student Body

Important areas of differentiation in the school are sex-gender and class; the students are predominantly white. I shall explore how teachers perceive links between structured inequalities and educational achievement. The second question deals with how teachers tackle issues related to structured inequalities. Race is now introduced, and teacher positions on racism are explored.

Social Class

The individualized progressive organization of Greenfield College stresses the worth of all students, encourages them to take charge of their futures and gives them considerable scope in self-determination and, therefore, social class is considered by the teachers as less significant in the school, though it is accepted that in general schools reinforce the class structure. Moreover, the relatively homogeneous position of students in the class structure is emphasized with little consideration of differentiations (chapter 5).

Teachers relate the significance of social class to the home background of students:

> *Julie:* It's obvious that the class background enables them to focus more clearly on objectives which will lead them to success and reward.

Or the focus shifts to parental attitudes, aspirations and motivations:

> *Susan:* I think there are obvious things that affect kids because of social class, and I think one of the big things is the influence of the parents, be that positive or negative, whatever class you come from, and I think there are middle class children who suffer terribly because of pressures from parents, which are counter to what they really want to do.

Parental attitudes are not necessarily considered class related:

> *Anna:* I feel that they can all do equally well if they have got the parental backing. It doesn't matter where they come from if they haven't got parental backing it makes it far more difficult for anybody to teach them, you know for them to learn anything.

Whilst the relationship between social class and achievement is noted by teachers, there is a significant trend to emphasize individual, personal and biographical aspects, and family constellations.

> *Julie:* I think the most critical factor actually is the psychological, emotional state of the family. Social class is a factor particularly with marginal kids. And it's a very important factor. But certainly the kids' school achievements are very much a reflection of their personalities and their parents' personalities.

Teacher emphasis on individual and family constellations in determining achievement is reinforced by the complexity of the specific features of the class structure in the local area. Teachers emphasize homogeneity and stress the middle class character of Greenfield, but focus mainly on one criterion: the relative affluence of the area. Teachers often refer to family homes 'with fitted carpets, colour television, and not a book in sight'; these are often families who have experienced upward mobility achieved through work rather than schooling. If children of such families underachieve in school, this is interpreted by teachers as an indication that social class is not particularly significant, as the one criterion that is related to is the affluence of the family. If children of such families are seen to have an instrumental orientation towards education, and if parents are concerned about school achievement, but lack the means by which to guide their children, they are easily interpreted as 'pushy', and the children's underachievement is related to the psychological pressure created. Teachers' conceptions about social class connect to their political perspectives, but also to their mode of working and organizing in an individualistic way.

The class structure is seen to assume reduced significance in Greenfield College by many teachers. Students who thrive in the school, academically and socially, are described by Jill:

> ... Well motivated students can do well here. I also think that very independent kids can do well here ... who would probably under-achieve in a more traditional school because of their repressive atmosphere and so kids who are very independent and perhaps who are also rebellious can do quite well here, 'cause there's ways of expressing themselves ... perhaps they don't do well academically, but they may do well socially in terms of being integrated people when they finish.

The organization and ethos of the school are seen to offer more scope for achievement by a wide range of students;

> *Edward:* ... if the student has an area of success within the school, and therefore a chance to gain status in the school's terms, they're less likely to be anti-school ... The job in the school is to broaden pro-school values until they are positive, until they include everybody who comes here and so in other words, stretching our range of activities that we can offer school approval to, until it includes everybody.

Though such concerns aim to address working class children as well, individualization in the school can, however, be argued to have specific affinity with middle class students. Bernstein (1975) argues that 'invisible pedagogy' (chapter 3) has specific links with the lifestyle and values of the 'new middle class'. Further, teachers acknowledge that schools impose a range of activities on working class students from the outside, whereas middle class students may have acquired these activities at home. But often the need for such activities is seen as externally determined, through the examination system (the need for writing for example) and it is felt that the internal organization of Greenfield cannot do much to counteract this.

There are contradictions in the aims of teachers in Greenfield. Because of the location of schools within structured inequalities mediated through examinations, the difficulties encountered by teachers in resolving the contradictions pose a necessity to rethink solutions anew for successive students. Given the individualized framework in the school, the characteristics of students which could be generalized with reference to their group memberships are seen as aspects of the personality of an individual. This is the level at which student characteristics manifest themselves to the teachers in their day-to-day work.

Sex-gender

When discussing sex-gender and its relation to educational achievement, again teachers tend to differentiate between schools in general and Greenfield in particular. Thus a great majority of them express concern about sexism in society, and sex stereotyping and differential treatment of boys and girls in schools, and men and women in the labour market. However, when discussing Greenfield College, the teachers' conceptions diverge: (i) some hold that girls and boys form two clearly differentiated groups within the school, and though they enter traditional jobs in terms of sex typification, the school itself has little influence on those patterns, and indeed makes attempts to break them down; however, it is faced with a difficult task, as the local culture is characterized by sexist values, and the students come to the school already conditioned to conform to the stereotypes; (ii) others emphasize sexism within the college, the practices of the teachers, the organizational features, and the lack of clear purpose and sufficient concern about the issue in order to prioritize it and tackle it through resolute attempts.

Whilst many teachers feel that sex-gender does not affect educational achievement as such, they think it is more significant in the channelling of efforts according to career choices, and in the social and emotional development, whereby girls are lacking sufficient aggression, confidence, and ability and willingness to question commonly-held assumptions and values, and boys are lacking a capacity to focus on their emotions and are locked in male-defined activities which give scope only to superficial self-expression. Their views on the role of the school differ. In terms of sex-typed subject choices, many teachers consider that there is little they can do, as they are committed to the self-direction of individual students, and are not prepared to impose on them; thus they could not, for example, order everyone to do at least one science subject. Whilst some teachers are particularly concerned about this, discuss the problem, and encourage girls to choose subjects other than the traditionally female ones, and try to support girls who face difficulties within subjects, the solutions have tended to be individualized. Feminist teachers feel that unless there are fundamental changes in the organization, practices and atmosphere of the school, it is impossible to tackle sexism in any real way. Julie remarks:

... girls do focus very much on the intimate social structure and school based on conversation doesn't actually do anything to divert them, though it may talk about the subject of sexism. But the very activity of talking about your feelings is actually repeating the process which marks off boys and girls. You know, I don't do anything about it at all.

Teachers who share this view find that tackling the problem is difficult as they themselves have been conditioned to act in certain ways. Particularly female teachers think that many male teachers are not prepared to accept and confront their own sexism; some form of positive discrimination, of prioritizing girls' needs, is considered necessary before any real changes can develop. In general the teachers feel that sexism is one of the issues that they wish to confront the students with. Phil remarks that the measure of their success is that most students are now familiar with the term sexism. However, on the basis of interviews and informal discussions it is evident that the teachers are not widely considered *anti*-sexist by the students. They do, however, consider the teachers anti-racist.

Race

The stand against racism adopted by the teachers in general has been sufficiently strong to communicate itself to the student body. Racism is an issue that teachers have wanted to discuss with students, whether they have initiated the consideration of the issues, or whether they have waited for it to emerge in student conversations. It is not only dealt with by team teachers within the confines of humanities; subject teachers do likewise.

Racism has, however, posed dilemmas for Greenfield College; it has not been easy to derive a way of dealing with it from the ethos and organizational principles of the school. This is particularly so when racism is linked to group-based collective activities. Teachers regularly confront racist remarks, talk to individual students, encourage projects to explore related issues etc. But such an individualized approach has not been very fruitful in handling the groups of lads engaged in incipient anti-school activities, who have actively and openly professed their following of the National Front.

When a group of lads distributed National Front leaflets in the school, a discussion which followed in a standing committee expressed dilemmas. It ranged from an emphasis on the need for a clear policy and resolute action to suggestions that tactically it would be best to ignore such incidents as the students would like the teachers to confront them; if NF was tackled, it would be important to be seen to be consistent, and therefore teachers should not, for example, put up Anti-Nazi League posters as some had done. Despite their anti-racist stance teachers are faced with difficulties to which they respond in different ways, when confronted with the necessity of dealing with racism outside the individualist, informal teacher-student interaction. Thus racism remains an ongoing problem as it is integral to the structures and culture in Britain, and as it is clearly reflected (if not reinforced) within the school.

Public Expenditure Cuts

Greenfield College exists within a context of restructuring with its increasing pressures. Most teachers emphasize the detrimental effects of the cuts; it has been more difficult to operate the curriculum because of the deteriorated staff-student ratios, increased student numbers, lack of properly maintained equipment, lack of technician help, of resources etc. However, some teachers also stressed that the cuts, though negative, had forced the teachers to take stock of the direction of the school, which they might not have done otherwise; consequently they had become more efficient. The ingenuity and flexibility in meeting the cuts was stressed by many; the school was still innovating, moving ahead, whilst some did point out that 'we are innovating on the cheap'.

I have argued that the restructuring process reaches schools mainly through the expenditure cuts (chapter 2). The changes have affected Greenfield College through the cuts, as well as through changes in examination policies,[16] and in legislation for parental choice of schools and publication of examination policies. Awareness of this process is evident in the college; teachers have been concerned not just to react to cuts, but to plan ahead, and to resist the effects through continued innovation. However, the atmosphere of the school has been affected, leading to demoralization of the staff, and strains in the informality, with friction between teachers and teachers and students, as noted in chapter 5. When less time is available for teachers to negotiate, persuade and insist, then authoritarian imposition is more readily resorted to.

Problems of resistance to cuts on the national level are evident. Teachers have participated in official NUT action, but many feel that this is not far-reaching enough, and not tackling the issues. How to deal with the cuts raised the dilemma of the relationship between the democratic structures and trade union action, in that the latter does not operate through consultation of the whole school and is seen to contradict the former, and in that the teachers are 'wearing two hats', on the one hand through the committees implementing the cuts, and on the other hand resisting them through the union.

Action also raised the dilemma of whether to adopt an isolationist position, safeguarding the aspects of the school valued by the staff; these would be jeopardized by taking action, particularly action whereby Greenfield College would be easily identifiable, and action would not be guaranteed to be successful. The question of survival (chapter 5) is important, 'I'd rather have this school than not', remarks Susan, who expresses the sentiment that it is preferable to attempt to accommodate the cuts rather than to engage in militant trade union action which, in the backlash it might elicit, could lead to the disappearance of the specific features of the College valued by teachers. However, another teacher expresses differing sentiments, 'we should forget seeing ourselves in that kind of precious way'.

Teacher Profiles

A student describes an ideal team teacher as an interesting superhuman able to hold conversations and capable of keeping students 'alive'. Many stressful aspects of the teacher's job in the school have emerged. S/he is in public view, and has to engage large parts of him/herself in developing relationships with students, and has to, in the course of his/her work, confront and solve many contradictory issues and problems: how to handle students, to encourage learning, balance all-round development and preparation for examinations, not to reify and objectify learning, not to legitimate the system by directing all students towards examinations despite the results they are likely to gain; how to assess the potential for achievement of students without labelling them and channelling them towards different positions in the labour market; how to reconcile the concern for individual autonomy with the concern for wider issues affecting all (such as sexism and racism), and how to encourage groupwork within the organizational framework of the school; how to satisfy parental expectations without compromising the principles of the school; how to balance the necessity to take action against the cuts with the necessity to safeguard the specificity of the school.

Given the range of problems the teachers have to tackle, their working conditions assume great significance. Many of the concerns within the committees can be interpreted as safeguarding and improving these working conditions. Finn *et al.* (1977) emphasize the importance of such occupational concerns in the development of progressivism, and argue that the educational thinking of teachers may not be as significant. In Greenfield teachers tend to argue for the importance of the democratic structures in terms of the removal of constraints that are normally expected in secondary schools; however they see a link between such occupational and educational concerns.

Thus the teachers do not make a distinction between their concerns for progressivism and democratic structures, and their educational thinking. They do, however, make a distinction between their educational thinking and their occupational concerns vis-à-vis trade union action. Though many emphasized that trade union action would, in the long run, benefit the students, they acknowledged that in the short term action could be against the interests of particular students. The child-centred teachers would thus argue against such action, whilst others may respond like Bill:

> people said hang on a bit, this may be democracy and all that, but I'm getting paid by County Hall and I'm getting pushed around by politicians and I'm a working person, I've got a family and all that.

> These kids are here for two years and we're trying, you know, to do
> certain kinds of experimental educational things with them, but in the
> end, I'm a working person and I want my working life sorted out, and
> I'm not going to leave it in their hands, 'cause they'll go off anyway.

Teacher trade unionism in Greenfield College is located within an interception
of occupational, educational and political thinking. The crisis of democracy,
the impasse, and differentiations in perceiving it are also located at such an
interception where several issues merge. The internal structuring of the
teaching staff has occupational implications; the concern about 'good practice'
and different ways of perceiving it raise educational questions; and the debate
on democratic organization — participation versus representation and consultation — have political implications.

The background of the teachers is predominantly middle class, though a
considerable proportion also come from working class families. Of those
interviewed, many had experienced social mobility, or their parents had
experienced social mobility. Few of those who, by their origins, were middle
class emphasized the liberalism in their background.[17] Several teachers experienced frustrations within their own schooling, and described themselves as
rebellious and critical in their school careers. Many are of the age whereby they
have experienced and been affected by the 1960s 'counter-cultures'.[18] Such
counter-cultures were characterized by critical analyses of the social structures,
but rather than postulating political action, they tended to emphasize the
creation of 'alternative' lifestyles and change from within at the level of the
individual. Other teachers, however, had been more influenced by radical
student politics. A majority of teachers share political positions to the left of
centre, scanning the spectrum from Fabianism to 'ultra left'. Only a small
minority are non-graduates; the rest have not undergone the lengthy process
of teacher training, during which students are more likely to assume a teacher
identity. Thus the general background of the teaching body contains a number
of features which have affinity with teaching in an innovative, progressive
school concerned to breakdown hierarchies and to rethink the processes of
thinking and learning.

Many teachers were attracted to the school because of a sense of scope and
possibilities, hitherto unknown within the state system.[19]

> *Sarah:* First ... I thought it was ... very exciting, it was trying to
> reform a lot of the worst aspects of schools ... I just thought it was
> absolutely marvellous ... I hadn't really thought about education as
> critically as I have since and ... I was much more sympathetic to a
> liberal point of view ... I used to think it was a marvellous,
> progressive move, and now I just think it's a nice reform.

Julie expresses a similar sense of scope that attracted teachers to Greenfield in
the early years, and a shift in viewing that scope; she no longer considers the
school 'a bastion of a whole new way of education; all it stands for now is

variety in education'. Janet expresses the same sense of limitations in terms of the wider aims of the school, and juxtaposes that with a sense of Greenfield having achieved something that in general schools within the state system have not done: 'I don't think we can change the class nature of society through schools like this . . . But I do think we make schools a more pleasant place'.

How do the teachers in such a school view their own futures? There is a certain degree of despondency in teacher conceptions. Many wish to stay on in the school, but fear the impact of the changing situation within it, through the pressure of expenditure cuts, of legislation concerning the publication of examination results and parental choice of schools, and through the changes within the staff (many teachers have been leaving, and the number of new teachers has significantly increased because of the increased roll as well as replacement), and because of an executive with a largely new personnel. Others feel ready to leave in the near future, having gained as much as they wish to or feel they are able to. However, the choices are not simple, and are linked to notions of professionalism even where teachers do not have 'career-ist' motivations. The teaching force is organized hierarchically, with inbuilt assumptions about movement from job to job along a career ladder. Even the emphasis on 'personal development', implying cumulative change and building on one's experiences is easily identifiable in professional terms. Those who have no wish to pursue a professionally constructed career have few clearly defined alternatives available.

Strands of Progressivism

Despite the overall cohesiveness of Greenfield teachers — they do not scan the whole political spectrum, and have shared perceptions about the school vis-à-vis constricting external influences — there are a variety of positions within the school. These have an impact on teachers' analyses of the school system, and the role of Greenfield and its teachers, and on the teachers' practices. There are descriptive surface divisions in the school (chapter 5); the day-to-day operation of the school is structured along such divisions in that informal networks and channels of communication are delineated by them. They are also influential in the decisions that are made about important issues such as staffing and resources.

Such an ordering of reality was powerful for me as a researcher as well; it seemed that a progressive school contains institutional realities and ethos which cut across any classification and analysis in terms of the strands identified in chapter 3 as distinct frameworks used to analyze and explain schooling as informing practices. However, through observation in meetings over a period of four years it was possible to begin to build a picture of divisions in terms of people involved and arguments put forward, crystallized in voting patterns.

The Liberals

These include teachers who emphasize child-centred, individualized learning, within face-to-face relationships. They have developed theories of learning, stressing personalization, meaningful learning, often realized through creative writing. The school is greatly valued — the curriculum, democracy, relationships and atmosphere. Because the positive achievements of the school are considered important, these teachers are reluctant to engage in militant action within the trade union, and are particularly concerned about the survival of the school, and prepared to adopt an isolationist position.

The Radicals

These include committed trade unionists and Marxists, emphasizing the significance of wider social structures the school is located in, thus engaging in generalized discussion not linked to particular features of Greenfield College. They emphasize the importance of solidarity between trade unionists, and consider it important to take risks over national issues in militant action. They draw attention to the limitations of the democratic structures in Greenfield, and its reformist nature. In the field of curriculum they are interested in group work and the introduction of issues considered important. They value the informal relationships within the school, but are concerned about the concealment of institutional roles.

The Libertarians

These include teachers who are child-centred like the liberals, emphasizing individualization. They are particularly concerned to avoid authoritarianism, and wish to respect the 'space' surrounding students. They stress the importance of student participation. Within curriculum they are prepared to introduce areas of study, through persuasion rather than imposition; they value group work, but hope that it evolves from student interaction. They note the limitations of the democratic structures, but nevertheless emphasize its significance in offering scope in day-to-day existence of teachers. They are likely to advocate trade union action and participate in it but they are influenced by the worries of the liberals about the vulnerability of the school.

The Pragmatists

These teachers cut across the above categories. Politically they have not got a shared framework; they may be liberals near the centre, or further left, encompassing those who have analyzed schooling with emphasis on the limitations and the small range of achievements possible given the role occupied by schools in a hierarchical society. They are the 'plodders' (chapter 5) who emphasize occupational and professional thinking notions of efficiency, realism and effectiveness. They see their work primarily as teachers rather than educationalists, as a job rather than a mission. How this job is perceived is dictated by an often astute analysis of the balance of power within the school and local politics. These teachers may engage in trade union action and may actively advocate it, but they are concerned that action should be effective. They are likely to be frustrated with democracy — its time-consuming repetitive inefficiency rather than its limited scope. Student and parent expectations are stressed, and questions about possibilities in divergence from values of the local community are raised.

In decisions relating to wider policies affecting the whole school in the long term, these strands are important. The main cleavage exists between liberals and radicals; the libertarians and pragmatists may shift on the basis of issues or the way in which they perceive the relationships between schools and wider social structures. Meetings in the school do not operate on the basis of divisions delineated by these strands; however, crucial policy issues affecting the fundamental structures and organization within the school, and important trade union issues force the cleavages to the surface.[20] It is widely believed by teachers in Greenfield that they have a tendency to 'polarize issues'. This refers to the fragmented nature of the school, and to an awareness that underneath the unity of the staff there are important differences and that the general ethos of the school contains contradictions which are glossed over, and to which the teachers have no jointly considered way of relating.

Practical decisions, which in the day-to-day existence of the teachers can be equally significant as wider policy issues, follow surface divisions, informal channels and networks; however, these surface divisions (chapter 5) tend to reflect the existence of different strands thus for example the 'plodders' tend to be pragmatists or liberals; the 'inspirationalists' tend to be radicals and libertarians.[21] Though no single teacher could be exclusively placed within one category, profiles with characteristics of one category dominating can be formulated. Teachers can shift over time. Thus libertarians may have become radicals, when their sense of scope for individualization has been eroded over the years. The radicals may have become pragmatists, when they have developed what is considered a more realistic analysis of the role of schooling.

Conclusion

In this chapter the focus has been on the teachers and their approach to significant issues within the school; the overall aim has been to explore how they view the possibilities and limitations within progressivism, and different ways of relating to these. The aim has also been to pinpoint the contradictions and tensions that exist in Greenfield College, and different ways of relating to these, and different solutions posed. When such differentiation is explored, it is possible to identify the existence of different strands in teacher thinking, having impact on their practices. Such a discussion links to the first part of the study. In chapter 3 I noted that the term progressivism covered a wide range of practices and ideologies; in order to analyze the changing status of progressivism within schools in Britain, and official educational thinking, it is necessary to try to disentangle the various aspects. This led to a postulation of the existence of different strands; the critique of progressivism has tended to focus on these unevenly. Thus criticisms from the left have identified liberal features of progressivism and have analyzed these in terms of flexible accommodation to the changing requirements within schools. Criticisms from the right have focused on radical and libertarian progressivism, particularly on what has been interpreted as lack of discipline and prevalence of Marxist teachers.

During the seventies and the eighties within the wider society (economic structures, social relations) a process of restructuring has been ongoing, and in chapter 2 I suggested that this process ought to be analyzed in conjunction with resistance to it. Developments within education during the same period have contained trends towards centralization and standardization. Such trends are linked to the general restructuring processes, but also, specifically, deal with features of the education system — the degree of autonomy of schools and teachers, containing spaces for work on the basis of an oppositional stance. Practical indices of the spaces were increasing teacher militancy and pupil resistance and rebellion. I argued that whilst restructuring was directed particularly towards the spaces within which such resistance (or its potential) was located, it affected both liberal (hitherto acceptable) and radical and libertarian (unacceptable) progressivism.

The changes within Greenfield College have indicated the difficulties of all progressivism; the continued pressures are eroding the basis of liberalism as well as libertarianism. The teachers are shifting towards pragmatism and radicalism.[22] Radicalism continues to be significant as a critique of schooling and the position of teachers and students within it, whilst ways in which it informs practice have become delimited. I have also emphasized that restructuring is not a straightforward, uncontested process. Though Greenfield College has responded to increased pressure mediated through cuts by demoralization, increasing concern for examinations and search for diffusion of criticisms of the school, it has also attempted to continue innovation and has tried to be flexible in its approach to the cuts. Such processes are still ongoing. It is possible to predict that the school will become increasingly conventional, and indeed out of the present crisis a more streamlined Greenfield College will emerge, but the maintenance of democratic structures, innovative curriculum features and informal relationships in the school throughout the seventies and up to the early eighties is in itself a powerful index of spaces. But limitations have been demonstrated as well; the school came into existence through a double paradox: the progressive policies of a Conservative local authority and the radical and libertarian progressivism in a school designed to demonstrate the culmination of liberal progressivism at the secondary stage. I shall focus on the students next, in order to clarify the organization and ethos of the school, and practices within it, focussing on the tensions and contradictions these entail.

Notes

1 This debate was sparked off when the examination board rejected the Mode III 'O' level syllabus when it was resubmitted for a review; this reflects a general trend against mode IIIs.
2 The individualized approach is so strong, that the concern tends to be for individuals in collectives.
3 Research in Leicestershire indicates that many employers do not give overriding emphasis to qualifications — for example KEIL (1976) and ASHTON and MAGUIRE (1980).
4 For example Jill discusses a student:

> I got one boy ... who's doing food and nutrition, an 'O' level, and really isn't capable of it at all, and I tried to talk him out of it, and ... the cookery teacher tried to talk him out of it as well ... but he's insisting on doing it and I — we can't stop him. I'm not prepared to say 'you will not do this exam', because he so desperately wants to do it, then he has to do it, and he has to accept failure if that's what happens. It may be part of his own education and he learns his own limitations.

5 In the team that I studied, out of 149 students only twelve took no examinations at all.
6 Such negotiations are discussed in chapters 8 and 10.
7 This is a generalization — varying degrees of cooperation between members of staff do take place.
8 This aspect of the school was experienced in the course of research, and contributed to the development of methods adopted.
9 One such marginalized teacher was ousted out of an Allowances Committee — according to her account she put her name forward at a meeting, when one more member for the Committee was required. However, she was not informed of the meetings, and was unable to participate, despite her attempts to do so.
10 Three members of staff participated, one of whom taught only part-time, and one of whom could be considered 'marginalized'.
11 For example David who refers to a student who has come from a rather traditional feeder school, and who is attempting to introduce patterns of disruptive behaviour learned in that school to Greenfield. The teacher acknowledges the sets of expectations of the student, but does not act according to the teacher role as defined by the student. David discusses this with the student, and offers an account of what is happening, but essentially does not adopt an authoritarian approach, outlining to the student an alternative set of behaviour and expectations, but wants the student to develop these himself.
12 This term is adopted from CORRIGAN (1979).

13 For example CRITHER, C. (1977) 'Structures, cultures and biographies' in HALL and JEFFERSON.

14 Thus in this context conceptions in terms of working class/middle class are not considered very illuminating — a more detailed picture, incorporating features such as self-employment, upward social mobility, the employment of mother as well as father, would be useful.

15 This is further discussed in chapter 7.

16 The number of Mode III examinations has decreased; during the research period the Mode III 'O' level in social studies was not accepted by the examination board when it was submitted for a review.

17 A couple had attended progressive schools.

18 *C.f.* CLARKE *et. al.* in HALL and JEFFERSON (1977).

19 For most of them, because of their left of centre politics and/or working class background etc. it was the existence of the school within the state system which was crucial.

20 When this occurs, meetings can be very acrimonious, with bitter comments and accusations.

21 The divisions are also reflected in notions of 'good' and 'bad' teaching — significant in the allowances debate about rewarding merit — whilst some common agreement does exist vis-à-vis the marginalized teachers, and vis-à-vis a few experienced, extrovert teachers wellknown throughout the school, overall, different groups of teachers have different notions of good/bad teaching, and include different people in each of the lists (chapter 9).

22 The shifts could be observed during the research period, or could be discerned from teachers' own comments about their views and practices in the past, or from the comments of others, as well as from written records such as minutes of meetings, internal papers etc.

Chapter 7

The Students

The focus here is on the experiences and perceptions of students[1] in Greenfield College. The criticisms directed at progressive education from the political left and the right lead us to ask whether students in a progressive school are propagandizing rebels or privatized ritualists; anarchical and undisciplined or subtly controlled; are there possibilities for radical learning and what are the limitations restricting these? The categories of curriculum, democracy, relationships and perceptions of social differentiation are utilized to continue the narrative developed in chapters 5 and 6.

Curriculum

The focus is mainly on teams, because these are a central structure in the school, within which the educational ideology and practices are forged; the teacher conceptions of autonomous learning have been developed in teams in particular. The subjects covered in a team — or the exams prepared for in a team — form an unofficial core curriculum within the school, encompassing all students.

Subject choices are negotiated between tutors and students (parental influence is significant) at the beginning of the fourth year. Whilst there is an aim to balance practical and academic subjects, and have all options open to all students regardless of sex and ability, all individual timetables are in theory 'tailor-made' according to the interests of specific students. The notion of autonomy, and the individualized interaction between teachers and students mean that in practice teachers attempt to influence student choices, but not impose on them subjects against their inclinations. The result is sexual differentiation, but also a kind of informal streaming. With increased roll and decreased staff-student ratio the flexibility of choices has narrowed, and determined students with determined tutors are more likely to fulfil their wishes with regard to demand subjects. Such patterns emerge from the school ethos and practices, and cannot be dealt with unless the individual negotiations exist within a framework of conceptions of desired directions with strategies for implementation.

Project Work in Social Studies

Individualized learning is developed in project work, which facilitates the construction of a close relationship between teachers and students, within which self-direction is aimed for. Social studies is focussed on to consider issues of student choice, teacher guidance, and possibilities for radical teaching and learning. Students choose project topics on the basis of their interests, but teacher suggestions also play an important role, and the 'profile' of the range of projects undertaken by different tutor groups varies.[2] But student self-determination is important; Kevin emphasizes that he makes his own choices and does not 'let the teachers influence me in any way'. Many teachers feel that the process of work is more important than its content. Thus, choices can be relatively random and the emphasis on student interests led to any topic being acceptable particularly when the students entered the school.[3]

The crystallization of the child-centred ethos is found in biographical and autobiographical work which encourages the students to explore themselves and their relationships to others — this is linked to interest in student 'feelings' (chapter 6). Feminist teachers encourage a focus on women, and attempt to transform descriptive projects on pregnancy, abortion etc. into an exploration of social processes. Radical teachers are interested in issues such as racism, politics, nuclear power etc. But many students do not take up teacher suggestions, and radical teachers are concerned that unstructured, individualized Social Studies work does not raise questions about political and economic structures. The process of work includes discussion between tutors and students, some discussion among students and, where possible visitors or teachers from outside the team able to discuss the issues are introduced to students. An interesting feature of the work process is a 'plan'. Students who find it difficult to structure their work are encouraged to explore issues of interest, and it is hoped that structure will emerge as they get immersed in the study. Often, however, a plan is constructed; through these a routinization of negotiated learning took place. The teacher is active in their construction, and though there was consultation, the plans were often written by teachers, and followed by students passively.[4]

Personalization

The students are encouraged to adopt different approaches, and boundaries between subjects are not prominently evoked. Such integration is typical of progressive schools. But the hallmark of Greenfield is the personalization of work; this is seen as positive by radical, liberal and libertarian teachers. Such personalization is related to the educational and political thinking of teachers, but also serves important functions in the school;

    (i)   it is the avenue through which a link between informal relationships and atmosphere and the work undertaken is forged;

    (ii)   it is the process through which the 'democratic milieu' is constructed (the students feel that their opinions matter, and that they as individuals matter);

    (iii)   it is the device through which the students are motivated, and through which their active involvement in their school career is sought.

Thus, overall, the ethos of Greenfield College is transmitted to the students through personalization; the discussion of this process is continued in chapter 8.

Illustrations

I shall recount observations on the process of learning as integrated, negotiated and personalized. The focus is provided by a consideration of possibilities and limitations for radical development.

Thomas

Thomas was impressed by a series of television programmes, *Holocaust*, and wrote a lengthy review of them. This led to work on discrimination, Israel, the Middle East conflict, and, finally, Cyprus (his father is of Cypriot origin) and the role of the CIA. He was actively involved in the direction of his work. He lacked materials, though, and was frustrated when unable to pursue his questions. His main resources were conversations with his father, his tutor and the researcher. His progress illustrates the flexible approach in Greenfield, in that he was able to pursue such directions, and link successive pieces of work in a way which he perceived as meaningful. At the same time a general interest in international politics was generated. Limitations were indicated as well, however. It is difficult to resource the work of individual students thoroughly — the more students undertake unresourced projects, the greater the pressures on the teachers. Personalization can at such times be a response to the lack of resources, or at any rate a partial solution to it. Thus Thomas was encouraged to construct a picture of the culture of Cyprus through his own research relating to his relatives.

Janice

The example of Janice and her project on the police illustrates a way in which the students use the notion of self-direction, if not always articulately, in order to resist some of the demands of schooling, or in order to handle them without a great deal of personal investment. Janice was doing a project on the police, and the resources used consisted of one book. She partly copied and partly paraphrased sections of the book, under the chapter headings. Her folder consisted of a random, unorganized collection of pieces of paper. I attempted to discuss her work, and asked what specifically she was interested in, aiming to consider her views both on the police itself, and on the work she was doing, and the meaning she vested in it. She was unwilling to be drawn into such a discussion, and her repeated answer was 'I'm just doing it on the police'. Though I knew Janice, and had discussed her work with her before, for example a project on reggae that she had been quite involved and interested in, at this point she grew increasingly irritated at the prospect of being asked to reflect on what she was doing. Janice, in a sense, was self-directing. She had no specific questions that interested her *vis-à-vis* the police. She had chosen a topic and was now doing the work, without any wish to get involved. She resisted every effort to read any particular meaning into her work. She was 'just doing it on the police', as something had to be done, and doing something without a big fuss meant, as far as she was concerned, that she ought to be left alone, and get on with what she was doing. Intrusions were seen as troublesome, and resisted through 'doing work'. Janice was using the notion of self-direction to try to avoid the imposition of schooling, however altruistic the teacher motivation.

Gwen

Gwen was working on a comprehension sheet from a past English examination — this activity was popular because students considered it 'proper' work and not much involvement was required. The sheet dealt with a kibbutz, and assumed some background knowledge which Gwen did not have. She asked for help and responded to information I gave her by further questions about the state of Israel, Nazi Germany, organizational aspects of kibbutzim such as childcare practices etc. She was interested in doing a project on these issues.

Her tutor Trevor was interested but doubtful because of the wide range of questions. He was aware of Gwen's lack of confidence and considered it related to gender-specific socialization. Gwen asked whether such a project was for 'brainy' people, or could she do it. She did embark on the project and acquired materials. Trevor gave her written questions to answer, which concentrated on the perceptions and feelings of a kibbutz inhabitant rather than on organization and underlying principles. Trevor regretted Gwen's impossible task of finding out 'all about the Jews', and gradually the project was dropped.

Gwen then worked on costume and dress; Trevor explained:

> that raised a lot of important questions and started from something
> in which she was herself very interested in — that preoccupation

with dress that that sort of girl has got, and actually worked that through to something which was really perceptive and I think that was valuable.

But Trevor also noted that the chances of Gwen expressing views on political issues was 'very remote; she would have decided that was something for clever people'. But by not encouraging Gwen's earlier project Trevor reinforced, without intending to, Gwen's feelings that politics is not for somebody like her. Whilst claiming not to be interested in politics Gwen, in the course of informal discussions and interviews did express political opinions, but also emphasized her lack of confidence; for example she thought the democratic structures in Greenfield were important, but did not wish to participate. Her project on dress may have encouraged her to consider important preoccupations, but her gender-specific socialization was not challenged, and personal concerns were focussed on and underlined in a way that did not encourage links with broader social political questions that Gwen did have some opinions on, but which she did not consider her proper concern.

Kevin

Kevin had thought there was unemployment because of the number of coloured immigrants arriving in Britain. He did a project on racism and immigration, found out facts and figures, and explored the political questions with the help of teachers. When discussing the project with me, he emphasized that he had changed his mind as a result of the work, and had discovered that his earlier opinions were prejudiced and misguided. He was, thus, able to explore political questions that were significant to him. This had a personal impact, in that Kevin readjusted his views.

Celia

Celia, together with another girl, became a vegetarian during her stay in Greenfield College, and attributes this to the influence of the school, and a couple of teachers. The issues were discussed with her, and during a lunch break a teacher cooked a vegetarian lunch with the girls in the home economics area. Celia's vegetarianism was not just linked to dietary questions, but to a total outlook which included an interest in the Ecology Party, opposition to nuclear power, interest in alternative energy, a concern for the underdeveloped countries, and criticism of technological development.

Student views

Students generally appreciated the chance to pursue their own interests. They often remarked how the work they did would not have been possible in their previous schools. Relationships were considered important, and students appreciated the informality of the school. But there were, of course, differentiations. First, some students considered there to be a link between the atmosphere and work, between teaching and learning:

> *Mary:* I do want to work and I actually enjoy working. I feel closer to the teacher and feel open to talk to them about private problems. I think . . . you are treated as one of the teachers and not as a little school child. (questionnaire)

Second, there were students who valued relaxed relationships, but wanted to be 'made to work' and disagreed with teachers who argued that this attitude to learning would preclude the informality:

> Teachers should push you to work, and actually teach you something, not just let you sit down and get on with it. (questionnaire)

Third, students emphasized the need for learning in a broad sense, and made a specific equation between style of learning and style of interrelating:

> Out of this school, I get confidence to face the world outside. It brings you up as adults, and teaches you besides work, to know what is going on in the world and not just like a computer who can tell you everything, but does not know how to act. (questionnaire)

Fourth, students adopt an instrumental attitude towards their learning and relate their choices to what they perceive as necessary in terms of examinations, and expect the teachers to help them in this process.

> *Alan:* 'I would never do anything like the murals on the walls of the team area. I can't see the point. I wouldn't get anything out of it. They don't get you marks in exams, and THAT'S what you're at school for.' (questionnaire)

Differences in student views on curriculum and pedagogy are related to various aspects, such as their attitudes to education and schooling, their world-view, and the ease or difficulty with which they negotiate their careers. These questions are further explored in chapter 8.

Creative Writing

Creative writing is considered, by the English-trained child-centred teachers, to form the backbone of learning in Greenfield. Educationally it is linked to theories of learning which emphasize the motivation and involvement of the learner, in order for the learning to transform him/her through personal impact. Politically it is linked to thinking emphasizing the importance of the individual, stressing the need to develop the ability of students to take control of their own lives and futures.

This approach was illustrated by a teacher who discussed the progress of Alan, whose thinking was characterized by contradictions; for example he emphasizes the importance of involvement in the democratic structures in the school and in broader political processes, but also indicates his own disinclination to participate (p. 121). His tutor believes that Alan will resolve these contradictions. Creative writing has been used to encourage Alan's growing social awareness. The tutor explains:

> Alan's had undigested and generally blinkered views about people who are poor. They began to come out in a way he described an old lady who was visited by a paper boy in his rounds ... and the conflicts in his mind and anxiety about people less well off than himself or older or in some sense less privileged. At the same time his sympathetic curiosity — they were both there in this piece of writing. I applauded it and encouraged and reinforced that and from then on most of his pieces of writing began to explore that kind of situation with a drug taker, a recluse, obsessive — and each piece of writing got better and better and in each he would draw a map between himself and other people.

A deliberate decision was made not to use social studies in developing Alan's thinking, that is, to consider more directly social issues, institutions and processes; such an approach is seen to give more scope to stereotypical, detached responses determined by student expectations of 'proper learning', formulated during their school career. The teacher continues:

> What I haven't done with somebody like Alan is to use social studies ... getting him to talk for example about the police or the law or whatever — he wouldn't have been able, I don't think, to talk about that in a detached way because of the conflicts there within him, he would have been too reluctant to get involved in talking in a committed way, because he's frightened of being committed. Now that would have been counter-productive.

The comments of this child-centred teacher manifest the scope for development of strategies for each individual student, based on teacher perceptions of him/her, in the context of a close working relationship, and attempts to avoid routinization of learning. Examinations, however, pose problems for such attempts; such problems have been noted by teachers (chapter 6); here I shall consider student perceptions.

Examinations

In general, students view examinations as necessary and/or positive, and most students do take examinations. There is concern for personal preparation and not much criticism of the examination system. Within the ethos of self-direction, and approaches developed by teachers to facilitate this, students often approach their work on the basis of assumed expectations contained in examinations. Many students consider examinations an important backbone to Greenfield, introducing clear objectives in a flexible situation, and providing the students with motivation — Marilyn:

> especially in a school like this, if you didn't have any exams, there wouldn't be any learning going on, because it's so ... casual round here that exams are the aim that people need to get things done and to learn things.

Marilyn holds this view even though she thinks that the pressure of examinations 'ruins your learning'.

The student prioritization of examinations leads to expectations towards assessment practices of teachers. Assessment, teachers feel, needs to take into account individual differences, and needs to provide encouragement and incentive for students. But at the same time teachers argue that the assessment of students vis-à-vis requirements of examinations is relatively easy, proceeding according to specific criteria acquired through professional practice. These assessments are not fed back to the student in a straightforward way. The students sense this, and ask questions about their work vis-à-vis GCE/CSE standards. Joyce criticizes teachers for 'buttering up' students. She gained her insights through a determination to succeed academically, and through the sense of struggle she experienced as a working class girl in the course of such career construction.

> I'd like to be criticized, told where I'm going wrong, and not just buttered up saying that's all right ... I think I gain from criticism — it doesn't put me off, it makes me work harder ... I don't think a lot of people realize (that they are buttered up). I think they believe the teachers are telling them the truth and ... when they take the exams (realize) that they've not been telling the truth. (It is) easy teaching not to criticize.[5]

Students who do not consider examinations important have secured jobs already, have no aspirations for jobs requiring examinations, or reject the common equation between certification and location in the labour market. Though generally students believe in this equation, there is an increasing awareness that it is not an automatic one, as recession has gradually been spreading to the area. Ralph did not take any examinations, and doubts their value: 'don't matter whether they take exams or not, still they can't get a very good job cause all the good jobs are going quick like, you know, cause there ain't many good jobs left'. Pete expressed rare awareness of the role of qualifications in different levels of the labour market:

> Interviewers ... like to see people who got good character and you know they got ambition, that sort of thing. And some people don't

even want exams, cause they might have too much ambition to get too far, and they probably can't offer them much.

Though examinations are considered important and an equation hard work = good qualifications = good job is believed in, a minority of students, often working class boys, question this equation and note the deterioration of the local labour market. For other students this observation leads to an increased emphasis on examinations as the crucial determination of the shape of their own careers.

Democracy

Though formally students are fully-fledged members of the democratic processes, their participation is not structured and they do not assume an active role (chapter 5 and 6). The crisis of democracy has not impinged on them a great deal. Here I shall consider the extent of student participation, the degree to which they are informed about the democratic structures, and their views on participation.

In a questionnaire returned by eighty-four students[6] twenty-six students had attended moots. Half the students knew reasonably clearly what a moot was; the rest had some understanding, except thirteen who did not know what a moot was. Only one-eighth knew want a standing committee was.[7] Nearly two-thirds, however, thought that student participation was a good idea, and many assumed that though they did not attend moots, other students did.

Student views on democracy are differentiated, though the majority is of the opinion that participation is important: 'we have to be taught here so why shouldn't we participate in making decisions about the running of the school' (questionnaire). Second, some students think that participation should be limited:

> Usually the decisions concern us, so I think we should have some say in them. However, I don't think students should have too much influence in these matters, because there is always the chance that they will make a decision just to please themselves, one that is obviously not practical. I think the teachers should always be there to suggest and help us. (questionnaire)

Third, students are of the opinion that, indeed, it is limited: 'the sorts of decisions we are allowed to make are for things like the minibus, the team-areas, nothing really serious' (questionnaire). Fourth, a few students think that teachers ought to make the decisions, students should merely be consulted: 'I think it's far too young to start making important decisions but they could certainly put views forward; then the teachers can go from that'.

Students consider participation important — why do they not attend moots more often? Some students refer to the characteristics of the structures and processes. They note the lack of sufficient information and the way in which formal procedures confuse and mystify. Large meetings with complicated procedures are intimidating. The teachers communicate in a forceful, articulate, often intellectual manner;[8] the academic language they use is directed at other teachers, and the students who attend have to try to 'catch on'. Because decisions which have not been reached through compromise and consensus should not be enforced, it is felt that many moots do not achieve anything, and decisions are not made.[9]

Secondly, they refer to characteristics of students — their apathy and lack of interest is referred to rather than structural and procedural aspects of democracy:

> *Stuart:* a lot of kids in this school — they're oblivious to it, they aren't bothered. I mean it's a great chance for them to decide for themselves what's going on, you know, who's gonna do what and what's gonna go where, but they just don't do it. I think they're too free, they've got too much freedom, and they just don't wanna know.

Student apathy is related to a lack of identification with the school, a lack of positive commitment to it, and a sense of detachment.

Personal orientations of students towards democracy are now considered. Descriptive categories are formulated to encompass student responses. First a small group, the enthusiasts, have been active in democratic processes, consider them important and feel that with confidence and determination it is possible to influence the proceedings. Second, the cynics have been interested in participation, have attended moots, but have become disillusioned: 'I haven't made any decisions for the school. I've stuck my hand in the air at a moot. But I don't think that's really making a decision' (questionnaire). Third, the uninterested feel that the issues do not involve them, and do not affect their career in the school: 'I have never attended moots because they bore me to death and I'd feel like those idiots in Parliament' (questionnaire). Fourth, the alienated are distanced from the school overall, and feel detached about processes there: 'I'm not bothered about what goes on here'. Fifth, the instrumentalists emphasize the pragmatic approach they have to schooling. They wish to study for examinations which are perceived to have specific links with the entry to the labour market, and do not want to be diverted of such endeavour.

> I don't bother with moots. I say leave the running of the school to the teachers and County Hall, I just get on with it. School is a school whatever it's like, you can usually get as much out of it as *you* want to, however it's run. (questionnaire)

Another student, Alan, notes that he is in the school to be 'educated', and leaves the running of it to others. He adds: 'I know this is wrong.' In the interview he is asked to elaborate.

> *Alan:*   I'm here to learn, pass exams and get out.
> *Interviewer:*   So why is it wrong?
> *Alan:*   Well the whole idea — everything's sort of set up for us, to make life easy for us, but all that really bothers me is getting me work done, passing exams and going to work.
> *Interviewer:*   Why do you think that is wrong?
> *Alan:*   . . . I suppose I'm not the sort of person that's supposed to fit in. I don't suppose a lot of the people are either. The idea is that the kids who come here, you know, take part in everything; go to moots, want to join in, but I don't. I just come here to learn for the exams.

Thus a sixth group, the passives, expresses support for the democratic principles, affirms their importance, but stresses their disinclination to get involved.

Such students do not perceive the democratic structures in terms of genuine participation and decision-making related to important aspects in their school careers. Participation is not seen to exist at the grassroots level. The formal structures seem distant and strange; students perceive their own situation in terms of powerlessness (see below). They share a sense of lack of control, and of limiting societal structures which ordinary people cannot influence. Therefore it is seen as meaningful to try to develop one's own situation, to be the maker of one's fate where one can. Further, students note the possibility of active engagement in political issues in the future; they have a sense of occupying a space between childhood restrictions and adult responsibilities, and want to make the most of this period.

Many teachers in the school emphasize the informal structures — the actual participation of the students in formal democracy is not as important as an atmosphere where the students feel that they are consulted, and make decisions about their own career in the school, and direct their own work. Most teachers feel that Greenfield is relatively successful in providing such an atmosphere. Not all students share this view:

> I don't really make any decisions about my life at school. I just think about what I'm going to do in team that day and that I'm going to work. (questionnaire)

> I don't make any decisions about my school life. I just take it as it comes. (questionnaire)

Thus whilst students emphasize that the decision of whether to work or not is theirs, that they choose their own work, and that teachers are interested in them and their opinions, they do feel that they exist within predetermined structures — Pete: 'It's not really freedom is it — you still got subjects to do, just that you got more choice with your timetable'. Students who do emphasize the importance of informal democracy feel that they make decisions about work — George: 'if you wanna work you work, if you don't wanna work you don't work, so it's your own fault if you get nowhere'. Indeed many students feel that they are not 'pushed' enough, and that there is a looseness in the patterns at the school: 'you can do more or less anything you like'. Second, students emphasize that they are treated as responsible individuals who have views and opinions:

> I think this school makes you independent and more mature. You are treated older which at first you ignore. Then it begins to make an impression on you. I think that it prepares you for when you go to work. (questionnaire)

The democratic structures in Greenfield are connected to the social relationships in the school, within which the students are given scope to explore. The formal democracy is characterized by problems and limitations, but it did provide a framework, the existence of which was significant; in chapter 5 incidents where students have used democratic structures were noted and chapter 12 develops the discussion of student involvement.

After the suspension of formal democracy in 1985 the participation of students has not been a significant issue; the teachers became increasingly concerned to resist the new structures proposed, or at any rate 'to defend their corners'. The executive proposals did not integrate students except peripherally and superficially: 'there could be more prominent student-staff groups like the Entertainments and School Fund Committees'.[10] The scenario offered is very different from that of a possibility of participation.

Relationships

How the ethos on staff-student relations has evolved in Greenfield over time was discussed in chapter 5. In chapter 6 I focussed on teacher perceptions. Here I shall consider student views and convey observations about relationships in the school. Student attitudes towards teachers and the implications of their views on first name terms are considered, and the discussion is developed by noting student views on teachers vis-à-vis other adults. The questions of ambiguities in interpretation of relationships and interaction are raised, noting the significance of control by teachers and dependence by students.

Teachers

Descriptions of teachers are, in the main, favourable. Their friendliness is emphasized: 'the teachers are some of the best friends I have' (questionnaire).

The teachers are seen to respect students; they 'seem to know you have a mind of your own' (questionnaire). Many students can identify with them: 'same sort of people as us'. They are seen as non-authoritarian: 'they are not always laying the law down and shouting out rules' (questionnaire). Such conceptions of teachers were seen to be of consequence to the communication and interaction between teachers and students: 'you can speak what you feel instead of being clamped inside and scared stiff of the person you're talking to'. (questionnaire) But students also had ambivalent feelings. They were critical of teachers who inspired little respect, were moody, untidy and lazy.

First Names

A symbol of the relationships between teachers and students in the school, and their informality, is the practice of students calling their teachers by their first names. Only a handful of students were critical of this custom. A few had been doubtful about it, but had changed their minds — thus a considerable majority of the students like the practice, and emphasize the implications it has for relationships.

> ... you can get to know them as a person and not as a teacher. (questionnaire)

> ... it is more friendly and the kids feel more equal to the teachers and not some inferior being from another planet which is how most schools treat kids. (questionnaire)

> ... it brings them down to our level and we see them as people and not as hermits. It also lessens the respect, though. (questionnaire)

Many students link the 'lack of respect' to social status. The significance of first names is their symbolic signification of teacher preparedness to question authority structures and hierarchical patterns. Jean expresses this as follows:

> It breaks down the prearranged social status. You don't feel like you're at school to be punished. For example you have to call police/prison officers etc. by their last names. I agree with the idea, as it brings you closer and makes teachers seem human. (questionnaire)

Teachers and Other Adults

Many students consider interaction between them and the teachers as comparable to that between them and other adults. But, secondly, a considerable number feel that teachers are special, and have a particular understanding of students which has evolved through experience and extensive contact.

> A teacher helps a pupil to make decisions because s/he knows how the pupil thinks and both are learning about each other. A teacher has had more experience with different types of children and is more helpful (than parents). (questionnaire)

> I think teachers will ask me my views a lot, whereas I don't think ... me parents would ask that.

> You can be ... brasher with the teachers than other adults that you know, even though you've known them for years, cause the teachers have a different attitude to us. They kind of believe we should say what we feel and not just respect someone because they're older.

Thirdly, some students emphasize that they respect other adults besides teachers.

> You are able to cheek and swear at the teachers, but when I'm with other adults I don't do anything of the sort, because I hold respect for them. (questionnaire)

A fourth group of students argue that the specificity of student/teacher relationships is gradually generalized to all relationships.

> Because I sometimes answer back teachers when they're nasty, I have started to do it with my parents more. I hate being bossed about, now, and have a mind of my own. I have lost respect for a lot of people. (questionnaire)

A fifth group of students emphasizes the unpredictability of teachers, compared to family etc., characterized by greater familiarity: 'other adults I've known longer so I understand their motions. Teachers seem a stranger kind of people of which I know little about' (questionnaire).

Clarities and Uncertainties

Many students, however, feel comfortable with the teachers and are of the opinion that the closer relationships affect the work of the students positively, because of the ease with which teachers can be approached when faced with problems. The dividing line between joking and friendly socializing and working is for these students easy to draw, and they consider this to be the case for teachers as well. A second group of students feels less at ease in knowing how to handle the relationship, and argues that this poses some dificulties for students, many of whom do not work hard enough, not because they don't wish to, but because they find it difficult in a relaxed atmosphere lacking in what they associate with discipline on the basis of their experiences in their previous schools.

The confusion about the nature of the interaction in general or specific exchanges between teachers and students crystallizes, in the case of some students, into development of techniques and strategies to avoid work, and to deal with teacher influence and/or imposition. Some students develop strategies with teachers which aim to maximize the relationship's instrumental potential, in terms of gaining teacher help towards an end more limited than they may have in mind — examinations.

Of particular interest is the fifth group of students, who feel insecure because of the perceived possibility of shifts in teacher/student interaction from informality to impersonal imposition. These students sense the contradictory and conflictual processes in the school, on the one hand tending to personalized relationships and on the other hand to impersonal institutionalized ones; the frame of reference for the former is the interaction between individuals, and for the latter the externally invested roles of teachers and pupils (this is developed in Part Three). Kevin describes the shifts in the content of daily interaction in the following way:

> ... some teachers have the idea of mucking about all the time, and when things happen to get out of hand they ... go mad, which doesn't really work; because the children don't know ... what to do really ... in my biology lesson the teacher's usually joking around most of the time, and suddenly he'll have a mad fit about something, you don't know when to laugh and when to be serious, which I don't think is right.

Rosie refers to some uncertainties and shifts, and expresses the fear that a relationship with a great deal of personal investment in its institutional context makes the student vulnerable.

> I do not feel that the teachers are so far superior that I should not talk in a friendly playing way or have jokes. I think that most of the pupils see the teachers as adults and a little higher than themselves, but not too high that they cannot be friends ... Teacher/student relationships like at the college help us to grow up as well ... I think that if you get on well with your tutor and he/she shouts at you, you could be hurt. I am fond of Julie, and think that she is a very good teacher, but if she were to really shout at me it would upset me. (questionnaire)

Students reveal more of themselves within a relaxed atmosphere, within individualized exchanges, than is typical in schools with greater formality. They do, however, sense the tensions towards impersonality and routinization within situations of conflict. Such tensions are manifestations of schooling as a site of struggles which take place through external mediations.

Control

Control assumes some specificity in progressive schools; this is evident in shifts from personalized to positional interaction. I shall illustrate this shift. Two students stand on the window ledge and hang out of the window — the situation is potentially dangerous, and could also be observed from the outside and related to criticisms about lack of discipline in the school. The teacher walks into the room, and a chain of events begins. First the teacher typically makes a joke containing a suggestion for the students to come down; the loudness of the joke draws the attention of other students. In most cases such mild pressure combined with a good humoured comment is sufficient to elicit the desired behaviour — the students are likely to respond with a joke. The next stage is reasoning and negotiation — 'come on, it's Friday afternoon, and you don't feel like this any more than I do'. When this fails, the teacher adopts a firmer tone, and an imminent threat is contained in a command 'get down!' (in an observed incident the students got down at this stage). The next stage might have been the teacher getting angry and shouting; either the teacher has made a relatively controlled decision to use anger as a strategy, or s/he expresses vulnerability in a stressful situation. The former entails the adoption of an impersonal posture and an appeal to the institutional role as a teacher, evoking the implications of the institutional role of the student.[11] The latter indicates that in a situation where more of the student is available for social control, also more of the teacher is available for student confrontation.[12]

Student views on control in the school are differentiated. First, they consider that it is possible to do 'what you want' in the school, and teachers are unwilling or unable to influence the students; some view this as positive, others as negative 'lack of pushing'. Second, it is considered that though students make important decisions, teachers' influence is significant, through persuasion, reasoning etc. Third, it is emphasized that students have to conform ultimately. It is interesting that disruptive boys who have tested the limits in the school still often belong to the first group, whereas disruptive girls who have done likewise tend to belong to the third group. This indicates that girls are more strongly controlled.

It must be added that warm, friendly interaction was constantly observed. A significant pointer of the relaxed interaction is the physical proximity adopted by teachers and students when talking to each other; they may stand face-to-face, with direct eye contact. Such informality, however, contains the contradictions and tensions expressed in student uncertainties. The greater the dependency on the teacher by the students, the greater these uncertainties are. Relationships in Greenfield encourage one-to-one interaction whereby the tutor assumes a central role in students' experiences of the school, and mediates its ethos and mores. When the students express worries about the possibility of teachers getting angry and adopting a disciplinarian stance, it is partly this dependency they are indicating.

Individualized learning is the guiding principle and organizational rationale of Greenfield College, as manifested in the concept of autonomy. The ethos of individuality emphasizes the unique potential of all students. Individualism characterizes the way both students and teachers work (problematic attempts at collective group work were noted in chapter 6). Personalization is the hallmark of the school, and assumes expression in the content of the work.

In the field of curriculum the notion of autonomous learning gives scope for students who want to develop critical awareness and to pursue political questions which enable them to consider social structures and processes in a way which leads them to radical conclusions. The flexibility of Greenfield allows, for example, girls to consider their own position as female, and link it to an exploration of structured inequalities on the basis of sex. Personaliza-tion can lead to a perception of the links between personal and social struc-tures (this is what Alan's tutor was working towards), (pp. 116–7) — when this occurs, some of the fragmentation and contradictions characteristic of consciousness in a developed capitalist society cannot be maintained, and the students have to consider the framework of their thinking in a broad sense and will be inclined to consider implications for practice as well — the illustrations above are pertinent here, notably those of Kevin and Celia.

But routinization of learning is also evident — a range of subjects does exist; there are processes which channel student concerns and fragment their learning experiences, and narrow the scope of work they are engaged in. A number of boys and girls do not confront many social issues; their work is chosen arbitrarily, and reinforces the concerns of young adolescents with little diversity in their experiences, and a particular interest in personal issues significant during this period (this affects girls especially); the social context of these issues remains unexplored.

The democratic structures have not integrated the students. The consen-sual ethos can encourage students to accept structures and practices which they might otherwise question; the ethos contains powerful unifying themes. However, importance of the potential of participation is emphasized by students, and has been utilized (chapter 5 and chapter 12). Moreover, indi-vidual students, or small groups of students who have participated in the formal processes have put forward proposals which have been accepted, or which have, at any rate, inspired debate. Such participation can provide a stepping stone for an active role in the future vis-à-vis social, political and organizational issues by affording experience and motivation.

The informal relationships and relaxed atmosphere of the school lead to a side-stepping of conflicts normally found in secondary schools. The preva-lent stance towards teachers is not oppositional, or characterized by 'guerrilla warfare in the classroom';[13] this can lead to unquestioning conformism. However, the informality of the relationships, and the symbolic relin-quishing of authority in the use of first names lead some students to question authority relations in general. An emphasis on student views is contained in the conversational approach to learning; this has communicated itself to the students, who consider their opinions to matter (p. 122). As indicated in the above discussion on teachers and other adults, this encouraged some students to question 'ageist' conceptions of adult/child relationships, and relations of subordination and domination.

We can observe pressures towards conformity as well as scope for radicalization in Greenfield. The latter possibility is perceived outside the school, and addressed by criticisms of progressive education in general, and, locally, of Greenfield College in particular (chapter 5). A student, Marilyn, ponders such a process; she notes that the school has

> a reputation for having a communist influence on people. I never got round to understanding that in my project (on the school). But afterwards I began to think the thing is that the school makes you want to change things, and when it comes to wanting to change things, that is left, isn't it. You know, the right is keeping things more as it is ... It doesn't make you rebel but you begin to look at things and think 'Oh God, that's not how it should be' and I think that's the way that this school is politically influenced ... it makes you stand up and think for yourself and then you begin to want to change things and people think that's communist, they think that's left.

Marilyn argues that being treated 'like individuals' leads to a critical consideration of social structures. Her perceptions are expressed (rhetorically at least) in a more negative vein by the critics of the school.

Social Differentiation

Student perceptions on social differentiation are now considered. Class, sex-gender and race are important axes along which inequalities are structured. The student perceptions of such inequalities, their assessment of their inevitability and acceptability and projections for future developments are considered, and contradictions in student thinking are noted. Student conceptions on political processes and their significance is explored. The influence of the content and processes in Greenfield on students is tentatively discussed; it is noted that students as thinking subjects evolve and develop on the interstices of several overlapping structures and processes.

Class

'Class' is used as an analytical concept when inequalities structured on the basis of social class are referred to. The problems involved in empirical definitions and their links to theoretical proposals are considerable. Indeed the aim here is not to chart the social class composition of students, but to focus on teacher (chapter 6) and student, conceptions on social class, though a simple classification on the basis of self-report by students in one team has been developed to contextualize their perceptions.[14] This classification indicates not a predominantly middle class school, though there is no significant representation of top and bottom categories of the Registrar General's classification. There are various areas of differentiation which have emerged as important during the course of the research, such as distinctions between:

    (i)   professionals, skilled tradespeople, and semi- or unskilled workers;

    (ii)   private entrepreneurs[15] and the self-employed;

    (iii) the educated and those who have worked their way up;

    (iv) those with a middle class background and those who have experienced social mobility;

    (v)   those who are owner-occupiers and council or private tenants;[16]

    (iv) various areas of residence.

This differentiation provides the framework of student experiences of class and enables us to consider their conceptions of class, and the shaping of their careers in the school and in the labour market, as discussed below.

Whilst accepting a general division of population into three classes, many students argued that they did not consider social class important, and a number emphasized that in the school and/or in the local area people were 'all one' and class distinctions were not significant, or the majority were 'in the middle'. Students were more likely to consider themselves middle class rather than working class. Criteria of definition used were occupation, income, dress and speech; several criteria were usually mentioned, and the complexity of definitions was often noted. Overall, the students do not find the distinctions easy to make, but generally those interviewed a year later had clarified notions of the meaning of social class, and the emphasis on closures between classes was stronger (chapter 10).

Class, Structured Inequalities and Social Mobility

Some students considered social class as crucial in structuring social inequalities: 'I think if you're working class you get a raw deal in this society' (Kevin). The role of education was emphasized by many in explaining how such inequalities may operate.

> *Bob:* ... if you get a good education, I reckon you got more chance of getting to a higher class. If your family's rich in the first place, you're probably going to stay that way, so you're not gonna move down. (Bob)

As well as material constraints, the parental attitude is emphasized as a determinant of success at school, and, consequently, positioning in the labour market.

> *Andrew:* ... if parents take a 'don't care at all' attitude then the child ... doesn't work at school and he doesn't do well (and) may fall into lower class jobs, whereas if he's looked after, pushed and helped, he'll get on better.

Whilst the closures between classes are observed by the students, the possibility of social mobility is also strongly emphasized:

> *Marilyn:* Often if you're upper class you're just born into money aren't you. That's bound to make a difference to your life — but there are a few people who were born in the lower class that really work hard and make it.

In a relatively prosperous, expanding area, where recession has taken longer to reach than most parts of the country, the students have observed social mobility, often in their own families. For these students the experience of social mobility in their families is not always easily turned into educational success (chapter 10). Their thinking is contradictory, structured obstacles are noted, but possibility of social mobility is nevertheless tangible. Several students begin by emphasizing equality of opportunity — the response nearest the surface is linked to their personal feeling that they can be successful. As discussion continues, the deeper responses relating to a sense of structured obstacles are expressed. The surface responses are reinforced by prevailing ideology; familiarity with dominant populist conservative ideology leads to its articulation in general references to political, social and economic issues. The notion of open opportunities and possibilities of individual advancement regardless of social class is prevalent in conservative thinking, predominant nationally and locally. The deeper responses are less influenced by such ideologies, and relate to lived experiences as a member of a class, and express a class identity.[17]

Students tend to consider social mobility desirable and discuss it in terms of 'bettering oneself', 'making it', 'getting on', 'getting out of the working class' etc. — but some students place positive emphasis on their working class background. Ralph describes his family background as working class, and when asked to project into his own future, he says 'I *wanna* be working class'. Brenda is not very ambitious; she works in a factory and has no other aspirations. This can be linked to her lack of confidence and low self-conception academically — 'I'm not very clever' — and to her low achievement at school. But it also relates to her definition of success, which does not equate social mobility and 'easier life': 'if you had a job, where you got paid a lot of money but you didn't enjoy it, it wouldn't be worth doing, really'. Brian indicates a strong sense of alternative values: 'working class people get working class jobs really. I mean if you go to a private school, you know snobs like, they probably end up being a vet or something'. When asked whether he thinks this is fair, Brian replies 'I wouldn't wanna be a vet ... I don't think working class kids want anything else really, you know, they're quite happy just to get a working class job'. Lack of instrumentalism and concern for social mobility do not preclude success at school, but other aspects need to assume strong significance to compensate for such a world view in career negotiations (chapter 10).

Student conceptions of the importance, inevitability and acceptability of class differentiations vary. Some students who observe inequalities argue that they do not concern themselves with these personally; Dave writes that 'the rest of the social world can get on and leave me alone, I'm allright, Jack' (questionnaire). Connected to this is a feeling that in order to ensure one's own success it is impossible to worry about others. Inequalities may also be accepted as natural and inevitable: 'that's just tough, if you're rich you're rich, if you're poor you're poor' says George, but others do not agree; Ken: 'people who live in slums, I feel sorry for them, and think that the ones who have got money should help them, but I don't think you would be able to make them do that'. Whether students consider the inequalities inevitable facts of life which one might as well accept, or feel quite strongly that they are unfair, there is a general, almost unanimous sense of powerlessness and lack of control.

Politics and Powerlessness

'Ordinary people' are seen as helpless, and those sections of society that are considered powerful enough to be able to influence the structure of society are seen to have a vested interest in the present situation; for example Celia notes that she could not do anything: 'people who could do something want it anyway, so there's nothing that can be done about it'. The general sense of powerlessness is linked to the fact that the majority of students have no conception of possible or viable alternatives. Celia is unusual in that her support for the Ecology Party provides some kind of set of alternatives which embraces her general political outlook and influences her practices (for example her vegetarianism, (p. 115) and tendency to send money to charities dealing with underdeveloped countries); however, she feels powerless nevertheless, as she does not consider the Ecology Party to be able to attract popular support. Many students express the need for alternatives, without having a clear conception of what the alternatives might be:

Philip: I wouldn't vote for any of them ... I don't think there's any way they can work it out, unless they bring a new system in, cause at the moment I think it's a right mess. I don't know ... I think they should find a different way.

Brian: I think they're all a load of rubbish.

Interviewer: What would you like to see happening?

Brian: I'm not sure really.

Such a sense of uncertainty contributes to the feeling of powerlessness these students experience.

The students who have a strong sense of the existence of structured inequalities, and of the unfairness of the situation, also perceive a weighted balance of power. These views are linked to their conceptions about the direction of their own life, which they wish to construct as meaningfully as possible. For many such a construction of personal futures is seen as a hard task entailing struggles against obstacles, and most of them have doubts about the success they hope for, and are apprehensive about the possible need to reassess their ambitions, which for some students during the course of the research becomes an actuality. Dave, when general political questions are considered, says that 'I'm quite ignorant and happy to be so', whilst he is able to discuss current issues articulately. Joyce considers at length the Conservative and Labour parties, explaining her dissatisfactions with each, but adds that whilst she is more inclined to support Labour, and criticizes a number of Conservative policies, she might fluctuate in her voting: 'when you get fed up with voting Labour, Labour aren't doing much good, I think you swop to Conservatives, just swop from party to party'. Joyce has criticized the Conservatives as interested in 'conserving what they got' and 'not bothered about the working class' etc. I therefore ask her whether she could consider any other alternatives — for example the Left. Joyce replies that she does not know anything about the Left, and adds 'I could if I wanted to'; she could ask her teachers, but, she says 'I want to keep naive, I don't particularly want to know'. She explains:

> (if you're Right), you're a bit more passive about your politics, but if you're Left ... further Left seems really fanatical ... it's easier to kind of fall in with ideals than to fall out ... isn't it.

The attitudes expressed by Joyce and Dave are shared by many students — it is easier not to be interested in politics, where involvement can lead to a commitment that affects one's life-situation in a fundamental way, when the context is that of a sense of powerlessness and lack of perceived alternatives. In general, students opt for individualistic solutions, and wish to construct their own careers in as positive terms as possible within a given set of opportunities.

Class and School

Equality of opportunity within Greenfield College is emphasized by students. Crucial aspects in the construction of careers are seen to be parental attitudes, and the attitudes and decisions by the students themselves.

> *Lesley:* it's not like saying clever people can do this, clever people
> can do that — everybody's got the same chance here, it depends

whether they mess about and waste their time or whether they take their chance, you know.

This is seen as a distinctive feature of Greenfield College: 'there's no equality in other schools' (Stuart). Philippa, who felt that her interest in music was not encouraged sufficiently (at home or at school), felt more restricted, and expressed a rare criticism: 'You can choose freely, but I think they can change your mind . . .'. Students thus feel that if not in general, nevertheless in their own school in particular they make decisions about their own future and, forge their own careers — work if they wish to, take exams if they wish to, etc. This is applicable both to those who do and do not achieve academically. This sense of scope within the school which seems to contradict the general sense of structured inequalities is linked to the process of individualization in Part Three.

Race

Students agree that some racism exists in Greenfield College, but tend to emphasize that only a small number of students are involved. This is explained, first, by reference to the ethos and operation of the school. One girl[18] argued that there is less racism in Greenfield than in other schools, because the open system did not encourage it. But, second, others feel that even though not much racism is evident, this is because the students are racially and ethnically relatively homogeneous — few evidently distinct cultural patterns are exhibited. Thirdly, students perceive the college to contain a lot of racism.

The reasons given by students for their racist views include arguments about over-population, housing, jobs and, prejudice towards different cultures. There are contradictions in their thinking; they have been exposed to a set of ideas by the mass media and their parents, and, unsystematically, another set of ideas in the school. The contradictions, then, express the confusion in integrating the sets of ideas together, without having been confronted by a definite need to do so, or been offered systematic support in doing so. The question of racism assumes pertinence, because the National Front received one of its highest votes in the 1979 General Election in the local constituency.

Teacher strategies were discussed in chapter 6; liberal tolerance is widely emphasized, for political or strategic reasons. A group of teachers argue that racism needs to be confronted with determination and vigour, but no overall policies exist on the issue. Thus liberal tolerance is communicated to the students. They consider the teachers as non- or anti-racist, but they are seen to adopt particular stances as individuals, not as a staff. Teachers' views, the general ethos of the school, and the individualism are reflected in student attitudes.

An illustration is provided by student views on distribution of National Front propaganda in the school (chapter 6, p. 101). First, they thought that these activities should not be allowed; the most common reason given was that some people would be hurt and offended. But clear-cut disapproval of NF policies was also expressed: 'it is against the law, racial hatred and racial discrimination and that, so I don't think it should be allowed'. Some of the students thought that groups such as the Anti-Nazi League should be allowed to distribute leaflets, but others thought that the same rule should be applied to all political information and propaganda.[19]

The second view is that NF propaganda should be allowed, as then no political propaganda needs to be forbidden: 'It's not fair to stop them from doing that when other political papers have got round, even though people disagree with the NF' (Pete). Or NF activities are seen as just one manifestation of the existence of individual freedoms in the school, and the scope for expression of all points of view: 'they should be allowed, if they know what they're doing' (Kevin). A third group of students were mixed in their views, and shifted their position in the course of the discussion, when the interviewer gave alternative arguments for them to consider. For example:

> *Stuart:* I think that if they want to do that, I think that they should be allowed to do it. Because everybody else is free to do what they want. I can express my view.
>
> *Interviewer:* Would your views preach such hatred towards a group of people like theirs do?
>
> *Stuart:* Yeah that's true, but — I don't like that, I don't like the hatred against people. It's a hard choice there; I mean you're being fair by not letting them do it ... I mean if they can't do it, then nobody else should be able to do it, I don't think. I mean if they can't spread their stuff around, I don't think — I mean — it's a very hard subject this — I don't know where to draw the line.

Student confusion and contradictory thinking, and the side-stepping of a range of political issues reflect the difficulties of the liberal position on the NF, combining tolerance and abhorrence, without providing a framework for the adoption of a clear policy. The teachers and students who emphasize the need to tackle racism in an open manner tend to be to the left of the liberals in the political spectrum. The liberal ethos on racism is mediated through individualized relationships and learning, and personalization, and is embodied in the notion of freedom — the uniqueness of each individual is emphasized, and the importance of self-expression in the development of the capacity for self-determination precludes imposition of an external framework which would provide a reference grid for anti-racism.

This account has focussed on confusions and contradictions, because the school has not been particularly successful in tackling racism: teachers and students of non-white ethnic origin were observed to be subjected to racism; prejudices were often rationalized in terms of problems of interpersonal interaction; no firm overall policy has been developed, and because of the school ethos and its individualization such a policy would be difficult to arrive at.

Sex and Gender

Sexism in the school raises broad questions which are addressed in chapter 11. Here the focus is on the worldview of students, and the way in which sex-gender roles are differentially conceived and evaluated by boys and girls. Boys tend to assume that there is considerable degree of equality between men and women, and that the direction is towards further improvement, whilst they themselves tend to be reluctant to diverge from the traditional male role, particularly in their personal lives. The girls are less optimistic about equal opportunities at present or in the future, and more concerned to try to introduce equality in their own lives, particularly in the personal sphere, whilst they still expect to get married, have children and care for them. I shall expand on these themes, and then consider how the teachers are seen to tackle issues of sexism.

Whilst many boys acknowledge inequalities based on sex in the labour market, they often qualify this by referring to legislation to ensure equal opportunities, and a clear trend towards increasing equality. They emphasize the disinclination of girls to choose occupations which are not traditionally considered suitable for them. The girls, however, consider the labour market less open, and emphasize obstacles, the lack of equal opportunities, and their lack of optimism for the future. Differentiation in the views of boys and girls clearly exists.

In relation to the family and the domestic sphere, some boys express liberal views; they expect to participate in household chores — they would 'help' or 'chip in', but a few are open about their beliefs in male supremacy — women are and should be 'second to men'. Bill would allow his wife to work, but expects her to do the housework. He showed little interest in considering the implications of the dual job for the woman: 'she'd do housework at weekends and that — can't you — I like a cooked meal, like, when you go home'. Dave expressed a more liberal view:

> Things like putting up shelves . . . I suppose she'd expect me to do . . .
> But, you, know, I'd have to chip in with washing up and drying pots,
> that kind of thing . . . clearing as well, I suppose, if she's not able to do
> it herself.

Andrew acknowledges how half-hearted such a commitment can be:

> you'd come home and you'd think well we both got to do housework;
> you don't just leave it to the women . . . Well I probably would in the
> end get a bit sort of — leave it all to the woman you know (laughter)
> . . . but now and again I suppose I would help out.

Stuart expresses an unusual conviction about the necessity to share jobs, and to break the traditional roles of men and women, and felt committed to this in his own life as well: 'a man and woman should share the jobs, each doing each other's jobs in the house'. Whilst boys talk as if it is up to them to decide the degree of their participation in the future household, girls tend to express hopes about their future roles, and the contribution of their partners; an equal division of labour was considered unattainable by most, and a couple of the interviewed girls considered the chores in the home their responsibility.

When the interviewed students were asked to project to the future, all girls except two expected to get married and have children, and be responsible for childcare; a small number said they would like to combine children and career. One girl expressed doubts about marrying and having children, but expected that she would do so because of strong pressures in that direction. The boys expressed stronger doubts about marriage; about half expressed a disinclination to get married. Marriage is seen in terms of financial responsibilities for the wife and the children, whom the wife is expected to care for at home (with the exception of two boys). At home there are few demands for participation, and boys have little conception of what is involved in the role they would expect their future wives to assume. Their doubts about marriage are not based on radical questioning of it as an institution, but on the restrictions that it would pose on their freedom of movement — going out, spending time in the pub, etc. Many boys have some involvement with youth cultures which prioritize collective leisure, and thus provide a 'magical resolution'[20] to the problems of working class youth. Such a solution does not tackle future responsibilities in terms of family and work, and does not develop any alternative conceptions; thus the boys tend to envisage the rest of their lives as kind of grown-up lads.

The girls, then, are more aware of inequalities than boys, because the traditional role of a woman is considered more limiting than that of a man. Whilst the girls wish to lead lives different from those of their mothers, they also map out their futures in terms of marriage and children as realistic prospects which they hope to make as meaningful as possible, and hope that their partners would participate in the process of creating a liberal relationship.

The teachers as a body are not considered anti-sexist by students, who in many cases say they are unfamiliar with particular teachers' attitudes to sexism. A number of girls do projects related to the position of women and equal opportunities between sexes, but only a handful of boys have touched upon such issues in their work. The personalization of the learning of the girls reinforces the importance they place in their future personal lives. Whilst specific teachers regret the disinclination by girls to carry the discoveries of their projects into their lives, as long as the sexism of boys is not confronted and as long as girls enter the labour market in its female sectors and emphasize marriage and children, it is difficult to see how they could engage in more than wishful thinking, particularly as the language used by boys suggests that it is up to them to make decisions without consulting their partners. Thus a girl like Marilyn who intends to have a career 'like any man' thinks she'll 'end up cooking the dinners'.

Conclusion

The question of radicalism or conservatism as characteristics of products of progressive schools is largely dissolved when student perspectives are considered. Along with the political right we can note the scepticism vis-à-vis authority, the concern for individual freedoms and self-determination and the critical orientations towards hierarchy. Along with the left we can note the lack of inclination to participate in the democratic processes in the school, the lack of interest in political processes, the laissez-faire attitude towards racism, the differential exposure of students to social, economic and political issues, and the individualistic striving for social mobility.

The attention is predominantly drawn to student perspectives which emphasize that they perceive a limiting framework structuring their existence; thus the experience of powerlessness is a strong determinant in student disinclination to be drawn into political processes as 'propagandizing rebels'. Hurdles to action are not considered worth transgression, when no feasible alternatives are perceived. Yet the naturalism of social structures is questioned, and passive determinism does not appeal to the products of a school with individualised ethos and practices, where teacher emphasis on autonomy is communicated to students in one-to-one personalized interaction. Students largely believe in self-determination, in the forging of their own careers, in the making of their own futures.

Student interests articulate with the Conservative ideology which emphasizes individual effort crystallized in private enterprise and market operations, and with social stratification locally, where social mobility and affluent 'self-made' workers affirm the possibility of constructing one's career. The students voice many conservative sentiments, and only when probed express the sense of struggle they experience in trying to convert their capacities into marketable commodities in the job structure. They sense that they need to work hard, and responses to in-depth questioning relate this to structured inequalities, but the surface responses find their reference point in the examination system rewarding individual efforts and abilities with certification and improved job prospects. Thus the ethos and processes in Greenfield assume their influential specificity in conjunction with the structures and forms of the school as a juncture of societal patterns. The interaction and mediations between the practices in the school, the forms of relations in the society, and the complex, negotiated, dynamic medley that ensues are discussed below.

Notes

1 It is illuminating to consider both teachers and students; *c.f.* WILLIS (1977) and CORRIGAN (1979) do not focus on teachers, whilst BALL (1981) considers students only through observation and surveys.

2 I have kept a record of projects undertaken by students in one team, and such tendencies are evident. This was also confirmed by a student who, in the course of her social studies project, conducted a review of two teams.

3 An example is provided by considering projects completed by four students by the autumn term in the fifth year:

    (i)   Girl: Navy, Western Europe, Law and Order, Italy, Railways;

    (ii) Girl: Smoking, Skin-care, One-Parent families, Sugar, Australia, Pregnancy;

    (iii) Boy: Energy, Industrial Revolution, Vikings, Ffestiniog Railway;

    (iv) Boy: Fish, Agriculture, Venice, Housing, Farming.

In later projects the notion of balance was often considered; it was determined by using the examination as a criterion.

4 Thus they, for example, worked through the plans section by section, without thinking about how these connected to form a 'project'.

5 Sarah responds to her criticism:

> Joyce thinks we ought to be harsh on kids, but that's a most difficult problem, because I don't see, given that we're kind of pledged to kind of jolly along the human system for as long as possible, how you can turn round to them and say 'For Christ sake what you've done is crap.' And yet on one level one ought to do that a bit.

6 The problems of administering the questionnaire are discussed in the methodological appendix.

7 This is significant, as in one of the coffee bars there is a notice: 'Drinks not to be carried away — Standing Committee'.

8 A student magazine considered which teachers had the 'lowest information content per 1000 words'.

9 'Not the *Leicester Mercury*', a student magazine, defines the word 'decision' as one not to be mentioned in moots.

10 An internal paper by the Principal, 19 February 1985.

11 The next stage, appealing to the Deputy, is indicative of the direction of this chain.

12 This was discussed in chapter 6, p. 96.

13 CORRIGAN (1979).

14 Information was gathered from 131 students in one team in the academic year 1979/80. In some cases the information was given by teachers, or by the peers of a few students. Out of the fathers of these students approximately 19 per cent were semi-skilled or unskilled workers (predominantly semi-skilled); 38 per cent skilled workers; 18 per cent non-manual low-level white-collar workers, and 23 per cent managerial or professional employees. About 13 per cent were reported to be self-employed. Sixty-one per cent of mothers were employed, 19 per cent were housewives; the information for the rest was missing.

15 Factory owners, shopowners, those with their own business.

16 Though EVANS (chapter 5) has shown the high percentage of owner-occupation in the area.

17 MANN (1973).

18 In an informal discussion.

19 For example the sixth-form students decided that they should not have an Anti-Nazi League poster in the sixth-form area, as this would mean that they would have to have National Front posters as well.

20 CLARKE, J. in HALL and JEFFERSON (Eds) (1977) uses the term, noting its initial use by COHEN, P. 'Sub-cultural Conflict and Working Class Community', Working Papers in Cultural Studies, No. 2 (spring), CCCS, University of Birmingham.

Part Three: Mediations

Chapter 8

Individualization

Through participant observation it became evident that individualization was a fundamental thread in trying to 'make sense' of Greenfield College. It emerges as a descriptive term which embodies many processes. In Part Two we discovered that individualization is at the heart of the ethos of the school and its organization, curriculum, democracy and relationships: the fostering of potential and interests of all individual students within a situation which allows for self-direction of students vis-à-vis their career in the school is a central principle. Individualization as a 'form' is discussed in this chapter — implications for interpreting fieldwork are considered. In chapter 9 I explore how individualization is mediated to and articulates with the practices which constitute the reality at the school level. Individualization as gender-specific is analyzed in chapter 11.

To address the macro-micro continuum three levels of analysis are distinguished: forms, modes and practices. Forms are defined through 'general theories' — they are abstractions within a conceptual framework. Modes are channels of mediation, empirically and historically defined. Practices refer to content at institutional levels — a reality shaped within the framework of forms through the mediation of modes in a negotiated manner. Marx uses the concept of form in Kapital. In Volume One he discusses value as a social relation of one commodity to another, not a physical relation. What is considered is a 'social reality' without 'an atom of matter' in it. A commodity assumes the form of value as opposed to its use-value in an exchange relation. Forms can only be discerned through an analysis of social relations using theoretical tools.

An incident in a Leicestershire school provides clarification. A group of students had been protesting about road dangers outside the College, after an accident involving a pupil. The local press was invited to a special assembly where the headteacher reprimanded the students who did not

> do what mature people are expected to do, go to the year council, to go to me, or to go to any teacher ... Instead they followed the example of demonstrators world over, and they caused trouble.[1]

He does not condemn the student sentiments, but the manner in which they were expressed: outside the avenues of legitimate dissent, connecting with a perceived alternative, oppositional framework. The action does not express itself in a form embodied in parliamentary democracy, based on representation, hierarchy, and division of activity and passivity, but it is immediate, commands a response, and involves a number of people in a collective action, where the significance is in the protesting group addressing an issue, rather than deflecting and defusing it through elected delegates pursuing bureaucratic channels. Thus forms channel activities, and in the course of doing so the issues become transformed and the site of anger and struggle remains marginal to the official, formal avenues.[2]

'Form' is a general concept referring to general, abstract features of the mode of production which shape social processes and institutions through various mediations. Here individualization as a form is considered. It is mediated through modes such as professionalism, compulsory school attendance and certification. These shape the content at the school level, where the structures and processes based on particular educational and political thinking assume unintended consequences and a contradictory reality. It is not surprising that a progressive school such as Greenfield contains ambiguities and conflicting tendencies, given the context of restructuring tending towards centralization and standardization of formal education, when progressivism is based on autonomy and flexibility. Further, restructuring is mediated to schools through public expenditure cuts, whilst progressivism relies on a variety of resources and a favourable teacher/pupil ratio based on curriculum needs rather than numerical calculations. However, it is useful to try to understand how such contradictions are shaped. How do macro and micro levels connect into a continuum? What are the mediations?

Individualization as a Form

In the discussion here I shall attempt to disentangle individualization as a form, normative individualism, and the problem of individuality, noting that the elusive medley referred to by these terms is reminiscent of the elusiveness of 'progressivism' (chapter 3).

Individualism in England has been, argues McFarlane (1978), a central feature for longer than is usually supposed; in fact within the recorded period covered by documents a time cannot be found 'when an Englishman did not stand alone. Symbolized and shaped by his ego–centred kinship system, he stood in the centre of his world'.[3] McFarlane's book draws our attention to the survival of 'individualism' from a previous mode of production. This survival contributes to its fundamentality; its importance lies in both the continuities and discontinuities. Williams (1965) notes that the term 'individual' used to denote a membership of a group; an individual was a unit, rather than an absolute. He traces the modern usage of the term without a reference to a social group. Abercrombie and Turner (1978) note that individualism was an ideology of the ascendant bourgeoisie; its oppositional qualities altered when the capitalist mode of production became established.

Lukes (1973) discusses different ways in which the concept of individualism has been used, as consonant with social and economic anarchy, lack of norms, prevalence of self-interest, self-assertion, independence, rejection of authority, self-fulfilment, free enterprise, natural rights, non-conformity in religion, self-reliance, and minimum of state intervention. The basic ideas contained are those of the dignity of the human being, autonomy, privacy and self-development. McPherson (1962), like Lukes, notes the connections between liberal-democratic thought and individualism; 'possessive individualism' is the theme unifying assumptions of liberalism. The individual is seen as the owner of 'himself' and 'his capacities'. But in a market society where skills are sold as a commodity, and are thus distinct from personality a fundamental contradiction is posed.[4] The assumptions of 'possessive individualism' are necessary because individualization is integral to the labour process in a capitalist society, and, further, it is constituted and maintained by the state. Individualization therefore is not just an ideological phenomenon, but, indeed, a phenomenon which reduces the significance of ideological integration of the subordinate class or groups:[5] it lessens the importance of repression in controlling those whose consent has not been ensured. It is a phenomenon through which the subordinate classes and groups are disorganized and fragmented into units; abstract individuals without a reference to the social groups of which they are members.

The atomization of people into 'individuals' is rooted in the social division of labour, argues Poulantzas (1978). Despite socialization of labour the direct producers are isolated from each other in that they have not themselves planned the acts of labour, and the mutuality of these. The state, through its practices, reinforces the process of individualization and its effects by atomizing the 'body-politics' into 'individuals', or 'juridical-political' subjects.

> The state here presupposes a specific organization of the political space upon which the exercise of power comes to bear. The centralized, bureaucratized state INSTALS this atomization and, as a re-presentative state laying claim to national sovereignty and the popular will, it REPRESENTS the unity of a body (people-nation) that is split into formally equivalent monads.[6]

The state completes and complements the individualization cited in the labour process by atomizing members of classes and groups into citizens, the unity of whom is then provided by the state.

Poulantzas emphasizes that the arguments do not pertain to 'concrete' or 'biological' individuals; individualization is rather the 'material expression' of the relations of production and the social division of labour, and a 'material effect' of state practices. Therefore, whilst it is an ideological process, it does not merely exist on the level of ideas; it is a process rooted in material practices:

how people's lives are structured through the process of individualization so that a collective, unfragmented grasp of their life-situation in terms of class, sex, race becomes difficult; individualization assumes a natural rather than a social and contingent character.

It is possible then to ask how the forms constituted by the process of individualization are strengthened and/or challenged within a state apparatus characterized by a degree of relative autonomy — in this case schools. Questions are raised about the possibilities and limitations of liberal/radical/ libertarian practices in unravelling the structured fragmentation of people's life-situation. Therefore, rather than just looking at the school ethos and its ideological expressions in terms of the curriculum, democracy, relationships, I concentrated on the realization of such thinking in practice, focussing both on teachers and the students. Similarly, the concern has not simply been with individualistic, ideological constructions of experiences and situations, but with trying to make links with the contradictory understanding of particularities and the structural, cultural and biographical locations of the people as thinkers and actors.

Poulantzas notes the separation between the private and public spheres, but argues that the state has considerable power in the former sphere as well. For example the family is a private space, but yet defined by the state.[7] Representative democracy and civil rights are expressions of the individual-private and its imprint on the state. Limits to state activity are posed, but these are achieved through class struggle, and do not constitute a locus external to the state. Gramsci (1971) also makes a connection between individualism and parliamentarism, and asserts that both are fundamentally linked, and the one cannot be abolished without the other. Anderson (1977) expresses in strong terms the mutual possibilities and limitations of representative democracy, through which the belief in ultimate self-determination is mediated to people.

Poulantzas suggests that individualization assumes different meanings and modalities for different social classes. When contradictions in Greenfield College are considered, the different ways in which individualization is conceived by teachers from middle class/working class backgrounds, students from middle class/working class backgrounds, Conservative local authority, and parents, are of significance.

Molina (1978) discusses the status of 'individuals' in Marxist theory. Marx focusses on human beings in their social connections — not as 'concrete' individuals. Individuals are personifications of, for example, a capitalist, but this personification is not a constitutive feature of them as concrete human beings. Thus Mr. Peel who, as Marx explains,[8] arrives in Australia accompanied by the necessary means of production is deserted by all the 3,000 working class men and women and children on arrival. Mr. Peel thus discovers that capital is not a thing, and not an aspect of his 'natural' character, but of his 'social' character; capital is a social relation between persons.[9]

The process of individualization and the problem of individuality — how concrete individuals are located in social relations — is considered by Holloway and Picciotto (and others).[10] The starting point is the capital relation, a relation of exploitation structured and restructured in negotiations and/or struggle between classes. Both the 'economic' and the 'political' spheres are instances of this relation. The state embodies the capital relation, though it apparently constitutes people as free and equal individuals (in chapter 11 I argue that gender relations are also significant in understanding state practices). The state individualizes people, and then unites them as a nation of citizens, and also as groups like tax payers, claimants, owner-occupiers, council tenants etc., that is, categories other than class; the question of exploitation does not arise.

Gerstenberger (1977) considers individualization as a fragmented process. The incorporation of working class in the capitalist mode of production occurs through 'control' — not integration or repression. The state established formal equality between people, ignoring the real inequalities between them. The neutral appearance of the state is the main integrating factor. The tendency by the capitalist class to transform the state into an open instrument of class power is resisted by the working class and the neutral appearance of the state is reproduced.

Consciousness develops within a framework of habits and activities that people's life situation leads them to acquire and perform. Individualization is a fragmented process. People are employee-individuals, owner-occupier individuals, rate-payer individuals and so on. Thus the process of individualization involves several overlapping tendencies and manifestations. The sceptical position on integration through indoctrination or simplistic socialization means that when studying Greenfield College we do not focus on the transmission of the school ethos to the students, but consider the way in which it is mediated to them through organization and social relations in the school, crystallized in the curriculum, democracy and informality in relationships. These co-exist in tension with professionalism, compulsion and certification. Hence we find in the school a multifaceted realization of the processes of individualization, in dynamic articulation with individualization as a form. But before turning attention to Greenfield, I shall frame the discussion by considering schooling and individualization, and progressivism and individualization in particular.

Individualization and Schooling

Gerstenberger (1977) names three controlling devices used by the state: [i] the 'canalization of struggles into modes of legal procedure'; [ii] 'forming the habits and outlooks' of a dominated class for example through schooling; and [iii] administration.[11] In relation to schooling, the form assumed by control is shaped, significantly, by individualization. The consideration of left/right critiques of progressivism and the disentangling of the different strands of progressivism these address (chapter 3) has drawn attention not only to control, but also to 'oppositional spaces' (chapter 1) and possibilities for radical educational practices. The analysis thus contains dynamism and tension, expressed in the mutual interaction between possibilities and limitations for radical action within schools in general and progressive schools in particular. In chapter 1 a distinction between state form/apparatus was made; the relationship between them is not one of constant determination, but is characterized by relative autonomy, subject to alternation in periods of economic expansion or restructuring. Indeed the term 'relationship' implies not a constant unilinear imposition, but a fluid reciprocity. 'Spaces' for radical practices are located in the disjunctures between state form and state apparatus, but the political action located in these spaces is contradictory. How these 'spaces' articulate with individualization is a complex issue; I shall deal with it below.

The connection between individualization and control can be noted in early debates about the need for education for the 'lower orders'. Johnson draws attention to the Victorian middle class concern for the 'ungovernable' behaviour of the working class, with its independent educational activities, collective endeavours and the spectre of sedition. The importance of the 'individual' was evident in the debates;[12] schooling was to channel the activities of the working class onto individualized forms. This individualization has assumed different expressions at the level of practices in schools, ranging from the anonymous atomization of monitorialism to the personalized child-centredness of progressivism. Common themes can be discerned, in particular certification: 'individuals' prepare for and take examinations, and succeed or fail apparently according to their individual abilities and aptitudes. The network of public examinations has widened; more than three-quarters of the school population now take examinations. Those who do not take examinations often study alongside those who do, in lessons conducted according to criteria constructed on the basis of the examinations.

With the development of progressive education at the beginning of the century (chapter 3) new ideas emerged in educational theory if not practice: a conception of the teacher's role as a non-authoritarian facilitator; integration of the curriculum; stress on the potential of children and their creativity; stress on self-government and/or self-determination in varying degrees; stress on 'freedom'; and, above all, stress on the individuality of each child. Hitherto individuality involved fragmentation of children into units, pupils, to be brought together again wearing uniforms, house-colours etc., having shed their characteristics as unique, concrete individuals on the way (though these would be re-established in classroom interaction). Individuality here was linked to 'uniqueness', notions of different needs and interests, and self-realization.

The expansion of the state education sector provided scope for progressivism in the sixties. The educational climate started to change in the seventies;

the Great Debate was followed by a concerted Conservative campaign to centralize, harness and restructure the state education sector within an altered relationship between central and local state. A new education/training system is being forged.

I asked earlier why this shift took place. Restructuring of the capital relation, and of the relationship between state form and apparatus during the 'crisis' were noted, and linked to the potential intensification of class struggle, opposition not structured along class categories by women, blacks, gays etc. and on a less organized basis increased desubordination (chapter 2). 'Oppositional spaces' assume greater potential significance. For example when Greenfield teachers resisted cuts in expenditure and the revision of staff/student ratios (chapter 5), their action was seriously treated; this indicates the potential attached to such action in mobilizing a wider network of resistance. But the endorsement and later 'crisis' of progressive education generated particular interest in a pedagogical theory and practice which became an object of criticism by both the political right and the left. The case study of one progressive school, Greenfield, led to the consideration of individualization.

But to address the significance of individualization in Greenfield, a distinction between individualization as atomization and individualization as personalization requires clarification. This facilitates the consideration of radicalism within progressivism. Greenfield College has been perceived as a threat to status quo on the one hand (chapter 5), but on the other hand radical teachers there are of the opinion that the school is only viable in so far as militant trade union action is not taken. Aspects of the history of the school were connected to observations confirming individualization as a fundamental thread in the shcool; however, in different observations this process seemed to assume different meanings and outcomes. One manifestation was the tendency by many students to express support for the Conservative Party and its brand of populist individualism, though in discussions on Conservative policies a generally critical stance prevailed. For example the students' experience of individualized learning made suggestions on core curriculum seem irrelevant and ill-founded to them. Either an overall critique of the party developed from specific criticisms, or the general affiliation led to an adjustment of the specific criticisms.[13] Tensions between radicalism and conservatism can be understood by considering different expressions assumed by individualization — atomization and personalization.

Atomization refers to individualization as a form under capitalism, to division of people into impersonal, solitary units. Human beings are constituted as abstract, general, de-individualized individuals. But these units have a shared social basis. In so far as this social basis, denied by Conservative populism, assumes 'visibility', individualization does not exclude radicalization, and has, indeed, historically enabled the questioning of traditional authority structures and the extension of rights of a citizen to everybody.

Personalization, here at the level of practices of a progressive school, is contradictory; it can either inadvertently reinforce atomization, or provide the means for 'making visible' the social basis of that process. Personalization refers to a process where people are treated as complex, concrete individuals with unique characteristics, rather than as impersonal homogeneous units — they are seen as specific, heterogeneous and differentiated. If personalization leads to connections being made between personal and social structures, it involves radical questioning of abstract individuals as units, and emphasizes individuals as social constructs with specific biographies within social structures.

Tensions between atomization and personalization can assume a variety of expressions; this is crucial in understanding radicalism/conservatism within progressivism. Before turning to Greenfield College it is useful to note that here teachers and students are not considered merely as 'bearers' of roles, externally shaped 'units', but as human actors, complex, contradictory social constructs. Though the forms within which they exist shape them, they do not determine them. Actors are unique and *thinking* individuals, not in an idealist sense, but in a social sense, constituted within structures but imbued with specific political thought and practices in negotiation with the structures.

Individualization in Greenfield College

Teachers

A politicization process of libertarian (and some liberal) teachers has been occurring in Greenfield. A number of teachers have shifted their position, and give more emphasis to the context within which Greenfield exists; they are more likely to participate in and support militant trade union action. The limitations of individualization as atomization were noted through practice:

> *Trevor:* I think really, we began to realize some years ago that there was a sort of hidden repression ... there wasn't a possibility of cooperative learning because of the way one operated and you could see it quite unconsciously — since one was a school, that sort of institution — being employed as a control device. (Trevor)

Tom describes his own shift from a liberal position, a developing awareness of the relationship between education and social stratification; he has become less prepared to accept an 'optimistic, liberal, possibilitarian sort of view of education and schools'. Sarah describes a similar shift and concludes: 'I used to think it was a just marvellous sort of progressive move, and now I think it's a nice reform'. First Greenfield teachers dreamt of leading the way for a wholesale transformation of secondary schools. Instead there has been a gradual shift towards a more authoritarian education system with a greater degree of standardization and central control, and an increased pressure on progressive schools out of step with such moves. Thus the teachers have had to reach a point of conciliation with this fact, and have had to adjust their thinking in order to cope with the realization that society not only did not want the transformation that Greenfield pointed towards, but responded with a 'backlash' which by 1985 raised the question of survival more intensely than ever.

The teachers have coped in different ways. Some have left the state sector, mainstream schools or teaching. Some have adopted professional, careerist solutions. Others have become pragmatists searching for realistic responses to the new situation, trying to defend the gains of the school whilst making compromises perceived as necessary to maintain the school as progressive and standing for variety in secondary schooling, if not providing alternatives in education. Others have adopted a more radical stance and have shifted attention towards national issues within trade union framework.[14]

The structures and organization of the school are conducive to trade union militancy and afford possibilities for radical action. But they also contain limitations which have found expression in the conflicts between the democratic structures of the school and trade unionism (chapter 6), whereby the democratic structures accord with the individualized school ethos, and trade unionism assumes collective decision making; the moot strives towards a consensus (chapter 5), in a union meeting majority opinion prevails. Trade union action has often raised the Greenfield problem of survival. In debates about action the individualized ethos has provided a reference point; is it possible for one school to maintain a profile different from the prevailing in the state sector?

Teachers have had scope to develop various ways of working in the absence of constraints usually found in state secondary schools, such as departmental and pastoral hierarchies, control by the head etc. But again these possibilities are framed with limitations. Individualization makes working alone possible, and increases a sense of control in daily decisions about teaching and students. But fragmentation contained in individualization affects possibilities; it is difficult to encourage ways of working not normally prevalent in the school, as for example teachers interested in group work have noted (chapter 6). Difficulties in attempts to formulate systematic collective approaches vis-à-vis questions such as racism, sexism, resources etc. have been noted.

Fragmentation can lead to random development as is evident in Duncan's description of his team which

> operates too much as a collection of amicable individuals. And there's no attempt really ... to get things to jell, with somebody actually taking an overview of the team ... I think that's one of the criticisms I'd throw against the team situation. I think the whole scene's too damn arbitrary; too much of a hit and miss affair really.

But fragmentation also signals flexibility. The teachers can respond to issues in various ways. The framework allows the existence of different strands and gives scope for radical teachers. Also particular teams have been able to adopt ethos and practices deemed unacceptable by the rest of the school. Though influence has been brought to bear upon such teams, authoritarian measures have not been adopted to channel their activities,[15] But the 1985 crisis of democracy raised questions about coordination and variety of practices; the new structures suggested contain pressures towards conformity.

Whilst individualization poses limitations in an ambiguous, contradictory way for Greenfield teachers, the fragmented informal networks have provided scope for radical action within the trade union, the curriculum and the daily organization of teaching. The framework and ethos of the school have provided radical and libertarian teachers opportunities for the development of an approach to education based on specific political and educational thinking. But attempts to develop practices and thinking not prevalent within the state sector are fraught with contradictions and tensions and indeed by 1985 the new organizational proposals confirmed the narrowing of spaces and teachers were called upon to shed what they 'presumed to be their power'.[16] Attention has turned towards individual accountability rather than collective responsibility; this has been evident in episodes where specific individuals have been singled out for attention and warning in situations where groups of teachers have acted collectively (Chapter Thirteen). Within the increasing pressures the search for progressive normative individualism by teachers becomes more significant. Julie attempts to develop possibilitarian notions of individuals:

'I think there are some things in terms of individualization which are valued in our society, which I don't personally value — like 'you got to fight for yourself' and 'sod everybody else', 'I am what I own' — but I do believe in self-exploration, knowing yourself, living with yourself, formulating a personal set of values which may be in conflict with society.'

Students

Greenfield College students are free from many trappings of atomization, such as uniforms, streams, houses, petty rules.[17] A fundamental aim is to encourage individualization-personalization, which for a section of teachers means connecting personal and social structures. The teachers try to match the education to the student, and treat them as concrete individuals with specific strengths and weaknesses. The school ethos has found organizational and structural realization in the formal democracy, in teams, in individualized curriculum and in the informal student-teacher relationships.

However, such personalization co-exists with atomization. The major device transforming the personalization experienced by the students is the process of certification, and the atomization it imposes. The students, through the ethos and atmosphere of the school, and through their dealings and negotiations with the teachers have, overall, come to the conclusion that they can make choices about whether to work or not, whether to prepare for examination or not, and, where students perceive closures and structured inequalities, they tend to see the school as detached from such external processes.

The students, even when they do not make a straight equation between intelligence and examination success, do make an equation between effort, choice, desire and such success. A large proportion of the students continue this by making an equation between qualifications and success in the labour market as was discussed and illustrated in chapter 7. The examinations atomize; the students prepare for them alone, take them alone, and feel the consequences in their own lives. The atomization imposed by certification is reinforced by the personalization in Greenfield; this personalization blurs the hierarchical, bureaucratic processes imposed by the examination system. The students do not think that their success in the College is linked to their location within structures of inequalities, whilst they may argue that one's location in general can determine one's life chances, as noted in chapter 7. A sense of the possibility of self-determination is communicated to the students in such a way that the students are not aware of the framework within which such self-determination takes place, or what the implications of the framework are for specific concrete individuals. To reiterate, then, the form (atomization-individualization) shapes the practices (personalization-individualization) in the school through the mode of certification, and the content in the school reinforces and strengthens the atomization process. The daily existence of students takes place within a fragmented framework; thus the generally acknowledged impact of social structures on lives and careers of people is not systematically extended to perceptions of their own particular circumstances.

Many students are willing to 'soak up' the individualization — personalization of the school; individualization is a process affecting them outside the school as well, as a form through which many experiences and observations are channelled and perceived. Linda expresses a brand of normative individualism which is seen to offer a way of resisting restrictive influences:

> I wouldn't like to attend a moot. They're just stupid ... Well you get some things done; just that I don't wanna go to anything like that. And different parties and things. I don't wanna be in a group. I just wanna be myself. I don't wanna go round being like everybody else. I just wanna be me.

Such individualistic views can leave the students defenceless when faced with an inegalitarian, atomized, dehumanizing labour market. Linda had no solutions for dealing with the impact of these processes, and no collective sense of working class or feminist solidarity to draw on — avenues through which to express her discontent were not readily available She could, in fact, only think of one: she wished she could have 'been in Brixton', 'throwing stones'.[18]

Students often seek individualistic solutions to problems posed by a specific location within the structures of inequality,[19] even though they may be aware of the non-individualistic nature of their problems.[20] The belief in the possibility of such solutions is partly an expression of careers of students in the school where they have little perception of the location of 'individuals' within complex relationships.[21] Thus the general sense of powerlessness experienced by students is contradictory with their sense of self-determination. But the search for individualistic solutions also relates to examples of social mobility many students have witnessed. Their belief in the possibility of upward social mobility in tackling problems experienced by working class girls and boys is not merely a fetish, an illusion, but is based on their own observations. Individualization becomes linked with the hard work ethic. Hence the recession and the reduction of social mobility are gradually leading some students to experience a sense of detachment from the ethos and practices in Greenfield. There is increased concern for examinations and/or job searching.

That the students are considered in terms of individual characteristics rather than group characteristics poses problems within the school ethos and organization. For example unless girls are seen as a group, it is difficult to devise positive strategies for dealing with their problems. Teachers aware of sexist practices are making headway in encouraging breaking out from traditional roles by girls — and by boys. But such headway remains limited unless forceful action is undertaken. There are difficulties in reconciling this with the school ethos emphasizing self-direction and choices by students, be it that these may be sexist and within a predetermined framework. This discussion continues in chapter 11.

The same problem applies to racism. The school is predominantly white, with the members of ethnic minorities usually well-integrated, born in Britain, and familiar and comfortable with mainstream culture. However, when black students and teachers have experienced racism, this has not been easily tackled, and difficulties posed by racism have not been clearly divorced from an individualized, interpersonal context.

I shall now consider possibilities posed by individualization. In Part Two I argued that oppositional spaces, in the sense of room for manoeuvre in the school, existed, and examples from the history of the school were chosen to indicate that such spaces have been utilized by students. The spaces are located within the relative autonomy and flexibility contained in progressive schools. In Greenfield specifically, the emphasis on the self-determination of the students, combined with the informal relationships and formal democratic structures gives the interested students scope to explore political questions, and to get involved in action. Oppositional spaces are not constituted by individualization-personalization, but the two are connected. Given the existence of spaces, and the restructuring process directed at these, and given the unsteady balance of forces and fragility of forms undergoing change, individualization-personalization can, in this context, lead to resistance with varying degrees of organization. Such resistance is potentially effective in challenging relations of domination during a period of restructuring, which becomes 'crisis' only when it finds expression in both 'economic' and 'political' terms; that is the link between the two instances visible.

> *Marilyn:* This school makes you stand up and think for yourself . . .
> It makes you independent, and I think everyone's different here —
> no two people are the same. And that is what I think makes people
> stand back and look and think something's wrong, and you get
> things like the NUSS.

For some students the scope for independence and self-determination seems very real, as is evident from Marilyn's comments. They are able to spend their time in the school pursuing their own aims, and feel that some scope is given to them in an otherwise hostile world. For socially successful students who perceive academic achievement as possible Greenfield College offers a haven within which to explore. They are likely to sense that it is a haven; that individualization outside the school is atomization, not personalization; that outside the school 'individuals' are stripped of their concreteness and uniqueness — they are deindividualized. Such students can 'afford' to be radical, to observe 'something's wrong'. But the sense of injustice experienced by Marilyn must find an expression within a collective organization in order to be effective. This step is not an easy one to take. Marilyn mentions the NUSS, she considers it a 'good thing', but is not a member. Radical organized politics is considered alien by her as by many others, with its distant structures, modes of action and personnel which contain routinization familiar from party politics. Marilyn explains:

> It's a good thing for the students to be independent, but in fact the boy
> who runs (NUSS), he's a — you could almost regard him as a teacher,
> anyway — he's so much taller than anyone else. I don't know what
> that's got to do with it, but you feel that he's not student with you; I
> don't anyway.

Big steps are to be taken by students who would choose to utilize the possibilities; they are aware of this, and usually do not take such steps. This attitude was clearly expressed by students wishing to 'remain naive' or 'ignorant and happy to be so' (chapter 7). Similarly a girl discussing sexism noted that though women teachers talked about sexism, this was unlikely to have much impact, if they 'went home and cooked dinners'. Non-sexist content was not seen as sufficient.

Despite the pressures introduced by cuts, student-teacher interaction and relationships in Greenfield are still relatively informal and relaxed; the use of first names is a signifier of this. Students consider teachers as 'human beings', and are able to joke with them, moan at them, 'answer them back' etc., though not all students do this with equal ease, or with equal lack of consequence. The nature of relationships leads some students to question authority in general (particularly adult authority, chapter 7). The use of first names acquired a symbolic significance in early criticisms of the school (chapter 5).

Yet the possibilities for critical analysis and power are partial. The teachers *are* an authority despite the fact that students and teachers do not always behave as though they were. First names tend to acquire a symbolic rather than real significance; their use represents particular views and attitudes about authority, rather than particular practices or impact. This is not to ignore that Greenfield teachers are seen differently by the students from the way teachers are seen in other schools.[22] But the co-existence of possibilities and limitations is indicated. One manifestation is the shifting by teachers from personal to professional styles of interaction (as indicated in the chain of control, chapter 6; this is further discussed in chapter 9).

A further tentative point can be made. Frith has argued[23] that an important response to 'state realism' is a 'defence of fantasy'. The approach in Greenfield emphasizes creativity, and indeed a number of teachers would argue that students gain more perceptive insights through creative writing than through, for example, their social studies projects. On the other hand, Ellis *et al.* (1976) argue that such creativeness can be devoid of content, and serves few other purposes beyond integrating the students to the school. Personalized, creative, fantasized appropriation of reality can potentially lead to a deconstruction of aspects of that reality, or within the institutional context of constraints in schools to routinization.[24] But, argues Valkerdine in her analysis of pre-teen girls' comics, the potent fantasies of these cannot be countered by presenting the girls with alternative images of reality; what is needed is 'other possible dreams and fantasies'.[25]

The discussion on teachers and students has indicated tensions at the school level. To further our understanding of these, I shall discuss different meanings individualization holds for different groups, as Poulantzas has noted. Though individualization-atomization constitutes all citizens as units, they remain members of class, gender and race. Atomization is realized through state practices, the social division of labour and the labour process. Different groups have differential relationships to these processes, which they argue have varied effects. The emphasis on subjects as thinking actors reminds us that they related these processes according to their political framework. Thus differential relations to individualization-atomization connect with different normative understandings.

When considering tensions in Greenfield College, three normative orientations are of interest. First, individualism of working class students emphasizes a sense of 'looking to no one but self'. Particularly members of the skilled working class with experience of social mobility and perception of the possibilities of individualistic solutions stress the need to be 'selfish' and to strive for the betterment of one's own position. They are, as working class, endowed with what Giddens (1973) calls class-awareness, but not with class-consciousness; they experience powerlessness, and have little belief in the possibility of collective solutions. Secondly, individualism pertaining to what Bernstein (1975) terms the 'old middle class' contains conservative middle class values, stressing possessive individualism and individual responsibility. In the school this finds expression through professionalism (chapter 9). Thirdly, individualism of the 'new middle class' emphasizes personalization, uniqueness, potential, realization; such values were prominent in the sixties counter-cultures.

Contradictions and tensions result when these different orientations meet within the general framework of individualization and the organization, ethos, structures and processes of Greenfield College. Professionalism as a mode (chapter 9) strengthens atomization and poses limitations for individualization implied by the 'new middle class' orientation; teachers attempting to personalize learning and interaction. A contradiction exists between framework and practice. Students who seek private solutions to collective problems are perceived by teachers to conform to traditional 'old middle class' formulations. But for working class students concessions to 'new middle class' concerns are difficult to make (chapter 10), and possible only from positions of relative strength (c.f. p. 191). Working class students like Kevin, as developed in chapter 10, perceived the closeness between the new and old middle class positions when observing shifts from personalization to professionalism (chapter 9); neither would share his urge for social mobility.

These contradictions and tensions find expression in the issue of vertical teams, discussed in chapter 12. Here teachers interested in developing alternatives within the school were frustrated when they saw students aligning with dominant, traditional middle class conceptions in their concern for a framework that would allow them to achieve social mobility and hence resistant to change. Because of the democratic structures teachers were faced with a dilemma which they attempted to solve through professionalism, thus sidestepping problems posed by student participation. The students perceived this response as a lack of concern for individualization-personalization they had come to expect from teachers who were thus now seen to be closer to old middle class conservative expressions of individualization as atomization.

Conclusion

Individualization as a form constituted in the labour process and by the state finds expression at the school level by inflecting practices through modes such as professionalism. In Greenfield practices have been characterized by personalization. But this personalization reinforces the process of atomization which it in many ways questions, as long as 'individuals' are not viewed in their social context. But, particularly during a period of restructuring, the progressive character of personalization is also significant, when it contains a critique of processes contained within restructuring (such as standardization and centralization), and may contribute to a perception of oppositional spaces. The conservative critique of progressive education relates to such possibilities. The critique of the left focusses on the limited framework within which such possibilities exist, and their contradictory manifestations, and the way in which dominant relations are reinforced not through coercion, but through persuasion. Personalization can, on the one hand, limit the scope for exploration and perception to predetermined, immediate reality of the students; on the other hand, it can provide penetrating insights when leading to an exploration of political questions about the limits to personalization, and its shift to atomization. It is to these possibilities that the 'backlash' against progressive education is related. Indeed 1985 discussions on 'good practice' and new management structures raised also questions about core curriculum, balance between teams, and an investment notion of education with pupils as clients, and have led some team teachers to be concerned about what would be made available to students. There are also fears that the new structures would remain without democratic features altogether, negotiation and self-direction would disappear, and, in the absence of the important, inter-connected ingredients of the school ethos the team would become administrative shells where atomization would give less scope for personalization, and Greenfield would have little distinction to offer in the network of secondary schools.

Notes

1 *Leicester Mercury*, n.d.
2 C.f. the WILLIAM TYNDALE enquiry, chapter 3, pp. 45–6.
3 MACFARLANE (1978) p. 196.
4 OFFE and RONGE (1981) also discuss contradictions in possessive individualism.
5 C.f. ABERCROMBIE and TURNER (1981) who emphasize the significance of the dominant ideology in organizing *dominant* classes.
6 POULANTZAS (1978) p. 63.
7 *Ibid.* p. 72
8 MARX (1974) p. 717.
9 This example was also considered by HOLLOWAY and PICCIOTTO (1984).
10 GERSTENBERGER (1977), Edinburgh-London Weekend Return Group (1980), CSE Cuts Group (1979).
11 GERSTENBERGER (1977) p. 9.
12 For example GRACE (1978) quotes Bray's discussion of a contrast between the existence of an individual and of a crowd:

> children who have acquired the habit of sharing the life of a *crowd*, find the routine existence of the *individual* insipid and distasteful; they become more noisy and uncontrolled in their ways, less tolerant of any restraint, less capable of finding any zest in pleasures of tranquil enjoyment. The crowd influence is one of the most potent factors in the environment of a town. (p. 170)

Simon (1974) quotes Roebuck indicating that concern was not merely expressed about the problem in behaviour control; education was seen to offer the

> necessary means and instruments for the acquiring of knowledge, but ... also the training and fashioning of the intellectual and moral qualities of

the *individual* that he may be able and willing to acquire knowledge, and to turn it to its right use. (p. 165).

13 Both types of shifts were observed.
14 The number of teachers supporting radical proposals in meetings is usually considerably larger than the (small) number of Marxists in the school.
15 Influence may consist of informal discussions, more formal negotiations with members of the executive expressing concerns and criticisms, certain staffing policies, and, at times the subtle encouragement of some of the teachers involved to continue their career elsewhere. By 1985, however, the pressures increased for example through allowances.
16 An internal paper by the Principal, 29 January 1985
17 For example about eating, going to the toilet, movement, mode of dress etc.
18 Chapter 10.
19 As was evident from interviews and informal discussions.
20 For example KEVIN, chapter 10.
21 *C.f.* WILLIAMS (1965).
22 *C.f.* CORRIGAN (1979), WILLIS (1977).
23 In the Socialist Teachers Alliance Conference (1978).
24 For example the discussion in chapter 7, p. 112.
25 VALKERDINE (1984) p. 184

Chapter 9

Professionalism

At the school level practices and organization assume unintended and altered outcomes and impact. This process is explored by discussing how individualization-atomization is mediated through professionalism. I shall discuss the term 'professionalism', draw connections to individualization, and note its gender-specificity. A distinction between cultural and structural professionalism is made. Professionalism is considered an integral part of the work experience of teachers. In Greenfield College the school ethos stresses equality, individual uniqueness and autonomy. But the practices of the school do not always promote these and many contradict them. *How* these contradictions find their manifestation in schools is discussed by considering professionalism as a mode mediating atomization.

Professionalism and Teaching

In sociology ideal-typical criteria of professions are noted, and existing occupational groupings are compared to these. Teaching does not fulfil all the criteria, and has been called a 'semi-profession', a 'bureaucratic profession' (Leggatt, 1970) etc.; the term is, however, widely used to apply to teachers particularly in the sense of an occupational culture and identity, a way of doing a job (Hargreaves, 1980; Deem, 1976). Teachers' organizations use the terminology and ideology of professions to emphasize differences from the working class (Finn *et al.*, 1977). Professionalism is used in an attempt to defend the autonomous sphere of operation of teachers; it is used as a strategy to improve their work situation (Ginsburg, 1980; Deem, 1976).[1]

A teacher enters a structured occupation after a process of training characterized by differentiation and domination (Mardle and Walker, 1980). Through this training the notion of *expertise* has been imprinted into teaching; it has acquired increased significance through the certification of teaching, and the moves towards an all-graduate occupational grouping. Remuneration and status are linked to notions of expertise and are hierarchically organized. The structuring of, and hence the control and influence over teachers' salaries by the central government is under dispute. There are tensions between increased professionalization and upsurge of trade union action.

'Progress' of teachers in a hierarchical occupation is tied to the notion of a 'career', the purposeful movement of individuals through salary scales for increased remuneration, and through graded posts of responsibility to increased status. Thus directions that teachers' careers can assume are predetermined by the way in which the occupation is structured. The overall opportunities within the hierarchical 'ladder' are determined by the position of the occupation as a whole, and by the development of schooling in the national context.

Impersonality is a further aspect of the predetermined framework of teaching as a professional occupation. Teachers work within an institutional setting, assuming roles with reference points within that setting, positioned at a specific point of a career, with a specific remuneration and status. As teachers they relate to children as pupils. The work of teachers is also characterized by *autonomy*. They are able to exercise their own judgment in the classroom, but such autonomy is limited, with specific constraints, as noted by Grace (1978); he discusses the development of the teaching profession over time, and concludes that autonomy is 'limited', but nevertheless 'real'.[2] Sharp and Green (1975) discuss limitations on teacher autonomy in a progressive school.

Within this institutional setting of structural professionalism teachers are faced with — often behind closed classroom doors — problems which they have to tackle there and then by themselves, and have to develop notions of 'doing a job'. The teachers, in concrete settings, have to interpret and act on processes in the classroom and in the staffroom. Strategies for survival are developed, and daily work is routinized through 'tricks of the trade', development of an occupational culture — language, humour etc. This is the second sphere of professionalism, cultural professionalism. Teachers formulate common sense, unexplained notions of what it means to act 'professionally' or 'unprofessionally' and evolve a sense of unspelt out 'duties' and 'responsibilities' involved in the work; in the course of their work an occupational culture and identity is assumed. Cultural professionalism evolves as a response to the demands of the institutional setting of teachers. Structural professionalism formulates the setting within which teachers work; in it are condensed tensions caused by struggles between teachers (as state employees) and the state over the control and financial rewards of the occupation.

The term professionalism, then, is used here to denote a loose constellation of practices understood through notions of expertise, hierarchy, career, autonomy, impersonality, occupational culture and 'tricks of the trade'. This is not an attempt to repeat sociological checklists of criteria of professional occupations, but to pinpoint what makes the term important for this research. Certain features have been observed in a school during fieldwork; these are descriptively best brought together under the concept 'professionalism'. A more analytical explanation of these features can then be undertaken through a theoretical consideration of professionalism as a mode channelling school practices. In order to do this, it is essential now to discuss professionalism and individualism.

Professionalism and Individualism

Johnson (1972) quotes Marshall (1939) who refers to individualism of professions:

> It may mean the belief that the individual is the true unit of service, because service depends on individual qualities and individual judgement supported by individual responsibility which cannot be shifted onto the shoulders of others. That, I believe, is the essence of professionalism.[3]

Links between professionalism and individualization are discussed by Larson (1977). Though professionalism is a collective project, those involved seek support for individual careers and dignity; the importance of individual differentiation stems from individualism[4] being a central process 'running across the whole social structure'. Larson notes McPherson's discussion of 'possessive individualism' contradicted by the market. The individualism of professionalism is a 'subjective illusion'; it is not real, but conceals 'collective powerlessness, subordination and complicity'.[5]

Expertise is located in individuals, and knowledge and competence become qualities of *particular* people with appropriate training. The hierarchical structuring of an occupation with differing remuneration and status attached to specific positions rather than individuals contains a process of atomization. For example in any school the number of points and positions of responsibility is predetermined and not linked to the number of particular teachers able to fulfil the criteria of these positions. Teachers as teachers within an institutional setting are units devoid of personal, concrete characteristics.

Thus professionalism as a feature of a collective occupational grouping atomizes the members of the grouping; it strips them of their particularities and brings them together as units with a setting of defined roles. Within cultural professionalism this process is reinforced and in some ways contradicted. The development of the 'tricks of the trade' involves routinization containing a personal blend of solutions but within the ethos of the school the teacher is in. Routinization implies an increasing competence to deal with problematic situations, thus reducing stress caused by the struggle for survival in classrooms when conflicting expectations of teachers and pupils are negotiated. However, the occupational culture and identity of teachers also implies scope for the introduction of personalization into the work situation through humour and informal interaction.[6] Before considering professionalism and individualization in the context of Greenfield College, I shall turn to the specific relationship between professionalism and progressivism.

Professionalism and Progressivism

Professionalism gave scope for progressive education which lacked a power base in political parties, national structures or local communities (for example Dale, 1979). I noted in chapter 2 that because of the teacher shortage a campaign aimed at male graduates was conducted. It stressed that teaching was a profession with scope for decision-making, independent action and appropriate financial rewards. Such representation of teaching as a profession coincided with the relative salience of progressivism in the education debate, training institutions and schools, particularly the primary sector. These two processes reinforced each other, and changes in the content of professionalism occurred. Professional expertise and client relationships were viewed from a child-centred perspective, and the role of the teacher was defined as a facilitator able to analyze the process of learning of individual children.[7]

Teacher enthusiasm for progressivism was opportunistic, and related to professionalization as an occupational strategy rather than to educational considerations, argue Finn *et al.* (1976). Willis (1977) sees the development of progressivism as a response to problems of control in the classroom, where child-centred methods were considered effective, and thus reducing stress experienced by teachers in the struggle for survival. These observations are useful, but do not take into account differentiations within progressivism. Here the aim is to move beyond generalizations by considering Greenfield College.

Progressivism requires teacher control of curriculum etc., and thus gave scope to Marxist, libertarian and feminist teachers to try to relate their political thinking and practices. Thus paradoxically professionalism, a mode through which the form of individualization-atomization is imposed on the content of schools also constituted a space within which individualization-personalization and concern for pupils as members of a class, sex and race could be developed by teachers. Attempts to develop radical 'aprofessional' practices were located in opportunistic utilization of spaces assuming fragile, contradictory expression through professionalism. For example the Tyndale teachers (chapter 3) emphasized their professional expertise. This entailed relative autonomy from the state but also detached or critical indifference towards (particularly working class) parents (Sharp and Green, 1975).

Professionalism in Greenfield College

Though Greenfield teachers do not view the school as just 'a sorting house for employment',[8] examinations play an important role; amidst controversy the school can derive legitimacy from success in examinations. The significance attached to examinations has increased as unemployment has been increasing and the policy to publish results have strengthened pressure on the school to prioritize them. Teachers have complex, contradictory views on certification (chapter 6) and many find it difficult to reconcile their political and educational thinking with what they see as instrumental learning towards external ends.

Teachers assess and guide students within a framework imposed by external demands mediated through examinations, Interactions do not, therefore, take place simply between teachers and students as individuals, but between teachers as professionals and students as the objects of professional procedures. The problems experienced by teachers in deciding the appropriate examination orientation vis-à-vis specific students were noted in chapter 6. Generally they adjust their expectations on the basis of how they interpret the aptitudes and motivations of their students as individuals (chapter 6, p. 85). Standards set for students have implications for their careers (for example, Rosenthal and Jacobson, 1968). How the judgments are made is crucial; the teachers were asked whether they found it difficult — Duncan replied:

> No. I mean there are obvious criteria, aren't there, i.e. according to the system of exams we have ... So for example it's very simple to tell if somebody's going to make it mathematically ... You can predict the student's exam results from the moment you have them, within limits. I mean ... after half a term or a term I could start making some sort of assessment of their future exam potential.

Sarch expressed similar thoughts:

> *Sarah:* I imagine most teachers ... gauge what kids expect from school and therefore ... my stardards are not the same for all kids ... You know fairly early on quite honestly ... whether most kids are going to be sort of capable — I'm not trying to argue a straight IQ argument here; I'm just saying one knows fairly early on whether some kids are going to get good enough grades ... to end up in the sixth form taking A-levels or not.
>
> *Interviewer:* So you trust your own judgment?
>
> *Sarah:* Yes — not entirely. You see it's an interaction. I mean I might be wrong in doing this — it's something we ought to debate about actually.

Professional practice and educational thinking of radical teachers can be contradictory; cultural professionalism provides a solution to daily difficulties, and is so embedded in that setting that contradictions do not readily surface. When presented with the question in an interview situation, the awareness of contradictions is spelt out by this teacher.

The process of learning 'the tricks of the trade' is illustrated by comments of a probationer who was asked whether assessment is easy:

I think it would be for me now, because I know the standard, but this year it's not been. I mean I had some help and talked to people, but I think I tended to overrate at least one person. I think that comes with experience, but also it's a thing you talk about with them.

The school ethos, and the educational thinking of teachers emphasize individual potential and the divergent possibilities for learning by all, but professional judgments are made on the basis of standards set by examinations; when these standards are used as a starting point, a good, experienced teacher is able to make 'absolute' assessments on the basis of criteria provided by them.

The three teachers quoted above have had access to socialist, sociological and feminist thinking and literature emphasizing the relationship between school achievement and social class and gender. However, the pressures of their work are such that day-to-day decisions may be made with little regard to the insights gained through educational or political theorizing. The imprint of professionalism is strong, because it is inbuilt into the very notions of 'doing the job of teaching' as well as into the structured setting of teaching.

Problems do arise in the daily practice when students do not accept teacher judgments. For example Jill refers to a girl doing an English 'O' level. Jill does not think she'll get it, and 'tried to put her off by saying it's hard work and that kind of thing, but she wants to do it, so she's doing it'. Teachers try to dissuade students from taking examinations which are considered inappropriate, but if students persist, particularly with parental backing, they may be able to do so. But teachers' approaches are not all uniform. Janet did not want Pat to take 'O' level social studies:

> She kept saying things to me like it's my right you can't stop me and I was sort of a bit persuaded by that at one point, well perhaps that is her right and perhaps I'm being very mean . . . but in retrospect I was absolutely right . . . In fact she didn't even turn up for the ones where she could have passed.

Janet thought that if she entered a student for an examination, it was her responsibility to ensure appropriate preparation; she did not think it possible for Pat to complete the project work required, and because of the pressures of the job 'did not fancy months and months of nagging'. Janet did not sidestep the issue by entering Pat for the examination she was thought to fail. This decision caused conflict, and possibly contributed to Pat's increasing detachment for school, and her disinclination to take any examinations seriously (chapter 10). Left critique of progressivism argues that it conceals contradictions; progressive practice can also render them visible.

The differentiation in teacher responses must be remembered when discussing the impact of professionalism. From a radical point of view Jill stresses final difficulties in assessing students, even in terms of examination criteria:

I don't think it's fair to say to them you will not pass this exam, I'm not going to let you sit that, when in the end they may pass ... we may have misjudged his abilities, and I think it's arrogant just to think of yourself as the final arbiter for kids' abilities, so I would let them sit it, yeah.

Progressive teachers must channel students to appropriate options and to ensure reasonable overall results. They have to make judgments and relate to students professionally. Paradoxically, the solution to this problem can be sought for through professionalism; training, expertise and experience allow teachers to develop competence in making accurate assessments with examination criteria as a starting point. Professionalism operates as a mode channelling individualization-personalization into individualization-atomization. When making judgments teachers do not have students with specific social class location, sex-gender and biographical constellations as their reference point, but individual students are related to specific examination criteria in terms of their exhibited attainment. During this process individuals in their concrete characteristics lose their significance — they become atomized units possessing particular skills to various degrees.

The day-to-day work of teachers does not allow them much scope to analyze this process, and whilst the majority of teachers relate to examinations critically, at the same time they feel able to make such assessments relatively competently. This lack of analysis does not indicate unawareness of such a process however; the quest for teacher control of examinations was very predominant in the sixties generally, and, in a school like Greenfield College, emphasis is on Mode III examinations. But one aspect of the impact of the process of restructuring has been that the number of Mode IIIs has decreased.[9]

Teachers are faced by young people under compulsion to come to school who may place little social, intellectual or instrumental value on formal education. In negotiations with them teachers rely on tactics acquired through training, experience, and the occupational culture of the school The question of control raises particular problems for teachers in a progressive school. First, they are engaged in negotiations with students to a greater degree than teachers in more formal schools where greater areas of teacher–pupil interaction are defined by established rules and practices. Second, they have to reconcile their practices with the school ethos, emphasizing the self-direction and autonomy of all students. Third, radical teachers aware of political and sociological arguments that middle class children are more able to benefit from a situation where they have to rely on their own motivation and initiative, are concerned with the impact of lack of 'pushing' on working class students; moreover, feminist teachers familiar with theories pointing to the contradictions experienced by adolescent girls (increasingly made aware of society's expectations of femininity, which lead many of them to attach decreasing significance on schooling) attempt to encourage them to view their own futures separately from the traditional role of a wife and a mother, and emphasize the significance of work and various locations in the labour market — they are also concerned about the impact of lack of 'pushing' on girls.

Duncan talks about the problems of dealing with reluctant working class students; he refers to Shane who has done 'little written work', and has resisted Duncan's efforts to involve him: 'he mucks around, he promises to do something, and never does it in the end, and I've tried to talk it through with him'. Duncan is reluctant to give up trying, but notes the choices he is confronted with; decisions about learning and control cannot easily be divorced from each other.

> You try all the tricks of the trade and they're not working, and I'm not sure how much more you can force somebody to work, without actually forcing them into outright rebellion against you. I mean in the end you make certain sorts of decisions. You've got a 45-minute lesson — if X doesn't start in the first five minutes, you can choose to spend the next 45 minutes sitting on him, and trying to get some work out of him, and ignore the other twenty-nine in the class, or you leave him, you cut your losses, you try and start the others, and you come back to him in five or ten minutes time, and you carry on doing that . . . but in the end you start making the options — well is X actually disrupting the class, and more often than not he isn't; you got to turn round and pay attention to the fact that there are other kids who need your time and effort, and you move on.

The teacher has to balance the desire to encourage each individual student, the necessity to control disruptive behaviour, and the responsibility for all students in his/her tutor group. When the teachers at the same time operate within a school ethos emphasizing negotiation and minimization of conflict, along with self-direction of the student, they may decide, in the case of some students, to pay more attention to their social and emotional learning, than their academic progress.[10] Such a decision reduces the likelihood of disruptive behaviour on the part of those students[11] and releases the teacher to deal with other students.[12]

The establishment of different aims for different students is based on the assumption that they have different needs. This kind of educational ideology and practice, however, assumes a particular meaning when individuals are not simply individuals, but members of class, sex and race as well. Through the 'tricks of the trade' in the work of teacher-professionals inequalities can be reinforced, when judgments through the role of circumstances become routinized 'despite' the teachers. The contradictions and necessities of decisions are now reaching the teachers sooner than before. Because of the expenditure cuts the teachers have larger tutor groups and less resources, and the pressure of time is evident in a school based on individualized learning.

An important aspect in the work of teachers as professionals in a progressive school is the tendency to shift from personalized to positional interaction.[13] The former is based on negotiation and mutual decisions; the latter on institutional roles of teachers and students, whereby teachers, on the basis of their authority as teachers, make demands on students as students. Students feel uncertain about such shifts (chapter 7), and about the possibility that teachers who have treated them as concrete individuals resort to professional interaction, crossing to the public from the personal sphere.

To encourage 'self-direction' of students teachers must help them to identify their own needs and ways of meeting these. Teachers think it important that students know 'who they are'; they are encouraged to write and talk about 'themselves' and 'their feelings'; the teachers like to know 'what makes the students tick' and 'what goes on in their heads'. When students feel vulnerable and express concern about shifts in teacher behaviour, it is this knowledge that teachers have accumulated about them that make potential conflicts dealt with in impersonal terms frightening, and, secondly, angry personal exchanges expressing teacher frustration are imminently threatening as well. When students lower barriers between themselves and their teachers, and reveal aspects which they might not do in a more conventional situation, they have a sense of personal interaction, of relationships between two individuals, but they also express awareness of the experience that teachers have accumulated over the years, having dealt with 'different types of children', and trust the teachers to bring this expertise to bear upon personal interaction. The students thus relate to the notion of 'expertise' within professionalism, whilst being concerned about 'control'. Their worry about a teacher losing his/her temper in a frustrated manner relates to the conception of power — the differential institutional setting of teachers and students, and the possibility of the teachers using such a setting. Thus students often refer to teachers being 'moody' and 'nasty'.

Personalized interaction, and the attempt to elicit information from the students which facilitates their incorporation into the school by encouraging activities that absorb them, whilst also facilitating control, leads to situations where personal information is elicited from teachers by students. This occurs for a number of reasons; the teachers are aware that they cannot expect personalized engagement from the students unless they are prepared to engage personally themselves. Thus the teachers have, over time, developed techniques which enable them to discriminate how to reveal personal aspects, to whom to reveal them, and when to reveal them. However, particularly before the intense cutbacks began to affect the school, the teachers have spent a fair amount of time with individual students, discussing a range of issues with personal implications for both. The mutual confidence in each other that such situations may generate remove the teachers further from the teacher role and techniques, and more of them as persons is revealed than is intended. This does not refer to divulging of precarious information as such, but formulation of bonds whereby the vulnerability of the teacher is increased as well, and more of the teacher is available for student scrutiny. The teachers' position in Greenfield is relatively demanding and stressful, when they are faced with shifts from individualized personalized interaction with specific students to depersonalized, institutional student/teacher confrontations based on divergent sets of expectations and conceptions about the roles of teachers and students.

At times students purposefully engage in behaviour intended to explore and provoke situations where teachers lose their temper in a manner which does not wrest the control of the situation, but vents anger and frustration. This strategy of students is a way of penetrating through the professional 'armour' — it is a form of resistance on the one hand, and a form of humanization on the other hand. Some of the lasses, for example Pat and Lesley, were particularly skilful in eliciting the vulnerability of male teachers concerned to establish interaction with them in order to integrate them into the team; the girls flaunted the ambivalences created, and some spectacular scenes ensued. [14]

A further impact of professionalism is some stifling of creativity and divergence through the 'tricks of the trade' leading to routinization. Julie discusses the changes in Greenfield over time, referring to Brian (chapter 10):

> In the early days obviously you might say that kids like Brian might have actually enjoyed the school much more ... the school might have been much more electrifying — I mean there were kids who did much more exciting things, but the bulk of kids were much more unhappy, because their backgrounds didn't enable them to value it, to take advantage of it ... it isn't the same school it was once ... It is overall much better, but there have been certain losses ... It couldn't have continued. It was amazingly anarchic in the first years.

These comments indicate the solidifying of practice, seen not as a retrograde step, but as dealing with the realities of the day-to-day life in the school. They also illuminate pragmatism as a response to the perceived realities of the teaching and learning situation, and to the needs of students with a particular cultural location and biographical constellations, which make it difficult for them to benefit from the opportunities available at school. This situation can be intensified by the structural location of students; thus, for example, working class students with a strong instrumental orientation are likely to experience more difficulties than middle class students with a similar orientation.

The losses implied by routinization are mentioned. Talented working class students like Brian do not receive sufficient stimulation in the routinized environment with a reduced range of activities[15] to capture their potential and enable them to develop it, whilst attaining the academic achievement they are capable of as well. The routinization is a response to the pressures of the job of teachers as professionals. Thus cultural professionalism provides solutions to difficulties posed by structural professionalism. The limitations of professionalism in the sense of occupational culture developed in the workplace is that it welds together with the more formal, external professionalism involving notions of expertise, career, hierarchy etc. The daily practices of teachers allow, in their context, the simultaneous erosion of these activities, routine solutions which in the context of the modes of professionalism, certification and compulsion strengthen atomized individualization.

Hierarchies are crucial in the way that professionalism influences practices in an innovatory school; the operation as a restrictive mode channelling the content in the school is evident. External formal imposition of hierarchy in the school is through remuneration, structured in scales and increments for specific teachers, and in a definite number of points for a particular school. The staff in the school have operated their own allowances policy within these parameters (chapter 5). The criteria on the basis of which the overall policy of the school is determined, have been subject to controversy and disagreement over the years. In the context of allowances the teachers have to consider their attitude to aspects of professionalism, which the salary structure determines. The liberal and pragmatist teachers tend to emphasize the need to consider market principles, whilst radical and libertarian teachers emphasize the cooperative nature of the school, which ought to be reflected in the allowances policy as far as possible within the external constraints. Otherwise the school would, Janet argues, 'promote teachers who were good administrators, who got here on time, and did their registers'. External indices of professionalism would gain precedence. The notions of 'good' teaching would become solidified and routinized. This is, indeed, happening as the allowances policy is disintegrating with the crisis of democracy. Teachers who do not fit external indices are encouraged to consider moving elsewhere.

Whilst I am emphasizing professionalism as a structural and cultural feature significant for the school as a whole, we must also consider the different ways in which teachers relate to professionalism, ideologically, politically, and in practice. Different teacher orientations are related to different strands of progressivism in the school. The tensions that find expression through attitudes to professionalism are indicated by the case of one team which during the main research period was considered problematic by others. Phil from the team noted the suspicion 'that in our team we are ideologically unprofessional'. This referred to a worry that the teachers were adopting an explicit line which they imposed on students without sufficient regard to neutrality, and without giving students sufficient scope to develop their own views. This approach combined with a more structured teaching learning situation was seen as a retrograde step.

Phil referred to a meeting between the Acting Principal and the teachers in the team. The Principal expressed worries that

> the general level of expectation of behaviour and discipline was less
> controlled than he would have liked . . . he didn't see this particularly

as being slackness from us — he saw it as being a difference to what teachers should be. He simply presented it as a kind of practical problem of running the school.

Questions of practical problems of running the school touch upon professional responsibilities, starting from specifics such as conscientiousness in registration and punctuality. The language available to teachers in talking about responsibilities towards students tends to centre around professional rhetoric. Worries about lateness are expressed in terms of insufficient regard for the needs of the students; the language of duties and responsibilities is integrated with a language of caring.

The cultural professionalism which develops through occupational practice and identity also implies responsibilities towards one's colleagues. Indeed a characteristic of a good teacher which is considered important by teachers across the school, despite political or educational orientation, is the ability and inclination to 'cover' and control all students in one's own tutor group, and, when necessary or appropriate, those of others.

Professionalism arises through an external structural setting and through practices in the day-to-day work. To clarify these points in connection with Greenfield College, I shall consider why teachers in the school are professionals in terms of role, identity and practice, whilst taking into account differential relationships they have to professionalism. First, struggle for 'survival' is a reality both for the school and the teachers. They are forced to produce results in terms of which the school is judged — certification. Second, through their training the teachers have been in contact with professional socialization. Third, many teachers are concerned with their own self-development, and though they may not see such development in career terms, their location within a profession provides an avenue for such a development, which otherwise might not find any opportunities for expression. Retraining, and remaining within the professional location, allows one to keep one's job, ensures the possibility of secondment and therefore gives scope for self-development without sacrifices.[16]

Fourth, the 'bread and butter' aspects of professionalism must be noted. Advancement in a career does not only mean development and responsibilities, but financial rewards. Parry (1974) notes that

> Many teachers find themselves in a position where they are trying to live middle class lifestyles on incomes which make that aspiration impossible.[17]

One teacher actually refers to the affluent self-employed parents of some students, who lack a 'professional life-style' and the contradictions and gaps of understanding created between them and teachers with professional life-styles and no affluence.

Fifth, the disadvantages of professionalism are not always clear, and an alternative political framework is needed in order to question professionalism as a practice and an ideology; even then, the above discussion on examinations and assessment indicates that links between perspectives and practices are not easily made. Professionalism is linked to normative individualism. This is linked to individualization as a form which runs across social structures of society. Larson (1977) argues that this creates a 'subjective illusion' to which professionals have a particular relation because of their special competences, and because of the notions of self-development being linked to the notion of career. Further, the changes in the content of professionalism, through official endorsement of progressivism, moved towards a greater emphasis on the student–client centred approach, and were seen to overshadow structural professionalism.

Sixth, autonomy, detachment and expertise implied by professionalism provide teachers scope to develop their approach in a local context which is, in part, hostile to the aims and practices of the school. There have been few consistent efforts to explain to the local community what the school is aiming to accomplish; it is assumed that parents would not understand, or agree. Parental questions and criticisms are often responded to in professional language not aiming to be comprehensible to them.[18] Moreover, the demands of parents, local education authority, employers and students themselves may be contradictory; to reconcile the different expectations teachers adopt a professional stance which enables them to acquire detachment from them all. Thus professionalism creates a space within which the teachers can develop their practices. Such a space, however, is contradictory and limited. It deprives the school of any real power base in the local area. Moreover, it involves the school in compromises when presenting an image to the outside which may not be entirely congruent with its aims and practices. But when the new Principal tried to encourage 'open debate' during a period of restructuring, the liaison with the LEA, governors etc. led to increased pressure on the school to mend its 'irregularities' in a situation where the Principal did not condone all aspects of Greenfield organization, practice and ethos anyway. Formal democracy was suspended in an effort to assure the teachers that new management structures had to be adopted.

The limitations stem from the structural location of teachers (Sharp and Green, 1975) and their role in the school (c.f. Grace, 1978) as well as the local constellations, whereby the College is seen to stretch the autonomy of a school and its head to its very limits, and as it is seen to abuse this autonomy, tighter control is called for. What has been considered the Messianic fervour[19] of the early days has been tempered through the major crisis of the school (chapter 5). The teachers are constantly engaged in a delicate exercise of attempting to interpret the political situation, the limits of local acceptability, the extent of support from the governors and the officers of the local authority, along with the strength of hostility of local Conservative opposition and the local media, as well as the prospective parents. Opinion in the school is divided amongst those who wish to develop what is possible within confines of 'survival'; those who are prepared to take the first tentative steps to test the opposition;[20] and those who believe in the necessity and possibility of trade union militancy.

Teachers relate to trade unionism, professionalism and the democratic structures in different ways. First, the background of the teachers is significant. Their original or parental social class location influences attitudes — trade union conceptions are more familiar to those with working class parents than those with middle class parents. For example Tom explains:

> I got a very sort of proletarian view of the job, you turn up, you do your work and you get your money. I mean some people have got a much more middle class sort of view of the job in which you got many more rights and privileges than I see in jobs. My whole view (is) very much how my father approached it ... your work is being in a subordinate role ... I'm always amazed how people can see it in terms of rights and privileges rather than obligations.

The view of teacher-as-worker can have different manifestations as well. A more militant NUT member argued that at times teachers' rights were more important than students' rights; the teachers work in the school for a number of years, whereas particular students only stay for two years.

Second, biographies of teachers influence their views. Jill talks about her attitudes to duties and responsibilities of teachers; her comments reflect the significance of her occupational experiences, and of personality constellations.

> I've never taught in a place like this before, and most of my experience has been in fairly traditional schools ... I don't go along with kids doing exactly what they want to do, in terms of behaviour anyway, because it would get on my nerves and I don't think I have that much tolerance in myself ... I'm always concerned when my students are not where they should be ... I see myself being responsible for them and don't want them being around causing trouble anywhere else, causing a problem for anyone else.

The concept of biography allows us to consider aspects and experiences which are involved in the construction of a 'person' as a concrete, unique individual.

Third, political views of teachers are significant. However the divisions are not simple. Thus some socialists are strong supporters of the democratic structures; others feel that these are irrelevant and devote their energies to trade unionism, and encourage students to participate in the NUSS rather than the moots. Whilst some socialist teachers devalue professionalism in terms of professional occupational culture and identity, and feel hostile to administrative features of their jobs, and/or neglect them, others consider consistency in these matters important in educational terms, establishing a steady relationship with the students, not alienating them through apparent lack of 'caring'. The liberal teachers appreciate the democratic structures, and see the formal processes as linked to an informal atmosphere of consultation. Their focus tends to be individualized and child-centred. However, along with the pragmatist teachers, they consider the democratic processes to be too time consuming, and are prepared to limit the democracy in order to increase efficiency. Trade union action is related to through the notion of survival. If action is judged as potentially effective and successful, these teachers tend to support it, but are not interested in militancy without tactical considerations about its effect on the school. Libertarian teachers are either not very involved in the democracy, preferring to get on with their daily practice, or feel that the structures allow genuine scope in their work. These teachers are also relatively anti-administrative, and disinclined towards professional routinization of the job.

Related to the political thinking of the teachers is their educational thinking. The libertarians and socialists tend to be interested in experimentation and innovation, whilst the pragmatists and liberals are more concerned with consistency in approach. The language of consistency, with the notions of duties and responsibilities is constructed within the framework of professionalism. Thus the latter are more likely to accept and adopt professionalism in their frame of reference, whilst the former tend to be more critical of such a framework, seen to imply the increase in structuring of the teaching learning situation, and a diminished scope for inspirationalism.

But the radical teachers (socialists and libertarians) have not lifted the question of responsibilities towards the students from the context of professionalism and constructed them within an alternative framework. The lack of such language has practical implications in the school. Whilst all teachers are involved in routinization through exigencies of control, and are implicated in professional practices through assessment, the avoidance of administrative procedures and organizational features aiming for consistency and efficiency by radical teachers leaves them in an ambiguous position. They may be considered anarchic and irresponsible by the rest of the staff, and the shifts in their behaviour, and their lack of conformity to student expectations leave a section of the student body confused and uncertain in their approach to such teachers, who are seen as unpredictable or uncaring.[21] In the present climate in Greenfield such features are focussed on, and the positive contributions of these teachers are not noted and valued.

Conclusion

Professionalism is a mode that channels activities in Greenfield College — the content of personalization assumes the form of individualization-atomization. In a progressive school professionalism assumes specificity; there is no uncritical acceptance of normative professionalism, but nonetheless in day-to-day situations problems are solved within the framework provided by it. The teachers enter a predetermined setting shaped by structural professionalism. This setting creates tensions in terms of control, legitimation of activities, construction of career and so on. Such problems are solved through cultural professionalism, developed in the course of occupational conduct. Cultural professionalism leads to routinization, and to the operation of meritocratic ideology with its hierarchical implications — this is reflected in student views based on a notion of the protestant ethic emphasizing hard work and achievement through one's own efforts despite notification of structured inequalities, and in student worries about shifts in teacher behaviour, from personalized to formal interaction.

Whilst the teacher attitudes to professionalism vary on the basis of their political and educational thinking, their class background and their biological constellations, all teachers are necessarily affected by professionalism, and may in their work practice be engaged in activities which their political thinking contradicts. Moreover, teachers have to relate to students who are under compulsion to attend school, and the majority of whom expect examination progress leading to a satisfactory positioning in the labour market. When progressive teachers in a school with an ethos emphasizing self-direction are placed structurally in a position of power *vis-à-vis* students, they theorize this in terms of ideology of caring, with implied duties and responsibilities. The radical teachers have not developed a framework for the analysis of the problems of subordinacy of students, and power invested in them as teachers, outside the professional language. Such teachers, thus, in their daily practice, tend towards pragmatism in their acceptance of professional responsibility for students, or are faced with a contradictory situation where their rejection of such assumptions, and habits and practices related to them leads them to assume an image of irresponsibility.

Larson (1975) considers the emergence of an awareness of limitations and frustrated sense of scope on the part of the professionals, if shifted from the personal to the public arena, a political and a collective one, can lead to a situation where it becomes possible to distinguish between 'the progressive human meaning of one's work' and the 'ideological functions' of one's role.[22] Larson argues that professionalism contains possibilities for overcoming limitations inscribed in it. However, the pressures in Greenfield towards increased professionalism with reduced amount of control are evident. The pressures are introduced through the public expenditure cuts, local criticism, and trends towards centralization and standardization in formal education, coupled with the policies of parental choice of schools and publication of examination results, through which the public campaign and its impact is mediated to the school. Internally there are controversies among the staff about the direction they should adopt when dealing with the pressures, whilst ensuring the survival of the school without compromising its fundamental principles. Such debates are focused by renewed personnel of the executive, with roots and experiences in the liberal progressive tradition of Leicestershire.

The teachers have resisted many pressures, but a general toning down of radicalism over time is observed, as Sarah comments:

> there are a lot of people who've got very radical ideas, but it's very difficult to keep them going ... because they're working within a

system and ultimately want to keep the sort of situation they're in . . . The more radical aspects of the ideas get kind of toned down to fit in what's basically a state institution. (Radical ideas) get sort of bought off or lost in . . . general struggles in all different directions.

The underlying concern for the interaction between possibilities and limitations for radicalization draws attention to contradictions and limitations in the social pressures within the school, which are also practically experienced by participants. To address these contradictions, concepts connecting concerns of theoretical and descriptive parts of the thesis have been developed in this part, and aspects of the reality of the school are returned to in Part Four to illustrate the explanatory power of the approach, issues of class, and sex/gender and an issue-based social process (organization of vertical teams) are discussed to cut differential cross-sections into the 'picture' of the school. For example the emphasis on negotiation of student careers indicates the construction of individual solutions to problems posed by the inequalities within a complex set of factors. The individual solutions occur in the context of tensions between individualization and individualism, or, more specifically, between atomization and personalization.

Notes

1 This is expressed by the General Secretary of the National Union of Teachers in 1964:

> I believe that teachers know the educational needs of children and the strength and weakness of present education provision better than any-body else, and that it is the duty, the professional obligation, of the NUT to correlate these views and to make them known. If we do not, we have no right to talk about being a professional organization.

2 GRACE (1978) p. 218.
3 Quoted in JOHNSON (1972) p. 13.
4 It is clear that Larson means what is here called 'individualization', chapter 8, rather than normative individualism.
5 LARSON (1977) p. 243.
6 For example WOODS (1980), WALKER and GOODSON (1977).
7 A client-centred perspective was also developing in other professions, for example social work.
8 This point was made, for example, by the second Principal in his retirement speech.
9 For example social studies mode III, chapter 6, note 16.
10 For example Ralph and Lesley, in the discussion on student careers in chapter 10.
11 *C.f.* Ralph's involvement in work experience and music (chapter 10).
12 For example SHARP and GREEN (1975); they discuss the concept of 'busyness' which enables teachers to deal with 'problem' children and integrate them into the class and school, and with 'able' children, who produce the results which legitimate the practices of the school.
13 These terms are used by Bernstein, for example BERNSTEIN (1975) chapter 5, 'On

the classification and framing of educational knowledge' and BERNSTEIN (1971) chapter 8.

14 The question of sexuality has not been touched here; this was an omission not in the fieldwork but in the text. The complexities raised by issues of sexuality were such that I felt unable to elaborate them in this context.

15 The school is attempting to tackle this problem through an extension of team activities, by introducing art and science into teams.

16 One teacher's comments indicate how self-development can be sought for in the professional context, even though she does not define it in professional terms:

> I feel that in a sense I'm not getting anywhere personally. I don't particularly want to kind of move up the career ladder in any way, but I don't think I'm developing all that much ... I would like to do some further studying ... I have considered the possibility of retraining as a proper maths teacher — get seconded for a year ... so that I could teach 'A' level maths and develop my interest in maths.

17 PARRY (1974) p. 183.

18 One teacher jokingly referred to this by saying that 'the thing to do is to make them feel sorry they asked', through the utilization of professional terminology and jargon. SHARP and GREEN (1975) also discuss relationships between teachers and parents.

19 This term was used by an officer from the local education authority.

20 For example one teacher described herself and another teacher as members of a group of teachers 'who charge through the first hurdle and then turn back and say we didn't mean to cross it anyway'.

21 Some of the negative references to teachers in the questionnaires (chapter 7) reflected this — teachers were described as moody, ratty, rude, scruffy, slack, unreliable, not hard working.

22 LARSON (1975) p. 243.

Part Four: Greenfield — Social Relations Considered

Chapter 10

Student Careers

Even though the class structure is reproduced within a capitalist mode of production, and 'working class kids get working class jobs' (Willis, 1977), and girls/boys get women's/ men's' jobs, reproduction is not satisfactory as an explanatory concept (chapter 1); I shall consider the complexities of structured inequalities. The discussion on student careers focusses on scope for decisions in a relatively prosperous area of skilled working class (not forgetting that with restructuring the scope diminishes), and on the structures of limitations based on class and sex-gender.[1] The connections between progressivism and social democratic education policies based on the tenets of equality of opportunity in the context of the educational expansion of the 1960s focus attention on student careers. The structure and methodology of this book, with its attention on concrete human actors embedded in social relations, directs attention to student 'negotiations' of these careers. In Willis' study of the lads' preparation for manual labour the 'ear'oles' remain shadowy figures. Here a broad range of career constructions is considered, containing discussion of world views, connecting to earlier concerns of understanding progressive education as producing rebels/conformists as alleged by political right/left (chapter 7).

The significance of individualization through state practices was noted in chapter 1. The child-centredness of progressivism as a medley of theories, philosophies and practices was discussed in chapter 3, and the role of individualization in one LEA was referred to in chapter 4. The emphasis on autonomy, self-direction and uniqueness of each individual child in Greenfield College provided an important focus throughout Part Two. In Part Three a discussion of individualization as a form and professionalism as a mode aimed to construct analytical tools considering mediations between macro and micro levels. A distinction between atomization and personalization was made. Here I am interested in the specificity of career construction in a progressive school, where personalization affords scope for negotiations, and atomization diminishes that scope.

The formation of student careers is complex; it involves negotiations within structures of possibilities constructed by social class, sex–gender and a range of cultural, structural and biographical factors. Problems, strategies, solutions and outcomes, and student conceptions of this process are considered here, with particular interest in perceptions by the students of choice and/or determination. The crystallization of careers at school is focussed on; a small number of students[2] is examined to consider confirmation/alteration of positions in class structure and sex–gender system. The shaping of the worldviews of students and their interplay with negotiations in school, and implications for career construction are considered. The influence of the school is not systematically separated from that of the student background — overall, the school is seen as an integral aspect of the cultural and structural location of students.

A 'career' refers[3] to 'a way of making a living', connected to the positioning of a person in the labour market or domestic production and 'a course through life', which can be understood as either deterministic 'following a course', or negotiated 'steering a course'. But a 'career' refers also to 'a spell of rapid progression', and 'going swiftly and wildly'; on the one hand a career advances stage by stage, but on the other hand, there are unexpected ways of pursuing a course. The term has different meanings which are considered in formulating a dynamic conception of student careers negotiated in Greenfield, within a context constituted by extensions between atomization and personalization.

The group of students were followed over four years, and shifts and crystallizations in their careers were taking place.[4] Nevertheless only tentative considerations of outcomes were possible in the case of 18-year-olds; particularly those pursuing further/higher education may shift their direction. But the longitudinal perspective has been helpful in illuminating and deepening understanding of careers and worldviews. No clear categorizations were developed. Focus is on the range of solutions young people can adopt, rather than on typical social patterns. Some powers of generalization are lost, but the complexities of careers are indicated. Thus the chapter discusses aspects of career construction,[5] and then focusses on the particular careers of interviewed students in order to illustrate negotiations within structures of limitations and possibilities. The consideration of perceptions of these careers introduces evaluations of them. Thus the students are considered in terms of the relevant aspects contributing to ease or difficulty in achieving 'success'.

The term 'success' consists of differing conceptions, again in order to allow for the complexity of negotiations and perceptions vis-à-vis career construction. Thus 'success' can be academic, as measured by certification, or, secondly, occupational, referring to particular locations in the labour market in terms of financial rewards, working conditions, status etc. But third, the perceptions of teachers are also considered, and fourth, the assessments of the students themselves. Thus all criteria of success do not concur in all cases; the career of a student can be 'successful' and 'unsuccessful' depending on the point of evaluation (c.f. Brian, pp. 195).

Detailed discussions[6] throughout the research with teachers about particular students, and with students about themselves have provided the material whereby the relevant ingredients in career construction in Greenfield have been disentangled. These are structural, cultural and biographical aspects, worldviews, attitudes about schooling and education, and sex/gender. The case study aspect of the thesis (Part Two) is further developed. Practices where atomization and personalization coexist in tension are noted. The implications of the context of negotiations are considered, and the mediations of the form of individualization through the mode of professionalism is returned to in the conclusion.

Construction of Careers

Structural Aspects

Middle class students tend to be more successful than working class students in the construction of their careers; so it is in Greenfield College.[7] A wealth of sociological literature has explored factors contributing to middle class success;[8] the parents are familiar with the education system and with the labour market, and are able to provide practical help for their children as well as material support through provision of resources, increasingly significant because of reduced expenditure in schools. Middle class homes are considered to have a particular affinity with the school environment.[9]

But 'class' used as a descriptive term is problematic. In chapter 7 differentiations within 'working class' and 'middle class' were referred to. I use the term 'structural aspects' to refer to student and parental location and experiences in the labour market and institutions such as schools; 'structures' are, as Critcher defines them,

> those 'objective' aspects of anyone's life-situation which appear beyond the individual's control, having their sources in the distribution of power and wealth in the society.[10]

When working class students are academically successful in Greenfield we can note structural aspects operating — for example, the parents, particularly the father, is in a skilled trade (Bob); they have experienced social mobility (Philippa); the educational level of one of them is relatively high (Rachel's mother); and the home is relatively affluent (Marilyn). Students successful in career negotiations in terms of academic, occupational and/or social criteria without evident structural factors predisposing them have experienced the negotiations as problematic, and their career construction has involved struggles (Kevin).

The student conceptions of social class (chapter 7) combine perceptions of structured inequalities and a belief in the possibility of social mobility, observed by many in immediate families. Equality of opportunity was perceived as prevalent in the school, and a sense of powerlessness and lack of control over structured inequalities in society led to an emphasis on possibilities of individualized solutions to problems posed by these. The sense of possibilities is linked to the notions of choice in the school, and the internalization of the school ethos stressing the importance of self-direction and conscious decision-making on the part of the students about their own future.

I shall provide an illustration of differing negotiations. Ken gained a few low grade CSEs; he had several jobs after leaving school, before settling into a job as a butcher. He discusses his school career:

> I was thinking work hard, get exams and get a good job, and halfway through I thought I just can't be bothered, so you go off skiving somewhere ... And that's how it was in the fifth year, even though I did all the work, it could have been better if I still kept the idea, working well and getting a good job and getting exams things like that — just didn't think it was worth it.

Ken emphasized that the decision was his:

> (The teachers) said it is up to me, it's my life I'm going to muck up, that's what they kept saying, but it's not mucked my life up. Kids have got ten 'O' levels and still haven't got a job — I've got nothing, and I've had four.

Andrew, whose father runs his own engineering business, secured good 'O' level results and refers to the sense of ease in his career construction; little conscious effort was necessary in negotiation of choices. He explains how he obtained an apprenticeship as a telephone engineer:

> I was lucky really — it was the first job, well the only job I applied for, and got it. You know again that's just like the 'O' levels, it was something that suddenly come up in front of me, I did it and it's behind me now. You know, I don't even think about it really. I've been very lucky like that.

Andrew's career construction proximated his structural position; he chose an apprenticeship rather than sixth-form and higher education, like his father who had experienced social mobility as a 'self-made' man.

A surface structure of choice is focussed on by teachers and students in personalized teaching-learning situations emphasizing self-direction in career construction. But this coexists with a deep structure of limitations. Thus both Ken who steered 'a course' and Andrew who underwent uncomplicated 'progression' were led to outcomes predictable in terms of their structural position.

Other aspects of importance in the negotiations of the students are disentangled, which particularly in the consideration of individual students, are seen to interact closely with the structural features. Therefore, for example, similar cultural features assume differential effectivity on students from a variety of locations.

Cultural Aspects

Critcher notes that people 'create, and have created for them, ways of thinking and acting which embody ideas, beliefs, values, notions of right and wrong'.[11] These are called cultures. The appropriate cultural background is not definable in a simple way in Greenfield College. Affluent and/or middle class background does not ensure success in the school, though it does so if combined with a relatively liberal parental approach, active when necessary, supportive of the school in general, so that criticisms address specific issues relating to one's own children. The problems in the career constructions of Bill and George indicate that high aspirations are not sufficient. Both have affluent, self-employed, self-made fathers without an appropriate educational background on the basis of which to encourage their children. Their own social mobility has predisposed them towards beliefs on the possibilities of individuals in private enterprise; their aspirations may be counter-productive in putting pressure on their children without being able to offer meaningful help. This problem has specificity in Greenfield, which, as a progressive school, diverges from the expectations of parents,[12] who are thus even less equipped to offer support conducive to success.[13]

The cultural milieu in Dave's home does not appear particularly supportive and significant in his career negotiations. Whilst his parents were reported to have aspirations for him, these did not encompass staying on in the sixth-form and entering higher education, which he did. Dave's parents, according to him, support the Conservative Party, and thus may have few positive indentifications of themselves as working class. Thus Dave's emphasis on individualistic solutions, on the importance of looking after oneself, and the interest in 'getting on' reflect parental thinking. However, Dave also experiences a sense of separation from his family; this, and the importance of appropriate peer group affiliations, are evident in his comments:

> I've always associated with the right people, to get on. I mean like my sister now, I don't think she'll ever make it this far. She might do, but she's not showing the right kind of attitude at the moment. She's in the first year at high school, and she's associating with all the wrong type of people to get anywhere.

Peer group associations thus provided an appropriate cultural background for Dave, whose relatives have all left school, and are either unemployed, or in jobs with few prospects.

Joyce, Marilyn and Rachel, all successful, and all from a working class background, provide an example of an appropriate cultural background.

Whilst they were all encouraged to pursue their social careers, there is little pressure (as in the case of Bill and George). Such an affinity of their cultural background is, in all cases, related to structural aspects (particularly affluence). The lack of pressure is also linked to their sex; in negotiations and career construction in the school this did not prejudice the choice of successful strategies. All have entered higher or further education, but in ways which point them towards predominantly female sectors of the labour market, with limited opportunities.

Aspirations then are not sufficient in themselves, but those and other cultural aspects interact with a number of features such as structural location, sex–gender system, worldview and attitudes to education.

Biographical Aspects

Biographical aspects refer to personal histories constructed in terms of familial circumstances, health, physical and emotional characteristics etc., which manifest themselves in various constellations; their significance cannot be separated from other aspects. Critcher refers to biographies as

> the network of personal circumstances, decisions and (mis) fortunes which occur within a situation already highly structured and with a limited number of available cultural options.[14]

For example in George various biographical aspects were important; the existence of an academically and socially successful older brother, his small size etc. contributed to problems in gaining status with peers. However, his cultural background (above) was inappropriate, and his worldview alienated him from the school. His involvement with the 'lads', and his attempt to secure acceptance through aggression meant that George shrugged off efforts to get him involved in the school. A whole range of factors, therefore, influenced George's negotiations.

Biographical features were significant in the case of Linda, again, however, in conjunction with other important features. Her fragmented biography was solidified when she was, rather late in her childhood, adopted into a working class family. In the fifth year, she wrote in the questionnaire:

> I want to get a good job and I definitely don't want to end up in a factory. I can see myself in a couple of years packing things in boxes. That scares me to death. There's nothing wrong in working in a factory, I just don't want to end up like everyone else and get into a boring routine everyday. After saying all that I know I'll end up in a dreary factory and I'm too stupid to do anything better.

She did 'end up in a factory' and disliked it. Her class position, her sex, her partly West Indian origin, and her inappropriate cultural background (her parents did not value educational success, and related to working class identification positively) combined with biographical features to lock her into a position in the labour market which she found unsatisfactory.

It is suggested, then, that biographical aspects can assume particular significance for working class children, especially girls, who have little space for tackling their problems, whereas middle class children can be successful despite biographical aspects, when other features combine to place them in a position of strength in career negotiations.

Worldview

The impact of worldviews of students assume effectivity in complex constellations; I shall illustrate this by considering ways in which both conservatism and radicalism gain *differential* significance in career construction when existing in differential combinations with other features. The emphasis on negotiations within a surface structure of choice and self-determination indicates, however, that worldview is to be accorded attention. The students as thinking individuals do choose, albeit within a deep structure of limitations and determinations. The fetishized nature of these choices does not make them unreal; it indicates that they are made within structures of possibilities, constructed in a complex manner around various axes which this discussion on the features significant in negotiations tries to unravel.

Conservatism in outlook can pose problems in some cases and not in others. What is referred to is traditionalism, manifested in a lack of 'generational consciousness', youthful rebellion in dress, style or mode of behaviour. In general, neither the teachers, nor the school ethos in Greenfield value conventionality, which is seen as an index of convergent thinking and conformism. Both Dave and Kevin are conservative in such a way, though particularly Kevin's political thinking is radical. In the case of Dave such conservatism is associated, by the teachers, with flair and ability, whereas in the case of Kevin, it is seen as a manifestation of his instrumentalism, and desire to please. Thus in teacher perceptions his conservatism assumes greater salience than that of Dave's.

Sustained political Conservatism can pose problems for students in their negotiations in Greenfield, but only if combined with particular cultural and structural features, and possibly educational thinking. Thus, in the case of Bill and George, their problems in career construction were linked to structural and cultural factors but also to a worldview with little room for liberalism — unashamed instrumentalism in the case of one, and open, hostile racism in the case of the other alienated them from the school ethos, and posed barriers in their interactions.

Radicalism, similarly, has different implications for the career constructions of different students. Bob negotiated his stay in the school with relative ease, despite his radicalism, and managed to secure success in examinations and entry to higher education. However, his radicalism combined with a favourable structural and cultural background. For Stuart radicalism posed difficulties, and though he constructed a relatively successful career, he did not do so with ease. The problems of staying on at school — lack of money, the consequent dependence on parents etc. — heighten the ambiguities he experiences. Materiality of life is not easily escaped by working class families. Whilst Stuart enjoys school, when looking at his employed friends he is led to question the purpose of continuing school; 'all I'm doing is writing on paper all day'. The problems of Stuart indicate the difficulties of working class boys when they choose to accept what the school has to offer, whilst not just struggling for academic success; from such a set of expectations a career is not easily forged. Bob's unambiguous adoption of an individualistic stance vis-a-vis his own career further facilitated his progress, unhampered by Stuart's questioning.

Brian's individualistic radicalism — he is a self-confessed anarchist — led him to question the value of schooling. Whilst he negotiated a successful career in the school — his perceptiveness and sharp social commentary were appreciated by the teachers — he was not able to turn these into academic success; he left without qualifications, and though he did not place great emphasis on social mobility, and did not value 'middle-classness' positively, he felt ambivalent about the lack of certification.

The three successful girls, Joyce, Marilyn and Rachel are characterized by radicalism to varying degrees. It may be easier for girls to combine radicalism with achievement in examinations, because their socialization pre-disposes them towards conformity, tolerance[15] and a greater facility to adapt to contradictions. That Pete, whose radicalism was to sustain rather than hinder him in his negotiations, was also able to sustain an unusually contra-dictory position bears this out. His tutor Janet remarked that 'he's probably the only student I have ever met who's managed to combine doing well academically with also being one of the hard lads!'.

Attitudes to Education

In a school emphasizing choice and negotiation within a framework of personal interaction, student conceptions of the school assume particular significance. A close relationship with one's tutor is an important factor in the crystallization of careers. A critical approach on the part of the students towards the informality and relatively loose organization in Greenfield is likely to be manifested in dealings with teachers, when in the course of one-to-one discussions more of the private student is brought to the public arena, particularly when shifts from personalized to formal interaction occur (chapter 7 and chapter 9). Further, student ambivalence vis-à-vis the school poses problems in their negotiations. Whilst overall the strength of positive student opinions is considerable, many encounter difficulties in attempting to balance both academic and social, emotional learning, and to achieve in each.

Positive orientations in the school emphasize the constructive setting provided, within which students with a clear sense of propose can pursue their own interests, using their own initiative, and availing themselves of teacher help when it is considered necessary. For example:

Marilyn: Because I can use my own initiative I enjoy it. I . . . can't stand being bossed around. That's what I like about this school; no-one telling me what to do and I just like that.

Bob: If I would have been pushed I reckon I would have rebelled and not done it, so I'm glad they didn't.

These students were relatively successful in their negotiations; they achieved academic success, their social interaction in the school was marked with ease, and they were satisfied with the shaping of their careers. Their success, whilst linked to their attitudes to education and to Greenfield College specifically, also related to other factors, such as their structural and cultural background, and their worldview.

A group of students feel positive about the overall framework in the school, but encounter difficulties in the negotiation of academic learning and examination preparation; consistent help is not seen to be provided. Such students, however, appreciate the informality and relaxed relationships, and argue that within such a framework non-authoritarian yet insistent attitudes towards students' work could be adopted.

Susan: There's pushing and pushing; I mean you don't have to be very strict about it, but they could have checked up more on what we were doing.

Susan achieved the examination results she hoped for by staying on for a year in the sixth-form; her problems in negotiations were countered by her overall positive attitude towards organization in the school, and by her structural location and cultural background. Without such features the ambivalence of students assumes greater salience and significance, as illustrated below.

Gwen's attitudes about the school were contradictory; she had not reconciled her notions of what 'proper' schools should be like with the informal aspects she appreciated in Greenfield. This is expressed when Gwen is asked whether she likes the school:

Yeah I do in some ways, but I wish they would make you work more, and I wish there would be more classrooms, I don't like the team very much. I can't get on with me work. I know I talk and distract other people, but nobody seems to work in the team area really.

When asked what she does like about the school, Gwen continues:

Gwen: Well if you don't want to work, I think it's right that you

> shouldn't be made to. I mean it's up to you ain't it . . . And I like
> it because the teachers are all friendly and that . . . and you can call
> them by their Christian names.
>
> *Interviewer:* . . . on the one hand you would like to be made to
> work and on the other hand you say that people shouldn't be made
> to work . . .
>
> *Given:* I would like to be myself, but I think it's up to you, but you
> know, I'm all right in this school. I like it.

Such contradictory ambivalence, combined with a gender identity characterized by a lack of confidence, and a cultural background without strong
emphasis on educational success led to relatively mediocre examination results, though Gwen herself expresses little dissatisfaction. Her gender identity
has been confirmed through her location in the female segment of the labour
market, as a telephonist. When she read the transcript of the first interview,
she remarked: 'I sound as though I don't like the school, don't I, but I did
like it really.'

The contradictions are more deeply experienced by others, and the
negative orientation receives stronger emphasis. Thus George, who left with
a few low-grade CSEs, stressed in his first interview the importance of the
choice to work or not. In the second interview he is less certain:

> I suppose I realised that I didn't have to work, so I didn't work, and
> then if anybody pushed me into working I didn't wanna . . . I had
> nowt against school. I was just lazy, I couldn't be bothered, I just
> didn't think . . . just didn't wanna work, just wanted to muck about
> or summit.

George feels that had he gone to a grammar school, like his older brother
did, he would have worked:

> cause it would have been strict and you would have been told to do
> it . . . you just would have accepted it, but when you realized you
> didn't have to work, you started not working . . . when teachers
> push you and tell you what to do, you think, oh you git, and you
> probably wouldn't work just to spite them.

His ambivalent attitudes towards the school, with the emphasis on negative
orientation, pose problems for career negotiation, particularly when combined with other factors contributing to difficulties.

A few students found the framework of the College difficult to handle,
and felt that they could not have achieved much in that context, regardless of
teacher effort. Ralph, who was unemployed at the time of the second interview, had not taken any examinations. In his first interview he talked about
the school:

> *Ralph:* It's all right — wanna bit more discipline though, you
> know, make people work . . . cause look at the way I've ended up

> — that's through people not making me work, like ... they tried, tried all sorts of ways, but, you know, you wanna bring more discipline back.
>
> *Interviewer:* What sort of discipline might make you work?'
>
> *Ralph:* I don't know. Threaten to take me to the headmaster or summit. If there were cane or something like that.
>
> *Interviewer:* Cane would make you work?
>
> *Ralph:* Yeah.
>
> *Interviewer:* Are you scared of the cane?
>
> *Ralph:* No but it would make me work ... sort of torture, isn't it, if you don't work, so you work so you don't get tortured.
>
> *Interviewer:* Have teachers tried to make you work?
>
> *Ralph:* Well — tried to tell me it won't help in the long run — I know that, but — I can't put me mind to it. They've done all sorts of things.

For Ralph the cane symbolized a different framework, a context which he would have understood; power based on masculinity, which talking could not replace. By his second interview, Ralph wishes he would have taken examinations. But a successful negotiation of an academic career would have been difficult for Ralph, because of his structural location and cultural background and, to an extent, biographical factors; particularly his educational attitudes, his worldview marked by workerist, trade unionist Labourism combined with racism and aggressive masculine values made negotiations problematic.

Sex and Gender

Most girls in the school enter the labour market in its traditionally female sectors, which require fewer skills and offer less opportunities for training and increasing responsibilities and pay. Thus sex-gender is a strong determinant of the direction of girls' careers. Girls from a middle class background tend to have more scope for a brief relaxation of the expectations related to them as female. Overall, girls with high ambitions, even when successful, experience a stronger sense of struggle than boys. Because of the significance of sex-gender as a factor affecting crystallization of careers, chapter 11 explores related issues further. But some remarks are necessary here.

In Greenfield College sex and gender assume significance in career negotiations in several ways. First, because of the informality, flexibility and fragmentation no clear policy of intervention in choice of occupations by the students exists. Second, because of lack of systematic intervention in subject choices of the students, there is a strong tendency for both boys and girls to study subjects traditionally deemed appropriate for each. Third, personalization of learning assumes particular effectivity with girls, and tends to reinforce their gender identities. Fourth, the masculine 'tone' of the school facilitates the career construction of extrovert confident students, often boys, whose sub-cultural orientations the teachers find easier to relate to than those of the girls, insofar as the latter focus on romantic love and feminity.

One girl broke into the male job market through her interest in vehicle engineering. Her tutor was pleased about her success, but little support was provided by the careers officer, and difficulties were encountered in a study of a subject dominated by boys, despite the helpfulness of the male teacher. Some scope, then, existed within the school for a pursuit of a non-traditional career, but strong interest was required. The girl explains:

> you see (girls) following the same patterns all the while. I didn't want to fall into that rut really, I wanted to find out what men did ... I wanted to do other jobs that when I look back when I'm older, I think yeah, I've done that ... I did what I wanted to do, I didn't fall into any job that came along.

Despite the isolated incident of success of one determined girl to negotiated a non-feminine career, sex and gender in general have considerable influence on the crystallization of choices.

The discussion of aspects of career construction indicates that constellations of ingredients articulate in influencing student negotiations in Greenfield. There is an interface between (i) differing conceptions of. individualism (chapter 8, p. 155–6) connected to structural and cultural background; (ii) student orientations to personalization-individualization, connected to their world-view, attitudes to education and sex-gender, as well as structural and cultural aspects; and (iii) academic and/or social success in career construction. It is at this interface that student negotiations are located.

Career Construction — Boys

I shall now illustrate career construction by considering individual students, noting the complexity of negotiations, and the interplay of aspects outlined above.

Boys and girls are discussed separately. The discussion is structured on the basis of differential 'success', and differential ease/struggle experienced in negotiations. A focal point is provided by Kevin, a working class boy who has worked hard to achieve a measure of academic, though not social success. His career construction indicates problems of working class students, and negotiations by other students can be viewed in the light of this illustration. It is noted, also, that in a scheme of 'lads' and 'ear'oles' (Willis, 1977) Kevin would be the latter, a conformist — it is interesting that he was a *radical* conformist. Kevin's orientation to personalization was one of avoidance. This posed problems for him in negotiating an academically successful career — yet he managed to do so. The discussion of other students can be compared to Kevin as a focal point, not because of his typicality, but because of the complexity of the problems he was faced with, and because of the consequent complexity required in an attempt to study his career construction.

Kevin

Kevin's structural and cultural background have not predisposed him towards school success, yet he gained '0' and 'A' levels and entry into a polytechnic on a degree course — but he negotiated his career with difficulties. His instrumental attitude to schooling and education, his class consciousness and his determination to achieve social mobility formed a complicated constellation posing dilemmas for teachers, who perceived his desire to be successful in academic learning without engaging in the social and emotional learning they considered important. As he was also assessed as limited in his abilities, early comments by teachers in the team were somewhat disparaging:

> Psychologically Kevin is one of the ten most disastrous kids in the team. He is lacking emotions, and is dislikeable.

> Kevin's not that bad. But you often suspect that he says things just because he thinks you would like him to say them, rather than because he really believes in them.

If Kevin's dress and behaviour was conservative, his political thinking was radical, and class conscious, containing elements of identity, opposition and totality, but no conceptions of alternatives;[16] he was engaged in a search for an individualistic solution to the inequalities he observed: 'you got to be selfish, you can't pull other people along.'. Schooling is the avenue through which Kevin pursues his goals: 'I intend to get the most out of my education, and I will not let anything stand in my way.'. His career construction is characterized by a sense of struggle: 'it's hard to fight your way through from being from a poor background.'. Kevin perceives the problems in maintaining his radical outlook if social mobility is achieved.

> If I work my way up into quite a high position, I'd be the same as all the others, and I wouldn't try to help anybody who was on the receiving end ... It's all self really ... Other people have pressure on them and it's up to them whether they want to accept their fate.

Through his single-minded efforts[17] Kevin achieved sufficient examination results to continue 'A' level study. Later comments by teachers indicated their shift in perceptions about Kevin:

> He used to irritate me a lot, I now feel rather contrite about that, and sorry for it. I think he's done very well in many ways ... obviously

education for him is some sort of liberation, except there's no intellectual liberation — it's a social liberation. He's still very mechanistic
in what he thinks education will give him ... I feel very sympathetic
with his need to climb. But it's a psychological need as well as a
social need, and he's still psychologically utterly crippled.

I got quite a soft spot for him really, and I like him ... he might just
get what he wants in the end ... I think it's going to take a toll of
his personality — I think it already has.

This shift is related to respect for Kevin's achievement and respect for the
sincerity of his radical thinking, which, because of its incongruity with
Kevin's conservative demeanour and instrumental attitudes had been interpreted as an attempt to please the teachers.

By the second interview Kevin's 'left-wing views' had strengthened; he
expected to maintain his radical thinking despite his search for individualistic
solutions. He laughed at some comments in his first interview: 'did I say that
— I wouldn't agree with that now'. His perception of possibilities open to
him has narrowed down, but social mobility is still important. He explains
what it would offer him:

I sometimes see married couples who ... got loads of kids and live
in the council estate I live in. You know, they don't go out any-
where, because they never got any money ... they're just trying to
live a comfortable life — as long as they've got a car and a colour
television and a telephone that's it ... I don't think I would like to
do that ... (I'd like to) go on holidays regularly and things like that
... not scraping for money all the time.

To achieve his ambitions Kevin has had to 'abandon' his background, and he
was in an isolated position in the sixth form. But had he not maintained his
single-minded career construction, he would have gained less academic success. It would not have been possible in the space of the fourth and fifth year
to forsake instrumentalism, benefit from affective learning, and produce
work both with inherent value *and* purposeful for examination preparation.
Kevin had no 'natural' flair for education, because of structural, cultural and
biographical factors; it is unlikely that he would have been able to shape his
career in a desired direction had he accepted teachers' definitions of what was
important. Personalization in the school posed problems for him; he found it
more difficult to understand than the atomized framework which he could
analyze, and solutions were negotiated for in complex ways.

Alan, Dave, Andrew and Bob — Successful Career Construction with Relative Ease

Alan's approach to education and schooling was also characterized by instrumentalism (chapter 7, p. 116), but his career negotiations were not problematic, because his structural and cultural background provided a conducive location for success. He did not need to prioritize social mobility; therefore his instrumentalism was less salient, and he was not forced to resolve contradictory aspects in his thinking (chapter 7), and was not led to question the ease with which he was forging his career.

Andrew was self-motivated, and not strongly instrumental. He refers to being rebellious at home; the school gave him an opportunity to consider issues which could not be raised with his Conservative parents. Thus he was sufficiently comfortable at school to negotiate his way without struggling (p. 181). Yet he experiences a sense of powerlessness, and articulates it particularly in relation to personal lives; he perceives struggle in constructing a meaningful framework for day-to-day experiences.

> They're all ambitious when they're young like me, and … I don't know really, it's probably you don't realize you've lost your ambitions till it's actually happened to you — well you probably don't even realise then.

All students have a range of concerns to juggle with when they are negotiating their careers in balancing aspirations for job satisfaction and personal fulfilment, both of these within structured sets of possibilities, the delimitations of which are more or less clearly perceived.

Dave was successful in his career negotiations. Because of his interest in science his instrumentalism was not salient; though he perceived schools in terms of social mobility, learning had inherent value for him as well. Like Kevin, he did not consider his working class background positively:

> I'd like to be different from my family at the moment, I don't like the way my family is organized, the way that my parents live. I think it's awful … we live in a council house and we can't get any kind of home improvements done or anything. They haven't got any money put by for later life. I feel quite sorry for them actually. I hope I don't end up like that … I'd just like to be more settled and have more of a future — you know, less dull, and, you know, wondering what's going to happen, wondering where the next money's going to come from to pay bills and so on.

Despite comparable structural position, Dave has not experienced Kevin's struggles, though his perception of closures has increased during the course of the research. He avoids questions acutely confronting Kevin by disassociating himself from the political system. He can discuss political issues at length and articulately; yet he states that he is 'ignorant and happy to be so'.

Dave's worldview, attitudes to education and cultural milieu he placed himself in (p. 182) facilitated his negotiations in the school.

Bob also combines instrumentalism with an interest in sciences. He was able to forge a successful career without revealing private areas explored in the course of teacher-student interaction in humanities work; his instrumentalism was not salient. Yet he is concerned for social mobility; he equates being rich with easy life; 'not so many problems to deal with'. But his political perspective is radical — he supports the egalitarian features of Labour Party ideology and policies. However, his own situation has to be solved through individualistic means: 'I can't see us getting to a (situation) where everyone's equal, so might as well do the best out of the system as you can'. Asked whether his thinking is contradictory, Bob replied:

> Well I suppose it is a contradiction, but I don't really know. I mean I'd rather be rich than poor, but — I reckon Labour have got the best policies. I don't know — what's wrong with being rich and voting Labour?

Bob experiences no personal sense of struggle. His structural and cultural location have more affinity with educational success than Kevin's. He did not appear as single-minded, and did not pose similar dilemmas for teachers, who nevertheless expressed disappointment about his lack of achievement in humanities. Several factors contributed to the relative ease of Bob's negotiations in pursuing social mobility. His sense of powerlessness, lack of conception of alternatives besides Labour reforms which he considered limited, led him to adopt an individualistic solution which he is pursuing with determination. Bob, Andrew and Dave in their choice of science and engineering have followed a career construction typical for boys — this contributes to the ease of negotiations.

Stuart and Pete — Successful Career Construction

Stuart and Pete were relatively successful at school, but their negotiations were more problematic. Their structural background had no particular affinity with educational success, but they did not experience a strong sense of struggle like Kevin — neither of them was as instrumental.

Stuart did not emphasize the importance of examinations in the fifth year but his position left him in some ambiguity (p. 185), and in the sixth-form he refers to a 'competitive streak' guiding his work; he is also more aware of struggling, and feels uncertain: 'I'm not sure if I will get the job I want. I'll try and I'll keep on trying — eventually I think I'll get the job I want'. Stuart is sensitive, interested in a range of issues, and less guided by masculine values than most of the boys. This also leads him to uncertainties about balance between his private life and work. He wonders: 'why aren't I happy all the while; I'm not too sure'. He questions possibilities, he ponders limitations, he refers to patterns of adult life characterized by routinization, and hopes to avoid these: 'I suppose that could happen to me, but that's all within me — I got the power to stop that —· I suppose'.

Though Stuart experienced problems, his career assumed a direction agreeable to him. His political outlook and interests in the fifth year led him to engage in his work with interest, and to look at the school positively. He was able to understand the school ethos, and to relate to teachers in the personalized setting. Thus he was in a position of strength in his negotiations. His growing awareness of contradictions in the sixth year, and the atomized framework helped him to consolidate his career construction through increased instrumentalism.

Pete placed himself in a cultural location oppositional to schooling, by being one of the 'lads' (p. 185). Yet he stayed on to sixth-form, and though his 'A' level results disappointed him, he is constructing his career in a purposeful way.[18] Unlike Stuart, he does not identify with the school: 'I'm not bothered about what goes on in here'. He is not particularly instrumental: 'I probably won't end up with anything much different from me friends in the end.' He is, however, interested in learning, and likes 'to know what's going on in the world'; in this project he is sustained by his radicalism — he has converted his 'generational consciousness' as a lad into studying the police, law and order, racism etc.

Pete's career indicates the importance of negotiations, the significance of political leanings, and problems caused by isolation, when all his friends had left school. His social interests, divergent thinking and lack of overt instrumentalism led to easy interactions with teachers. The combination of teacher support, and his own independence have ensured the development of Pete's career in a direction meaningful to him, yet not diverging far from the structures of possibilities — thus he was able to pursue it despite difficulties.

Ken, Brian and Vince — Unsuccessful Academic Career Construction

Ken gained low grade CSEs, but did not consider himself unsuccessful (p. 181). He was pleased to leave school, but did not feel alienated during his stay. Despite being a 'lad', he had few conflicts with teachers; he felt they 'understood kids' and were 'on their side'. Ken devoted himself to music, which is 'all his life', and he entertains an ambition to be a popstar. He was interested in social issues — in school his political thinking was marked by increasing Conservatism, but a shift had taken place after a year at work, because of the influences of the materiality of life; 'you don't really know much about it, until you're out there, earning a living, then you know what's happening'. Because of a strong sense of powerlessness, lack of conception of alternatives led him to disassociate himself from politics.[19] The choices he has made have remained within structures of possibilities. He has constructed a framework for his life characterized by enjoyment and a sense of satisfaction, facilitated by engagement in generational sub-cultural activities providing a 'magical solution'[20] to problems of working class boys. His career construction has been socially successful in terms of perceptions of teachers, peers and himself.

Brian did not take examinations; yet his career in school was successful in many ways. The teachers considered him perceptive and able, and unusual in his willingness and capacity to pursue ideas in discussions. Despite teacher encouragement he was an early leaver, taking a job as a knitter, with awkward shifts and low pay. Brian was one of the lads, but his work experience has led to the paling of 'magical solutions':

> I'm not the same as I used to be, because I used to worry about things when they happened at the last minute. And I know I've changed because now I've started worrying about things, long before it happens, that's one thing.

He is ambivalent about his lack of academic success, but feels that he has chosen and negotiated his career. His interest in music reflects his disinclination to pursue social mobility, and his alienation from main stream politics — he likes 'working class music': 'I play because I like it ... I won't go out of me way to try and make it, I don't really believe in that.'.

Though Brian positively valued being working class, his tiredness, his low wages and his dependence at home made life seem like a struggle to him.[21] Thus having rejected notions of achievement widely held by others it was not easy for him to negotiate a satisfactory outcome. Poor prospects in the labour market for the development of skills through training at work have left boys like Brian with narrow sets of possibilities. Despite his working class pride, his generational consciousness and belief in anarchism, and hence lack of recourse to collective patterns shaped by experiences of working class, contribute to difficulties in constructing a meaningful career.

The structural and cultural location of Vince point to school success; yet his examination results were poor, but he did secure an apprenticeship in printing. He was one of the lads, whose generational consciousness separated him from his parents' Fabian, liberal outlook, which he in many ways shared, except the interest in education. He is critical of representative democracy; he would not vote. His main interest is music, and he writes 'protesting' songs with his friends about the way 'they make you do things, government and things like that'. The songs express views, but do not aim to change anything — Vince is not very interested in the future, 'just where I'm going to be tomorrow night or something'.

Though Vince's location in the labour market seems unexpected, he did secure one of the few available apprenticeships in printing, and is learning a craft within a relatively strong occupational grouping with a degree of status. His relationship to the lads is marked by some tensions as his background has predisposed him towards characteristically middle-class 'counter-cultures' (Hall and Jefferson, 1977).

George, Bill and Ralph — Problematic Career Construction

Bill (p. 182) wished to solidify the success of his self-made father through schooling:

> After the sixth and seventh year I want to go to a polytechnic/
> university, studying law. Law appeals to me because I think if I
> attain my law degree I will have achieved something in life. My
> father first discussed law with me and I liked the idea right from the
> start. I hope to eventually get my own law business — (High
> Hopes)! (questionnaire)

Bill was not successful in his career construction.[22] Like Kevin he was instrumental in his negotiations at school, but he was not prepared to work as hard. The inappropriateness of Bill's cultural background (p. 182) meant he had little affinity with the school, and his Conservative political thinking offered him few possibilities for understanding his own situation. Having witnessed his father's success, he believed in equality of opportunity, and did not experience a sense of struggle; he believed luck was important in determining people's positioning in the class structure and the labour market.[23] This set of beliefs did not provide him tools with which to negotiate a successful career. The personalization in the school allowed him to remain unaware of the framework of atomization. When he realized that he would have to struggle in order to realize his aspirations, he felt that his opportunities had already passed, and he accepted this with a sense of resignation, rather than frustration or anger.

The cultural location of George was inappropriate (p. 182); his worldview and attitudes to education were not conducive to successs, and biographical aspects locked the patterning of the sets of possibilities. The contradictory sense of frustration and choice in the second interview expressed the difficulties he had in negotiations. Despite being assessed 'bright' he was unable to pursue through schooling the self-made success of his father.

Ralph was an early leaver. He is stridently working class, with little interest in academic learning. He found the framework at school difficult to cope with (p. 187–8). The strategies used by teachers with Ralph were typical for the school; they tried to discover Ralph's interests — the only one expressed was cranes. Teachers had no information, and Ralph reaffirmed his pride in his manual background by turning to his cranedriver father for help. His project included photos displayed in the team area; he tore these up during the first term, and symbolically rejected academic negotiations. The teachers also changed focus to affective learning, and Ralph spent considerable periods in the music block, and in work experience in a garage.

Teacher strategies indicate problems and contradictions in dealing with students like Ralph; they involved an acceptance of his choices, and avoided disruptive behaviour, and gave Ralph scope to explore aspects he enjoyed. But they confirmed his position in the class structure. But because of his lack of examinations, and the increasing local unemployment, Ralph was not successful in constructing a skilled manual career. He describes his first job: 'all I were doing is standing up all day pulling two levers about ... I got the sack really'. Since then Ralph has been unemployed, and his pride and aggression have subsided, giving room for resignation and accommodation. He takes 'each day as it comes' and expresses surprise when he reads that in the first interview he said that 'the world's a tip. I'll be laughing when I'm going'. This view has been tempered: 'life gets boring after a while, but, you know — that's just it'. Ralph has increasingly accepted his tightly locked position, to which cultural and structural factors had predisposed him. His tutor thinks that 'the limitations on Ralph in the end were some of the limitations he set on himself', thus emphasizing a surface structure of choice. The deep structure of determinations was, in Ralph's case, so strong, that alternative choices would have been difficult to sustain, and would have required strong struggles and the ruthless instrumentalism of Kevin.

Career Construction — Girls

Entry to the labour market from Greenfield is differentiated on the basis of sex-gender. Crystallization of structural, cultural and biographical factors assumes significance in the negotiations of girls as well as boys. Here I shall focus on the way in which sex/gender influences the shaping of the careers of girls.

Lesley, Pat and Sandra — The Lasses

The lasses created a space for fun within the school; they enjoyed limited freedom to avoid the duller aspects of the female careers they were embarking upon — this space was located within the flexible structures and the personalized practices of Greenfield. Gradual adjustment of expectations is particularly clear in the case of Lesley, who in the fifth year expresses her ambitions: 'I keep saying that I'm not going to get married and be a little suburban housewife in a semi-detached house and things like this'. But she did not wish to struggle at school, and having fun seemed easier;[24] she left after the fifth year, and took a clerical job. Later she talks about readjustments she has made, focussing on marriage and children:

> I must have grown up so much to realize that that's probably what's going to be in store for me anyway. You know, I'm not clever or anything ... and now I've not got any qualifications to say yeah I'm going to be managing director of such a firm ... I think you come down to earth a bit and you realize that you can only do so much, there's only so many opportunities open for you. I mean if I wanted

to I suppose I could be a career girl, or whatever, I could go to nightschool for so many years, and learn whatever, but, you know, I'm quite happy as I am at the minute.

Lesley was disruptive at school, and negotiated her career with difficulty. She was assessed bright, but not 'pushed' to take examinations; affective rather than academic learning was considered more important for her, because of biographical factors, relating to domestic difficulties etc. These factors were largely shaped by sex/gender; the greater control exerted on girls in the home[25] makes them more vulnerable to disruptions there. Therefore teachers are more likely to focus on the domestic context of girls and thus reinforce the location of girls within the family. Boys are generally allowed more independence, their family circumstances are less likely to impinge on them, and these are focussed on less by teachers, and are thus not open to scrutiny to the same extent as is the case with girls' situation at home.

Pat does not express any clear ambitions, but several job shifts after leaving school indicate her unwillingness to settle in an unfulfilling job. She does not articulate what she is looking for, but her sense of having more talent than has been required of her is indicated when she discusses one of her jobs, an assistant supervisor in a factory: 'when I went to the interview ... it looked good, but when I got there it was just boring, you are not like an assistant supervisor, you're just like a run-around and it wasn't really what the job said it was'. She was a nanny in London, but 'it was just all lunch parties and dinner parties, the children were just for show'. She is unemployed and looking for 'anything', but qualifies: 'Well I say anything, but if there is a job that I could have and I wouldn't like it I wouldn't do it, so it's not just anything; I don't know!'

Pat's lack of certainty makes her regret not having worked at school: 'I just thought messing about would be easier'. And it was fun: 'the other night with Helen and Nicole we were laughing about what we used to do at school and we just couldn't stop laughing all night, so it must have been good'. Difficulties in career construction were related to biographical factors, sex-gender identifications and resistance through femininity (McRobbie, 1978); a middle class background would have provided Pat more space for negotiations. It was difficult for Pat to channel her creativity and perceptiveness; by the second interview her feminine career was confirmed;[26] she regrets her lack of success at school but notes that scope for alternatives was limited: 'it's just not me'.

Sandra's gender-typed career construction with negotiations characterized by feminine resistance assumed such significance that despite her lower middle class background she got a factory job.[27] Her attitudes were coloured by resignation, but she expressed a sense of regret about her school career, assuming that success would have been possible had she chosen it. The deep structures of determinations are not clear in Sandra's case, but biographical features relating to the family have assumed sex-typed significance. Despite her own convictions of choice, the personalized practices must have been difficult for someone whose family circumstances gave little back-up[28] for individual negotiations.

Joyce, Marilyn, Rachel and Rita — The Successful

Joyce, Marilyn and Rachel share a working class background with fathers in skilled jobs, mothers employed, and families relatively affluent. All achieved well in their 'O' levels, stayed on to sixth-form, and gained 'A' levels. All were self-confident, but also expressed a sense of struggle, of having to forge their careers, of being determined to achieve as women. For example Marilyn intends 'to do as good a job as any man'. They hope to get interesting jobs, but are not instrumental in a narrow way, and have specific interests which they wish to pursue in terms of their intrinsic value in personal terms. All can discuss political issues at length and articulately, and with enthusiasm, but try to conduct their lives without giving much thought to the realities they observe, thus Joyce wishes 'to remain naive' (chapter 7). They experience a sense of scope which can be utilized through determination, but also by a sense of inevitability (Marilyn: 'I bet I end up cooking dinners', when discussing future roles), which they try to adjust to. Part of their negotiations is an interest in constructing a meaningful personal life, at times at the expense of political awareness, including their awareness of structured inequalities in terms of sex-gender and social class.

Because of their interests, self-confidence and independence they found it easy to fit into Greenfield, and to negotiate the direction of their careers in the context of the school, but felt they had to be determined and more self-conscious than boys. All were familiar with feminism, and participated in women's groups in the school when these were formed. Teachers perceived each of them as successful and respected them a great deal. When I mentioned one of Joyce's observations on sexism in Greenfield to Sarah, her tutor, she remarked: 'did Joyce say that — then I expect it's right'. But all were orientated towards the female job market; fashion design, occupational therapy and languages.

Rita's work in the team was marked by personalization. The results of the focus she adopted were successful, in terms of examination results and teacher assessment. The personalized nature of her work, however, led her tutor to doubt whether Rita should study for 'A' levels, as personalized work would not be possible. Rita decided to stay on, enjoyed the work, and developed her social awareness in the course of the year between the two interviews.[29] She was uncertain about the usefulness of her team work, but considers that she had to have a personalized focus 'because I wanted to find out more about myself and the people around me', but she now wanted to 'probe deeper into history, geography and sociology'. Had she left school at

16, she would have been 'naive', and without the insights she was developing in the sixth year. Her views became more radical, she questioned her own racism etc. For some girls schooling affords a space to disassociate themselves from traditional notions of femininity, though their resistance may prepare them for future roles (Lesley, Sandra), and for others schooling can offer a chance to explore issues beyond the usually defined confines of femininity. Whilst some girls are encouraged to undertake such explorations in Greenfield, the school's more distinctive feature is its flexibility in allowing girls to follow their own interests, and they are not consistently encouraged to diverge from sex-stereotyped patterns within personalized structures.

Linda, Celia, Sylvia and Philippa — Problematic Career Construction

Linda's structural and cultural location, her sex and biographical factors contributed to formation of a pattern which she was dissatisfied with, but unable to change. Personalization in Greenfield confirmed Linda's individualistic thinking, which led her to feel frustrated with her own lack of abilities. But she was unwilling to readjust her expectations, which led to depression: 'there's not much point in living, there's nothing to do. Can't do anything about it, you know it's really frustrating'. Linda is not instrumentalist, nor does she identify with working class culture, nor is she interested in constructing a feminine career. She has no political perspective within which to perceive her apparently personal problems, save vague conceptions about a world recession; she does not connect personal and social structures. She struggles to forge a worldview explaining her own situation and guiding her own strategies:

> I don't care about anything, as long as I'm all right, I don't give a damn about anybody else. Nobody wants to know my problems, I don't wanna know anybody else's.

She tries to accommodate her problems through escapism, for example through music, but

> I'm listening to music that's about not getting a job, about being bored, and I got a group shouting at me get out, get up ... don't be in a factory, don't let them push you down ... but you can't get out, you're just trapped.

She is tempted by aggressive expressions of her frustrations, but she perceives these as aimless, mere sources of relief:

> Remember those riots in Brixton, I felt like — I wished I'd been there, I could have helped ... to throw bricks as well — I wanna get out and smash something.

She contemplates with aversion the traditional avenue open to women:

marriage and children: 'sometimes I get a feeling I might . . . get married just to get out of the way I am now, just to do something different.'.

Linda gained a couple of 'O' levels, which was more than had been expected of her in the high school, and which pleased her, but the deep structure of limitations posed strong determinations, and successful negotiation of a career in the school in academic terms would have been difficult.

Celia enjoyed school, and negotiated her social career to her satisfaction, was able to pursue her interests (chapter 7, p. 115) and got a lot of support in personal problems, but was not successful academically and felt that she was not 'pushed' enough. For example she regrets that she was not persuaded to carry on with science. Because of a range of domestic difficulties her tutor felt that Celia's argument that she would have been more successful in a traditional school was not accurate. Celia counters this: 'but I would have probably come out with more — better exam results'. Despite Celia's interest in certification and job prospects by the second interview she is about to get married and have children. She claims that the readjustment has been positive, and a conscious choice on her part, but such an adoption of a traditional female role was a clearly available option to her within the structures of possibilities limiting the direction of her career construction.

Sylvia has specific interests which led her to enjoy her stay at school. The flexible structures suited her, as she was clear about how she wished to construct her career. Social mobility was not uppermost in her mind, but she did stay on to sixth-form. She did not, however, gain any 'A' levels; her structural and cultural location will have had some impact, but biographical aspects were crucial, relating to her health and domestic problems. The latter assume gender-specific implications (p. 184).

Philippa's career construction was problematic. She was interested in music, but was not encouraged to pursue a full-time career in it, but her parents were also reluctant to allow her to continue her studies after the fifth year. Her sense of struggle is manifested in the lyrics of a song she wrote with other girls, including Rachel; they had a band in the school:

> You can't tell us what to do, we've got nothing to lose, when we women fight back, we know just what we're gonna do.

Her family has experienced social mobility; her father 'worked his way up'. She feels ambivalent about her class position; she talks about various jobs her mother has done, and mentions that she is cleaning 'in a big house' — 'I don't like that, because really she's like being a servant to the top rank'. She is also torn because of her own interests; on the one hand she thinks you should not work too hard at school, because it 'ruins your social life', on the other hand she's got 'so much to do in such a short time if I want to get to the top so to speak'; she'd like a career the same as a bloke would have a career'. Despite the lack of support from her parents she was relatively successful and managed to negotiate (with the help of her tutor) a compromise with her parents, enabling her to study knitwear design, which she thought connected with her interest in art.[30] At the same time she continued to develop her interest in music, hoping to construct a career in it in future.

Brenda, Joanne and Gwen — The Gender-oriented

All the girls encompassed a gender-orientation and identification. But these girls have been categorized separately, because of the relative ease and lack of contradictions they experienced in the construction of a career marked by femininity.

Brenda's working class background and sex-gender manifested in school by low achievement and a lack of confidence linked to low ambitions. She talks about her experiences in schools; she was well set on a feminine career by the time she entered Greenfield having interacted with teachers she remembered as harsh and unsympathetic. Moreover, she did not value social mobility in itself (p. 130), and was interested in developing her career in traditional feminine terms; she goes to beauty classes, has a steady boyfriend and conceives of her future in terms of getting married, having children, adopting a housewife's role, and returning to unskilled part-time work after staying at home. Thus she does not experience Pat's and Linda's problems.

Joanne achieved good 'O' levels, but left after a brief stay in the sixth-form having secured clerical work, and thus tackled her worries about unemployment. She was not particularly concerned about social mobility — once she joked about becoming 'a revolutionary working in Waitrose'. She enjoyed school, and pursued a range of interests there, but was not an instrumentalist. She was lacking in confidence and felt it was too risky for her to stay on at school; her desire to secure a degree of independence led her to enter a characteristically female segment of the labour market.

Gwen's career construction was marked by relative ease; she enjoyed her work as a telephonist. Her negotiations at school caused few frustrations, as she did not have particular ambitions, and had not consciously questioned the validity of a traditional female role. Her school learning was marked by personalization, which underlined her lack of confidence and assumptions about the inappropriateness of her engagement in broad political issues (chapter 7). Gwen's tutor tried to tackle her gender-specific socialization through projects on dress etc., but it may be that within this feminine sphere she was unable to question the patterns of traditional femininity she conformed to. Her interest in broader social questions, which she considered inappropriate anyway, did not receive much encouragement. Though Gwen is happy, it seems that the school could have done more to help her to examine sex-typed career construction.

Conclusions

The chapter has indicated the ingredients of negotiations through which the surface structure of choice and a deep structure of a limiting framework crystallize into a particular career. The importance of the structural location and sex-gender were emphasized. First, individualization as a form 'declasses' people into units. Second, individualization in schooling has constituted a feature of control through eroding collective patterns of working class culture. Third, working class students, whose structural location and sense of powerlessness related to that location leads them to individualistic solutions in terms of looking after oneself; to teachers with the new middle class conceptions of personalization this is reminiscent of old middle class instrumentalism which they oppose. Individualization, then, poses problems to working class students who may find the ethos of the school difficult to relate to, and negotiations characterized by academic *and* social success are marked with tensions.

The discussion on professionalism indicated how such problems find expression through emphasis on certification, shifts in teacher behaviour and interaction with students from personal to impersonal, the former drawing predominantly on concrete characteristics of participants, the latter on their institutional roles. Hence despite the existence of social mobility, working class kids tend to get working class jobs — where they are socially mobile, other factors in career formation (biographical, cultural aspects, worldview) have been conducive to this.

The extent of social mobility in Greenfield is not striking.[31] However, the sense of scope, the self-determination and the range of opportunities for self-confident, extrovert students with a variety of definite interests makes social and academic success possible in the case of few students from a working class background. Their positive experiences in the school, and their sense of affinity with the structures, processes and ethos of the school indicates specific adaptation to a progressive school. When girls are successful, they nevertheless enter the female sectors of labour market. Hence an examination of sex-gender is appropriate.

Notes

1 Race is not considered as Greenfield College does not contain a significant multi-racial element.
2 Thirty-one students.
3 *The Pocket Oxford Dictionary of Current English* (1961), Oxford, Clarendon Press.
4 Many of them felt that their future work patterns were relatively established; this was borne out by the information I obtained about a half of them at the time of writing this.
5 These aspects were arrived at through observations and discussions with all students in one team, as well as the data on the interviewed students.

6 These included informal discussions, and recorded interviews of all the team teachers, who were asked to comment at length on particular students.

7 Information was acquired of parental occupation of the majority of students in one team; information was also acquired on their examination results, and their initial location in the labour market on entry. No significant trends of social mobility have been discerned.

8 For example HALSEY (1981), JACKSON and MARSDEN (1962), DOUGLAS (1964).

9 For example BERNSTEIN (1975) chapter 6.

10 In HALL and JEFFERSON (Eds) (1977) p. 168.

11 *Ibid.* p. 168.

12 A note from the high school records commented on George's father: 'keen to support the school, but too authoritarian with an over-riding concern for discipline'.

13 *C.f.* SHARP and GREEN (1975).

14 In Hall and Jefferson (Eds) (1977) p. 170.

15 Research on the socialization of girls reviewed for example by DEEM (1978).

16 MANN (1973).

17 And with the help of a part-time teacher who 'saw himself' in KEVIN.

18 He was retaking an 'A' level, and his job was useful preparation for his interest in horticulture.

19 For example he would not vote.

20 See chapter 7, note 20.

21 According to latest information Brian was working in a warehouse, having been unemployed.

22 His examination results were a disappointment to him. He tried to retake them, but left half-way to join the navy.

23 'It depends on what they have. I mean if they go into a job and that and they start their own firm up and if it does well, they make money; then again they might go bankrupt, you know, so you don't know how you're gonna end up.'

24 She recounts:

> 'we used to sit down and Pat would say right girls we're not doing any work today, we're going to annoy everybody today, and everybody used to go along with it ... it's good fun isn't it. We didn't stop laughing. I don't know, you just sit there and get fed up and you think you'll have a laugh.'

25 For example DEEM (1978) and SHARPE (1976).

26 She got pregnant, had a miscarriage, and was looking for a job in childcare. When I spoke to her whilst writing this she had a baby, and was not employed.

27 A threat of redundancy was hanging over during the second interview. She is now married and has children and does not work outside the home.

28 Father's correspondence with the school emphasizes the need for rigorous, traditional discipline.

29 She expressed amazement at her own naivety when she studied the transcript of the first interview.

30 Her tutor described the course as more technical and vocational. She finished the course, and worked in design, but at the time of writing this is concentrating her energies into pursuing a career in music.

31 See note 7.

Chapter 11

Sex-gender and Sexism

Salient sexist features found in many schools are missing in Greenfield College. Gender is not an explicit administrative, organizational category in the school. There are no distinct facilities (beyond toilets), no uniforms, registers are not organized according to sex; if seating arrangements and student groups are single sex (they are not exclusively so), this is because of student choice. Tutor groups are not balanced in terms of sex, though teams are. No explicit channelling of students in subjects takes place. This does not preclude the possibility of implicit channelling, but no mechanism for it exists. Teacher hierarchies are narrowed and altered through the absence of departmental structures. There is no clear academic/pastoral split. The allowance policy operated by the staff is committed to reducing differentials by promoting teachers from scale to scale on the basis of number of years worked, whilst discriminating against graduates in favour of non-graduates. Moreover, the overall ethos of the school is committed to giving fair and equal treatment of girls and boys as individuals, and would not expect girls to simply be prepared for their traditional female roles.

Nevertheless, however, the subject choices of boys and girls are based on traditional models of appropriate areas of study for each (chapter 7). When moving from overall male/female subject divisions into consideration of the timetables of individual students, girls tend to study a mixture of subjects confirming aspects of their femininity and female career; boys tend to study a mixture of subjects confirming their masculinity and male career. The job aspirations and actual job choices of boys and girls are clearly differentiated according to sex. Many students leave the school with explicitly sexist attitudes (chapter 7), considering children and housework as women's responsibilities. Those who would like to see equality between the sexes do not pursue the implications of this, or feel resigned to external pressures. Moreover, it was noted that whilst the students tended to see their teachers as anti-racist, there was no widely spread conception of them as anti-sexist.

The practice and content of the school do not resolutely tackle sexism, and reinforce differentiation between boys and girls despite contrary intentions embedded in the school ethos emphasizing the development of the potential of all students as individuals. Therefore we can assume that there are aspects in the 'hidden curriculum' in Greenfield which contain and mediate traditional patterns. In order to explore these analytically, rather than descriptively, further theoretical discussion is necessary. A consideration of individualization and professionalism as gender specific provides us with tools which allow us to turn back to the school and to discern patterns and explain their significance.

Capitalism and Patriarchy — A Dual Analysis

The concept of patriarchy has been employed in various ways in feminist literature.[1] Patriarchy has been analyzed as founded on biological differences between men and women, or on the different values placed on these (Firestone, 1970); as universal and predominant in explaining the position of women in terms of 'sex-class' (Millett, 1971); as ideological, expressed in a patriarchal culture (Mitchell, 1975) and as material, based on the domestic mode of production as separate from the capitalist mode of production (Delphy, 1977). Thue use of the concept is problematic (Beechey, 1979; Barrett, 1980), and particularly Barrett suggests it should only be applied in a narrow way to refer to a particular form of household organisation. 'Patriarchy' has been used without clarification as to whether the rule of the father, or dominance of men over women is referred to. Analysis, in posing patriarchy as independent of the organization of capitalist relations becomes universalistic, transhistorical and biologistic. Barrett advocates instead the concepts of reproduction and ideology.[2]

But the concept of patriarchy is not abandoned here. Though the analytical separation between patriarchal and capitalist relations is important, an analysis of their joint articulation or an historical study of building of capitalist relations on patriarchal structures is not precluded. Patriarchy need not be understood as a universal concept; patriarchal relations can be considered in their historical forms, presently enmeshed with capitalist relations. No alternative satisfactory approach has been developed. Barrett's suggestion that reproduction should be used contains problems: the concept has been used diversely and with inadequate rigour. Moreover, reproduction is not an explanatory concept, but is itself problematic — it does not provide a starting point, if functionalism is to be avoided, but can be arrived at (chapter 1, p. 8). The prioritization of ideology hampers the understanding of the lived experiences of subjects within capitalist patriarchy.

Hartmann (1979) analyzes patriarchy in articulation with capitalist relations, whilst positing an analytical separation between them. The categories of Marxism, she argues, are 'sex-blind', and do not explain why women are subordinate to men. Patriarchy is a social and economic structure to which capital accommodates itself, and which it perpetuates. Patriarchy has a material base, which Hartmann relates to the control of women's labour power by men, both at home and in the sphere of production; it is a 'set of social relations among men',[3] creating solidarity and interdependence, even if hierarchical, between them. The social division of labour provides an 'underpinning' for differentiated sexual subcultures. Hartmann notes the difficulty in separating patriarchy from other social relations under capitalism, as both are enmeshed because of capital's historical accommodation to a perpetuation of patriarchy. Nevertheless she sees such an attempt as necessary in order to analyze the position of women in its specificity.

More contentiously, Hartmann argues for a 'coincidence' between male characteristics and those of capitalist society — for example competitiveness, rationality, domination etc. — men absorb the capitalist relations at work. The forms of their existence are shaped by these social relations, discussed by Hartmann in terms of values and ideology, but, within the theoretical framework adopted here, they are better considered as forms which channel experiences at work. The concept of form weakens the possibility of reading a deterministic, mechanical relationship into Hartmann's argument; *channelling* implies an uneven process of formation of subjectivities.

A dual analysis, then, is considered possible and necessary here.[4] The concept of patriarchy is taken to refer to power of men over women; this power extends to children — thus the authority of the father within the family is seen as part of such power. Development of compulsory schooling has involved an articulation between capitalism and patriarchy, at times in contradictory forms. Shaw (1981) discusses the concept of *in loco parentis* and indicates the assumption by the state of parental duties and responsibilities, implying models of patriarchy; *in loco parentis* and the idea of parental authority within it is derived from rights of fatherhood. Thus some of the parental rights are removed and located within the state.[5]

Individualization as Gender-specific

Fragmentation in the lives of people through the labour process and the practices of the state was noted in chapter 8. Here I shall discuss the gender-specific character of individualization as a form and the sexist impact it has on the content and practices within Greenfield.

Female domestic labour, argues Dominelli (1978) is fetishized through the marriage contract; ideas of romantic love 'mask' women's dependency within the family. Individualization is a double-bind for women, existing both in the public and the private sphere in a gender-specific way. Hobson (1978) notes the isolation of housewives, shaped by privatization of work at home; it is 'collective isolation' through the consensual position of large numbers of women being in the same situation in a privatized world. Hobson also touches on the gender-specificity of personalization by noting the position of housewives and mothers as 'a focus of the modern aspirations of personal happiness'.[6] Brunsdon (1978) argues that as women are defined primarily as wives and mothers, they are 'politically, ideologically and economically' placed on the personal sphere of the family, which is emotional apparently 'apolitical' and 'natural'.[7] Women, because of the culturally limited representation of women and the exclusions of their experiences as women, tend to think in terms of direct experience and common sense.[8] But, Brunsdon continues, the women's liberation movement attempts to draw on individual, personal experience, and construct explanations from the point of view of women, aiming to understand how this experience is shaped by the subordinate position of women as a group. Thus personal experience is not only seen as 'individual' or 'unique', but as 'gender specific'. The personal is defined as political; questions can be raised about the structures of women's experiences and subordination (for example it becomes possible to perceive the collectiveness of women's isolation). Hartmann notes that the women's liberation movement slogan 'personal is political' is not a 'plea for subjectivity', but a recognition of men's power and women's subordination as a social and political reality.

Winship (1978 and 1981) notes that the male labourer is 'freely' able to sell his labour-power; thus the ideological form of individuality is gender-specific. Winship (1981) focusses on the process of consumption as an articulation of patriarchal and capitalist relations, which constructs women ideologically as individuals. It is not clear what Winship's definition of ideology is; it does not seem to reach the status of an analytical concept, but tends to be used descriptively. However, her analysis of gender-specificity of individualization gives the sharpest of insights. What she calls the ideology of individuality and femininity could be considered as forms firmly grounded in the articulation of capitalist and patriarchal relations, rather than somewhat loosely floating superstructural constructs.

An illustration of the implications of the construction of feminine individualism and the personal, private sphere to careers of girls is found in McRobbie's analysis of *Jackie* magazine (1978). *Jackie* frames the world for readers in a way that it occupies the personal private sphere.

> Hegemony is sought uncoercively on this terrain, which is relatively
> free of direct state interference. Consequently it is seen as an area of
> 'freedom', of 'free choice' and of 'free time'.[9]

The articulation between patriarchal and capitalist social relations is alluded to: 'Jackie' is both a product of a privately owned industry, and a representative of the world of personal, private emotions. Capital, notes McRobbie, needs to control this space, but it is to be removed from direct contact with the state.

McRobbie discusses the salient characteristics of *Jackie*. First, the magazine deals with isolated individuals. The picture stories deal with characters outside their social and historical context; in the problem pages this isolation is symbolized, maintained and nourished. Second, *Jackie* is concerned with the construction of the feminine personality, with 'knowing yourself', your personality and that of significant others such as friends, boyfriends and members of one's family. Third, the focus is on romance, the girls' response to male sexuality; this defines girls' lives through emotions. Fourth, problems of girls are seen and dealt with as 'personal' even though they may be shared by large numbers. *Jackie* encourages 'conventional individualism' and conformist independence', both of which have bearing on the construction of the careers of the girls during the period of adolescence, when the future direction of such careers is being negotiated.

In discussing the impact of *Jackie* McRobbie refers to it as 'ideological work' on the 'raw material' of 'preexistent femininity'. But when she refers to the 'level' rather than 'ideology' of femininity McRobbie notices the significance of material practices rather than merely their ideological representations. It is useful to consider how this 'material' is shaped by forms of gender-specific individualization. I shall now consider mediations through the mode of professionalism.

Professionalism as Gender-specific

professions … are the non-ascriptive achievement-based elite … they are the elect, in a true sense of the most knowledgeable and morally superior of *men* whose dealings are with other *men* in the conduct of practical affairs. (my emphasis)[10]

Hartmann's definition of patriarchy (p. 207) refers to male interrelationship, these are expressed in the above quotation: professionalism is a mode stamped by masculinity. This is evident in teaching, where the differential position of men and women has been noted (Leggatt, 1970; Parry, 1974; Deem, 1976). Centred on the notion of a 'career' is one of the differences. Women in general relate to the construction of a career in a specific way because of energy and time required by familial responsibilities. This has implications for the position of women in the hierarchical structuring of teaching. The higher up the occupational hierarchy one focusses, the fewer women are found (Deem, 1978).

The notions of 'expertise', competence and rationality embedded in the thinking about professions have a particular affinity with masculinity. Contentious as this point may be, it is supported by the concentration of women in primary schools, where their expertise has been founded in a different way from secondary schools, and is based on generalized, pedagogical skills. Another significant distinction between secondary and primary schools exists, relating to the notion of teachers as *'in loco parentis'*. In primary schools the model of the parent is predominantly that of a mother, but in secondary schools it is predominantly that of a father (for example, Bernstein, 1975; David, 1978; Deem, 1978). Historically, the skills required in primary teaching were seen to be those of a good mother, whereas expertise and competence related to the knowledge of a subject developed within the secondary sector. Before the advent of primary schools as a specific stage in schooling, teaching in elementary schools was regarded as 'feminine activity' (Purvis, 1981).

Gender specificity of professionalism is evident in discussions considering why teaching does not fulfil all the criteria of professions (Leggatt, 1970). The answers commonly refer to the large proportion of women in teaching, and an overall attachment of material qualities to it (Lightfoot, 1975). The growing emphasis during the sixties on teachers as professionals with autonomy, initiative and expertise was linked to the development of progressivism and to the recruitment of new teachers; already trained married women teachers were encouraged to return to teaching, but the focus was also on attracting particularly *male* graduates (chapter 2).

The advent of trade union militancy aimed to safeguard and improve teachers' position directed focus to the ideology of caring as a significant aspect of professionalism. Teachers are seen as responsible for the children they teach; their welfare should be placed above concerns for working conditions and remuneration. Teaching is seen as a vocation whereby the rewards relate to satisfaction attained through the conduct of one's duties in the interest of those for whom one is responsible. Thus the ideology of caring contains a strong element of social control within it. Whilst in the 1960s there was a move to increase the professionalism of teachers, and also their autonomy, in the early 1970s, with the wave of teacher militancy, there was a shift away from ideological aspects of professionalism expressed through 'caring'.

Teaching, in so far as it is a profession, is a mode stamped by masculinity; women and men exist in a differential relationship to it. But teaching also contains the notion of feminine activity; it is conceived of as an extension to parenting, 'caring'. However, within the concept of *in loco parentis* two models of teaching are found: teacher as a father and as a mother. The significance of these arguments will be illustrated in connection with processes of sexism and gender differentiation in Greenfield College. Teachers and students are considered separately, for clarity of exposition of complex *interwoven* themes.

Greenfield College

Teachers

Male teachers tend to outnumber female teachers in Greenfield. Women are disproportionately concentrated on scales one and two.[11] The operation of the allowances policies has led to a high correlation between teachers' pay and their work experience.[12] Thus women, in so far as they have familial responsibilities, are in a disadvantaged position in the construction of a career. Because of an overall shortage of points in the school, the application of allowances criteria has not always been straightforward. But considerations have not taken into account the specific position of women; thus a section of women teachers have felt that insufficient discussion about unjust operation of allowances has taken place.

Differentiation between men and women exists vis-à-vis the democratic structures and processes. Meetings tend to be chaired by men;[13] and are dominated by men who tend to speak, whilst women tend to listen.[14] A female teacher asked to be a member of an allowances committee felt that she was going to be a 'token woman'. Another woman teacher who wanted to participate felt that she was ousted out by not being told about the meetings. In an election for an allowances committee there were fifteen candidates, three of whom were women. One of these candidates checked the ballot papers in order to discover whether those who had not voted for her had not voted for the other women either; this was indeed the case. Though such information appears incidental, piecing together of observations is one way of questioning the assumption of equality among the teachers. It is not argued that men teachers simply dominate women teachers. The question of women being, to a degree, complicit in their own oppression has to be raised.[15] Further, for those women with small children and domestic responsibilities attendance at meetings after school is difficult, and their presence as well as their voice is missing.

More diffusely and more importantly, male teachers set the 'tone'[16] of the dealings in the school, among teachers, and between teachers and pupils. Female teachers find themselves in difficult positions, when they are unable or unwilling to emulate that tone. An example was given by a woman who recounted an evening in the school disco concert:

> I was the only woman (teacher) there, and I'd come partly because I wanted to hear it, and the bouncers were Tom, Rob and Phil. And particularly Phil was extraordinarily heavy. I really objected to it, because if he sets the tone at that level there's nothing I could do. I cannot maintain a heavy tone, because I'm not going to heavy kids. Physically I'm not capable of it ... Sharon runs discos, Jill does, and they're little ... It's really easy for certain men to fall into that trap without thinking about it — being an incipient physical threat.

The notion of men as 'incipient physical threat' was borne out in discussions with male teachers who had supervised discos, and who frequently referred to the sizes of the boys attending.

The existence of an overall, masculine tone in the school is borne out, symbolically, by the Deputy Head of the school being called Hacker. He was clear of the implications of the name:

> it certainly implies an idea that physically — I mean it started on the football field that physically I was stronger than them and the chopping down idea ... Well it also was a reputation amongst the staff. Then it's a thing that gets built up in stories of playing for football teams, and I'm known as a person who carves people as a very heavy

tackler indeed, who wins the ball, who comes out with the ball every time it's necessary, and it built up with the kids like that, playing football with them.

There is no doubt that this image has been effective:

> I can stop kids who are known as very tough in the local district, and who are tough, tougher than me, and now probably could beat me into a pulp — six feet two, they have been labouring now for five or six years. And something is happening concerning some of our kids, and I go and see them, and they are quite meek and mild because they still remember me as they remember me when they were fourteen.

The 'mildness' referred to may not just be due to an experience of a superior physical threat, but also due to the location of that threat in a status authority figure at the top of the school hierarchy. It is certainly not incidental that this figure is also man and masculine, physically and socially.

The deputy was prepared to use this image and reputation when dealing with situations perceived as difficult.

> Now the idea that I actually lay a hand on a kid, is absolutely common in the district. I mean O.K. I break up fights and I may do that very aggressively — if the kids were not taken aback by that I would probably slam a kid up against the wall, but that is as far as it would go, but the reputation exists. And let's face it if a kid is bullying I will have him in here for a large number of hours and when they come out psychologically they might be in a pretty beaten down state if I felt that was actually necessary to stop them — and they might have been crying, although they come in here as very tough kids ...

Certainly the heavier aspects of such physical control are not engaged in without thought and without some regret, but are utilized if it is felt that the realities of the situation are such that pragmatically choices are limited. Where capitalist social relations may not be sufficient for controlling the situation (teacher-deputy/pupil), patriarchal authority is invoked as more effective (male adult/child).

Three dimensions of complexity must be added to the above discussion of the tone of control. The masculine tone is not confined to men. I shall illustrate: an informal discussion took place between three teachers. Janet suggested to Duncan that the discipline and control operated in the school placed women at a disadvantage when dealing with difficult or disruptive children. Duncan disagreed and noted that Julie had no particular problems in controlling students, and in fact was very successful. Julie replied that she had a very 'masculine self-image', and therefore her ease in handling situations did not refute the point about the position of women teachers in the school.

Thus I am not suggesting that masculine control is operated by all men teachers, and by no women teachers. Sex is a biological attribute; gender, with masculinity and femininity, is a socially acquired attribute. Though the concepts of sex and gender overlap considerably, masculinity and femininity are not sex-specific in a clear-cut way, but gender-constitutive. Though masculinity and femininity are constructions affecting most features of our lives, and though differential value is placed on them, and differential power and influence is attached to them (for example, Lightfoot, 1975; Clarricoates, 1978; Smith, 1978; Sharpe, 1976), men are not singly defined by masculinity, and similarly women are not singly defined by femininity.

The second complexity is that though the mode of control is predominantly masculine, the content of control and of interactions is also feminine to a significant degree. Bernbaum (1973) pointed to a coexistence of 'expressive' and 'instrumental' orientations in the school, the former mainly among women, the latter mainly among men. Greenfield College, as a progressive school, has an ethos in many ways akin to primary school; the model of the teacher as a mother has more significance there than in a formal secondary school.

The third significant feature is that teachers shift between masculine and feminine models when both are available. The nature of the different models is illustrated in a quotation from the Deputy Head; this quotation also indicates the shift in teachers over time.

> There were all sorts of things that I wanted to do that you could call in many ways a very sort of masculine, aggressive approach . . . As I saw teachers whose work I respected taking a very gentle approach with students, and some of these were men teachers, and that being very successful I have changed my own ideas in a way from that sort of rather aggressive approach that I had. People laugh about that in the school, as I am seen as pretty aggressive, having gone into teaching very starry eyed indeed and having some of that starry-eyedness knocked out of me, and realising that you have got to be a very tough customer yourself, and I brought that with me here, and I began to realise that in fact probably I had slung too far in one direction and the whole thing of getting through to students required a very soft approach. The setting of standards, implicit standards and goals for students didn't even necessarily require an aggressive approach either, it could just be done very implicitly . . . and I began to change my mind about that.

The deputy's comments also illustrate something about what the perhaps ambivalent constructions of teacher as a mother/father, femininity and masculinity are taken to mean.

Thus teachers in the school may shift over time towards the expressive content of Greenfield, reflected in its ethos. The shifts can also be situational, depending on teacher perceptions of best available strategies. This is illustrated in Julie's account of two incidents of touching. The first concerned a male black student who felt he was not integrated in the school, and found communication with the staff difficult. Julie felt that one could relate to this student through touching, and that he himself communicated in this way (slapping of shoulders, tapping of arms, brushing of elbows) — this is personalized, expressive touching. The second incident concerned a white male student, whom Julie encountered outside the teaching area he should have been in — the boy did not make a move in that direction when asked to do so, and Julie grabbed him by the arm and walked with him arm-in-arm through to the appropriate area. The boy was embarrassed, and pleaded with Julie to let him go, as she was 'showing him up'. Though this incident was not without humorous overtones, it is nevertheless an instance of instrumental, 'depersonalized' touching, as a swift response to the realities of the situation, rather than a response to the perceived or communicated personal needs of the student as an individual. But it had personalized implications, and indicates the ambiguous fusing of the public and the private in a progressive school (for example, chapter 9).

Teachers, in their dealings with students, individualize them, because of cultural processes and structural constraints (chapter 9), either through personalization or atomization. The masculine mode of control through atomized stock solutions to problems and pressures encountered in day-to-day teaching contradicts the feminine content, concerned with personalized interaction, addressing individuals as concrete persons with particular characteristics. A diffuse, gender-specific effect of individualization is that it hinders teachers from seeing divisions amongst the staff. It is difficult for female teachers in the school to raise issues relating to their position as women. Inequalities between men and women cannot be seen unless there is a preparedness to look at categories, to look at groups, and to see generalities. Thus whilst forms of individualization are gender-specific, this very gender-specificity is hidden through individualization as a process fragmenting group formation and identification.

Students

For the girl students individualization assumes its gender-specific character, when personalization is transferred into atomization, and becomes linked with their future roles entailing isolation, domesticity and privatization. The mode of transference is certification. This affects all students, but on girls it interacts with the raw material of pre-existing femininity[17] and developing sexual and gender identities. But personalization can also be liberating, if it involves exploration of the 'personal as political' (Brunsdon, 1978; Winship, 1981).

I noted above that many students consider the treatment of boys and

girls in the school to be indistinguishable, but equally prevalent is the view
that they are in fact treated differently:

> Ken: I reckon some girls are treated better by some teachers. The
> girls ... don't get shouted at, and don't get told to work so much
> like we do. When we're in Julie's class, we say one word and we're
> out ... (the girls don't get) thrown about (so much).

> Brenda: Duncan is nice to us. And the boys — he just — he's not
> very nice to the boys at all in our class. He's always pestering them
> and ... if they don't wanna do a subject, he makes them do it ...
> but if any of us didn't want to do something then he'd just say fair
> enough.

> Joyce: I think the boys are controlled more than girls, or tried to be
> controlled more than girls, you know. (Girls are) allowed to get
> away with more. (They're) treated softly ... they're kind of
> hardening up the boys, you know, for later life. With the girls
> they think oh you're gonna have an easy easy life, we won't treat
> you too hard, you know, just be at home.

Thus a section of the students, particularly girls, feel that boys and girls
receive differential treatment. These feelings stem from their experiences and
observations.[18]

The phrase 'throwing about' is used by many students. It reflects the
existence of masculine mode of control, and the existence of 'incipient
physical threat'; in reality no such incidents have been observed or alluded to.

> Joanne: Trevor ... doesn't shout that often, but when something
> really gets him mad, he gets dead mad and he goes to them and
> picks them up and throws them — well, not throws them around
> — just puts them down where he wants them to sit because he's
> been telling them for about ten times, and it shuts them up.

Shifts in a teacher's behaviour are indicated — he does 'not shout very often';
thus this manner of ensuring control is reverted to during periods of pressure, when more feminine, personalized ways of dealing with students appear
ineffective. The quotation illustrated the combination of professional authority, insisting that the student do as s/he is told, and patriarchal authority,
even if the masculine power is largely symbolically expressed (throwing
around).

Subject choices in Greenfield occur along sex-specific lines, but no
formal mechanisms channel students towards traditional choices. Thus many
students and teachers are of the opinion that deeply embedded conditioning
and sex-stereotyping outside the school influence subject choices, and there is
little that the school can do to tackle this problem — the onus is on the
outside world. But there are aspects within the school that perpetuate the

sex-specificity of some subjects and student choices. First, the sex of the teachers of 'sex-biased' subjects tends to reinforce the bias of those subjects. Girls who do choose 'male' subjects often drop out fairly soon from lessons taught by a man, populated by boys, and with a consequent tendency towards a masculine orientation;[19] the girls cannot identify with the content and procedures. Second, because of the pressures of the cuts in expenditure, and increased roll in the school, combined with a deteriorated staff/student ratio, the 'demand' subjects, where all interested students cannot be catered for, introduce an element of covert streaming. When girls *have* remained in male-dominated lessons, they have been particularly determined, or have had particularly supportive tutors. Third, there is a strong experience of sexist teaching in sex-biased subjects:

> *Joyce:* I think the men teachers treat the boys with a lot more enthusiasm about the subject ... The teacher thinks oh she doesn't want to do physics or chemistry. I won't force her to do them, just leave it, whereas they encourage the boys to do them.

Individualization makes systematic tackling of the problem difficult (though some action has been taken); the school ethos emphasizes that students should be self-directing. Teachers are faced with a dilemma: on the one hand they feel they have to respect the choices of students; on the other hand they are aware that those choices operate within a set of determinations outside and inside the school. When teachers attempt to be forceful, they may not be successful anyway, as many students have internalized the school ethos, and adopt an active stance. 'They won't let me give up science' said a girl to her friend. 'Just give it up' was the advice she received from her.[20]

The school ethos values independence and autonomy; a successful career is more likely when students have these qualities. But observations of differential treatment of boys and girls suggested that teachers tend to curtail boys' independence in choices related to academic work. But girls' independence does not receive particular encouragement; careers of disruptive girls indicate that 'deviant' independence is more consistently and insistently dealt with in girls. Lesley, a girl perceived as 'difficult' thought that teachers were 'more lenient with the lads when they're fighting or they're arguing'. Other discussions with 'difficult'[21] girls suggested that they experience the control in the school as tighter than disruptive boys who had not lost the sense of scope for making their own decisions — 'you do what you wanna do in this school'.

An incident illustrates this. A large number of students went on strike when teachers took trade union action, refusing to do lunchtime supervision. Those on strike congregated at the school gates where a couple of teachers were also located. It was not suggested that the student action was unacceptable, and that they should not be there. When a group of girls after a great deal of hesitation decided to join them, somewhat self-consciously, they were seen and pursued by a male teacher who accused them of not being where they should be, and called them 'silly little girls'. The girls were indignant and after the teacher left argued that he had been wrong because they had been 'on strike' and not missing a lesson.[22] However, they remained in the team area doing artwork. Only later did groups of girls join the boys at the school gates. This observation, though incidental, adds weight to the tentative suggestion that in practice deviance of boys and girls is differentially defined.

Curriculum differentiation is evident in the content of work in humanities. The girls' projects tend to be more personalized than those of the boys. This is a result of interaction and negotiation between students and their teachers. Personalized learning is encouraged by teachers, but boys tend to shun it, and the girls may adopt it to the exclusion of other ways of looking at issues. For example, girls' interest in personal appearance is considered legitimate in the school; teachers aim to guide projects dealing with fashion and make-up towards questions about the position of women in society. Some teachers nevertheless feel that girls' perceptions have been allowed to remain narrow, focusing on the domestic and personal arena. These teachers feel that, ironically, no matter how such topics are approached, they restrict girls to the sphere of the private, the personal, the emotional.[23] Even when the projects draw feminist conclusions, they have little impact in the lives of the girls.

Personalization in the school can be compared and contrasted with McRobbie's discussion of *Jackie*, which many girls in Greenfield read. The curriculum content thus operates alongside the kind of ordering of 'raw materials' or 'existing levels of femininity' found in *Jackie*. Teachers, generally, are concerned that the students should 'know themselves' and those around them; in *Jackie* there is also concern for 'personality'. Both in school and in *Jackie* there is concern for being 'an individual'. In the latter the scope of this individuality is severely limited. Thus, though the feminist slogan 'personal is political' points to the potential liberating influence of personalization, and though the teacher's concern for personalization is indicative of the 'expressive' content of teaching in Greenfield, and signifies the feminine aspects of the model of a teacher, the impact on girls and boys is different. Even if there were no sex-specific mediations within the school, the raw material of femininity brought in by the girls ensures that they perceive and relate to individualization-personalization differently. Moreover, because of the predominance of men in the school both numerically and in terms of the 'tone', there is a tendency to place differential value on 'masculinity' and 'femininity', which is communicated to the girls. Jill noted how teachers in her team were more tolerant of boys' 'inane' discussions than those of girls.

The girls start behaving in a way that those characters behave in magazines, you know, sobbing about this boy who doesn't love me anymore. I mean I find it pretty difficult to take, but I'm prepared to tolerate it, I find football just as offensive, and I'm still prepared to tolerate a football conversation ... Not one of the men actually ever will talk to the girls about something that they got as a problem, particularly if it's what they would consider to be trivial ... Yet they will always relate to the boys about football.

Career aspirations and choices in the school are sex-specific.[24] This is a reflection of the local labour market, differentiated along sex-specific lines (Ashton and Maguire, 1980). But for choices to cross sex lines, new procedures and explanations at each stage are required, and the schools play an important role in this (Keil and Newton, 1980). In Greenfield nothing systematic is done to break the notions with which girls and boys operate, though it is acknowledged that girls fare worse in the local labour market.

Differential treatment of boys and girls poses problems; but so do attempts to treat them in the same way. The school ethos emphasizes students as individuals; this entails the rejection of sex-gender as a salient category, for example in formal organizational terms. But the significance of gender crystallization in adolescence (for example, Chandler, 1980; Sharpe, 1980) this approach with its supposition of equality of opportunity does not tackle gender-structuration. Thus, for example, in mixed-sex discussion on sexual morality boys were loudly and defensively joking, and girls had few opportunities to express their views. Their comments were trivialized and transformed into humorous cracks by the boys. The needs of boys and girls and their mode of approach were different in this situation. The mixed-sex situation was based on liberal thinking aiming to avoid reinforcing of differentiation. Instead the situation underlined existing divisions and development of diverging gender identities among boys and girls.

Girls themselves are a differentiated group. Adoption of femininity is a class-specific phenomenon (for example, Sharpe, 1976). This was evident in Greenfield in girls talking about adolescence. Links emerged between how youth was viewed, and what the girls' ambitions in terms of future location in the job market were. If the future was perceived in terms of a traditional female role, then going out and having fun was considered important, constituting a breathing space, which at the same time contains the possibility of ensuring one's prospects in meeting potential boyfriends. Ambitious girls concerned with achievement tended to experience youth as a time of difficulties and hard work, and, as Joyce argued, 'particularly hard on a girl' because 'you have to compete with the boys'. The sense of girls struggling against the odds was prominent when it was manifested. The differences between girls were based on class divisions in terms of parental background and/or they were linked to class positions aspired to in the future.

I shall reiterate the line of argument pursued here before considering attempts to break down sexism in the school. Sexism is not merely a reflection of external pressures emanating from the wider society, but is embedded in the internal practices in the school. Even the supposedly 'sex-neutral' content and processes assume different meanings for boys and girls, and reinforce their differentiation. The search for explanations led to the discussion of individualization as a gender-specific form, mediated to the level of the schools through modes such as professionalism and certification. Thus the practices in Greenfield, though characterized by personalization, are transformed into atomization, so that human actors are stripped of their concrete characteristics. The intersection between capitalist and patriarchal relations ensures that the units are nevertheless sexed ones. Professionalism as sex-specific was discussed, both in terms of the available orientations of men and women towards it, and in terms of the masculine and feminine content within it, and the particularity of Greenfield as a progressive school was noted in employing both models of teacher as a mother and a father. The impact on students was discussed in terms of shifts between the two models, and in terms of the overall tone of control in the school, linking teacher authority pertaining to their institutional position to patriarchal authority, based on incipient physical authority symbolizing the power of men and/or masculinity. Teacher student relationship, curriculum and subject choices were then considered on the basis of the assumption of shifts, and the transformation of personalization into atomization.

I shall consider attempts to break down sexist patterns by first noting difficulties entailed. A student, Marilyn, makes pertinent comments; she begins by describing a female student campaigning against sexism in the school:

> She's so strong in her attitudes ... maybe if all the teachers were the same as her, it would be inbuilt in them to change things, then it would happen. But teachers came to school — the women teachers are going to come to school and argue about sexism, and they're still going to go home and cook the dinner. It's just the way it is, whereas for Tina it's more clearly from the inside; it's her whole life.

Fundamental pressures are seen to be part of the daily lives; reorientations of values and beliefs and thinking are difficult or ineffective because of the determined framework of existence. Joyce: 'it's easier to kind of fall in with ideals then to fall out'. — the dominant ideas are powerful, because of the structures and relations supporting them.

Action on sexism has included joint teacher-student meetings (initiated by a student, Tina). These have called for separate introductory sessions to sex-biased subjects for girls and boys and across team timetabling for those who have chosen a subject where the majority are of another sex, thus bringing girls (or boys) from several teams together. These suggestions have been followed in a partial, but not in an organized way.[25] Students wrote introductory leaflets on sex-biased subjects and distributed these in feeder schools in order to reach students before they had to make decisions when entering the upper school. A number of teachers have become actively supportive of students crossing sex-lines, encouraging them when convictions weaken and problems are encountered. There has been no overall review of resources in the school in terms of their sexism, but anti-sexist resources do exist. However, there is no general and systematic effort to supply them; action has been team based or teacher based. The overall ethos and organization is reflected in the attitude to resources and poses limitations to anti-sexism. A further problem is the orientation of the subjects, but some men teachers have begun to consider how they meet the needs of girls, and encourage their participation.[26]

Tom describes himself as 'a convert of feminism' who always questions sexist behaviour and attitudes. Male teachers can also adopt feminine strategies which can be traced to the model of the teacher as a mother, and to the ideology of caring within professionalism. This can be difficult when sexist expectations of students form stumbling blocks. For example one male teacher who adopted a soft, understanding attitude to a group of disruptive boys, listened to them and reasoned with them was described by these boys as a 'poof'.[27] When faced with external pressures intensified by the cuts, and with 'difficult' boys who respond more positively to masculine than to feminine control teacher shifts from one to the other occur.

The many observations of the louder and more demanding boys distracting the teachers' attention away from a quiet girl can be contrasted to observations such as a teacher discussing a feminist story with a group of girls, evidently consciously ignoring a group of boys 'dossing'; she refused to be diverted. There were also observations of teachers questioning students' aspirations, roles adopted by girls, and notions of masculinity and femininity, and some indication of teachers addressing their own behaviour. Two women's groups were formed in the school, one for teachers and one for teachers and students. The latter group floundered when teachers attempted to address girls through it, rather than tackling sexism in the school as addressing both female teachers and students as women. The girls started their own group, but this ceased when girls active in it left. Since then women teachers have organized out-of-school girls only activities, and a girls only slot on the timetable is planned, where girls do assertion training, self-defence, listen to speakers, go on trips etc. The women teachers' caucus provides a large forum for a whole range of issues affecting the school to be debated and sexist processes to be monitored and opposed. Practical changes are more difficult to achieve and a sense of disillusionment among women teachers has not disappeared; women as feminists and radical activists have the tightening grip of restructuring to contend with.

> *Sarah:* the trouble is what one needs to argue now is the whole thing that you have got to have positive discrimination in favour of girls ... an argument like that is streets ahead of most of them who are way back in the old idea of treating boys and girls identically and equally, you know you have got such hell of a long argument ... We are trying to just keep where we are in terms of

education cuts etc.; to tackle the problem of sexism as well just seems too much like hard work.

Conclusion

Though personalization is easily transformed into atomization encouraging isolation and privatization among girls, on the other hand it has radical potential because of the possibility of conceiving 'personal as political'. This would facilitate the perception of one's situation in a non-fragmented way, as a member of a collective group, be it based on class, sex or ethnicity. Attempts to link personal and social structures reach incipient success, where effective strategies vis-à-vis individual students are developed, and where their daily experiences, and the framework these are located within, allow for action and the expression of altered perceptions (for example, Celia, chapter 7).

The school ethos emphasizes that students are concrete human beings with particular, unique characteristics. But there is also a growing concern for viewing them in their social locations as members of sex and class and an attempt to discuss practices to bring students together and give them a sense of collectivity in their academic, cognitive learning, as well as social and emotional learning. Interest in group learning has increased. But the in-creased pressures caused by cuts, Conservative policies of parental choice and examination publication, along with moves towards centralization and stan-dardization of education, and a renewed momentum of local criticism tend to stifle changes in the school or make the teachers more hesitant and cautious in what is considered feasible.

In this situation the privileging of the concern of sexism appears dif-ficult, as such a fundamental aspect of the school cannot be tackled without prioritization, which is considered only by feminist teachers.

Notes

1 An overview is found in BEECHEY (1979).
2 For example GARDINER (1977) analyzes the dual relationship of women to the class structure through their role in the sphere of production.
3 HARTMANN (1979) p. 11.
4 Another approach considering the coexistence of capitalist and patriarchal relations and the dual articulation of these in subordinating women is found in BLAND *et al.* (1978). Women's relationship to capital as wage-labourers is complemented by their role in the family which is shaped by patriarchal relations. The contribution of the state in women's subordination is also considered.
5 The significance of a theoretical feminist analysis of the state is evident — state practices assume a gender-specific form. Rather than just describing or noting this, it is constructive to develop ways of analytically exploring the foundation of such practices.
6 HOBSON (1978) p. 87.

7 BRUNSDON (1978) p. 23.
8 A more detailed discussion of women's exclusion from 'man's culture' can be found in SMITH (1978).
9 McROBBIE (1978) p. 6.
10 LEGGATT (1979) p. 159.
11 In the year 1980/81 58 per cent of the scale 1 teachers and 40 per cent of the scale 2 teachers were women. Of women teachers 39 per cent were on scale 1 and 33 per cent were on scale 2. These figures were made available to me by a teacher.
12 An analysis conducted within the school, in 1979, found a high correlation between teachers' pay and their work experience.
13 A female chair of the Standing Committee argued that men found it difficult to relate to her seriously, and found the situation odd and amusing.
14 The male domination was evident from detailed minutes kept during the course of the research of various meetings, such as moots, Standing Committee, National Union of Teachers, sub-committees etc. A considerable proportion of the contributions of women were from a deputy, who as a member of the executive occupies a specific position in the professional hierarchy, which intersects her position as a woman.
15 C.f. MACCIOCCHI, M-A (1979), 'Female sexuality in Fascist ideology', *Feminist Review*, 1.
16 This term has been initiated within the school.
17 This expression is used by McROBBIE (1978).
18 The hardening up of boys is referred to elsewhere as well; for example CLARRICOATES (1978).
19 When sexism in the school was debated by the staff, it was noted that attempts had been made to appoint women to teach three-dimensional design; however, there were no suitable applications. The response by some women teachers was to encourage the men themselves to tackle their own sexism.
20 I overheard this informal conversation during participant observation.
21 That is, missing lessons, truanting, doing little work, formulating groups joining together in these activities; using the vulnerabilities of teachers, revealed in personal interaction.
22 These girls (including PAT, SANDRA and LESLEY, discussed in chapter 10) were considered difficult and 'hopped' lessons — but so had a number of boys participating in the action.
23 A female teacher expressed this in the following way:

> girls do focus very much in the intimate social structure and school based conversation doesn't actually do anything to divert them, though it may talk about the subject of sexism. But the very activity of talking about your feelings is actually repeating the process which marks off boys and girls. You know, I don't do anything about it at all.

24 Information on career aspirations was gained from questionnaires, interviews and discussions. Information on career choices was available for the majority of students in the team, from students or from tutors.
25 Thus for example some teachers do separate introductory sessions for boys and girls, others do not.
26 Conscious thought has been given to the kind of science teaching that girls might respond to. It must be noted that this concern is part of a general discussion and consideration of problems in science teaching, and its ability to attract a larger number of students, and a concern to improve examination results. The music teacher in the school has given thought to what girls want out of music, and how their expectations could be met.
27 In a discussion with a tutor.

Chapter 12

Vertical Teams

I shall return to the question of restructuring in the context of recent developments at Greenfield College. In this chapter a process relating to an earlier research period is discussed, indicating the contradictory existence of possibilities and limitations for radical teaching and learning within progressivism after the considerable tightening up of the centralization and standardization process and the public expenditure cuts in recent years. The students operated the democratic structures of Greenfield to overturn a decision made by the teachers to introduce vertical teams.[1] The themes of this research can be illustrated by considering this process; it provides a case study of the politics of school organization, and illuminates tensions in progressivism and professionalism, and the ambivalence in spaces; the limitations in utilizing them, and the shifts from personalization to atomization mediated through professionalism, undercutting the existence of different strands of progressivism within the school.

The sequence of main events was as follows. In 1974 a resolution was passed in a moot that 'vertical teams are the next step to take in the development of the team idea'. These teams were not introduced because of the practical problems that their implementations was seen to entail. In autumn 1979, in the context of staffing difficulties[2] the Staffing Committee raised the possibility of 'going vertical'. After a week-end conference, several Staffing Committee meetings, informal discussions, team meetings etc., the Staffing Committee met in the spring of 1980 to decide whether one fourth and fifth year team would be given a go-ahead to form two vertical teams, as the staff of these teams requested. The voting was inconclusive, and a moot was called, where the teachers who attended decided that the two teams could 'go vertical'. Two weeks later students called a moot (about eighty of them attended) and this decision was reversed, with the majority of students voting against vertical teams, and teachers voting for them.

I shall discuss the implications of this process, and issues thrown open by it. The lines drawn cut across the ethos, practices and structures of Greenfield. It is possible to analyze several features of the school:

223

(i)   the contradictions and difficulties entailed in the notion of student participation;

(ii)   the tensions in teachers acting as professionals, on the one hand formulating a long term view of the needs of the school as an institution, and, on the other hand, being preoccupied with their own work situation;

(iii) the problems of taking into account the needs and interests of particular students, and the interests of students in general, as abstract entitites;

(iv)   the expectations raised by the ethos of the school in the students, and their willingness and ability to act on the basis of these expectations in specific situations;

(v)   the existence of spaces contained within the democratic structures and processes of the school; and

(vi)   tension between differentiation of teachers as thinking persons with particular frameworks of educational and political perspectives crystallizing into different strands, and the unity of the teachers as professionals 'doing a job'.

The thread of exploration is provided by the consideration of the following paradox: the teachers made a radical decision but their action and organization were conservative; the students made a conservative decision, but their action and organization were radical.

The Process and the Paradox

The significance of oppositional spaces within progressivism rests on the convergence of different strands within it, with radical teachers being prepared to search for and utilize spaces. During a period of restructuring such action has potentially increased significance, for example, in opposing public expenditure cuts. The vertical teams are argued to have provided a possible dynamic within the school resisting the qualitative effects of cuts. The positions and actions of teachers and students are then considered, noting the structural positions of each. The teachers resort to professionalism in an attempt to side-step the contradictory problems posed by student participation in these issues: this leads to a situation whereby polarization occurs between teachers and students, and students are locked into institutional positions emphasizing their differences from the teachers, and assuming a sectional profile. The students respond in a way channelled by teacher professionalism, drawing on the ethos of the school and its democratic structures to defend their own interests.

In the teachers' debate the advantages of vertical teams were stated: the mixing of the age groups would facilitate the adoption of new fourth year students; older students could guide and help the work of the younger students thus also group work would be facilitated; catering for non-examination students would be easier;[3] yet early orientation towards examinations by the fourth years would be possible at an earlier stage; the age divisions in schools were unrealistic and not beneficial outside the school; the rather conventional unexciting sixth-form could be reorganized and benefits of team work extended to this age group; new thinking about curriculum and resources would be facilitated by the continuity in teams, instead of the present two-year cycles; the introduction of vertical teams would provide a dynamic for a school struggling against outside pressures; and attempting to maintain its progressive ethos and practices in a rather hostile educational environment.

The disadvantages were seen to be numerous: timetabling would be less flexible; the development of science in teams would be jeopardized; the induction of new teachers would become increasingly difficult; the variety of skills demanded from a teacher would be considerable; examinations would become a constant concern, with students preparing for examinations in each team each year, whereas in the two year cycle of horizontal teams the fourth years are given scope to develop work not solely orientated towards instrumental ends; the energy required by the organization would be more than the teachers were able to expend in a situation of considerable pressures and difficulties; students, parents, governors etc. would not be enthusiastic about the change; introduction of vertical teams would divert people away from developing their teaching skills, and encouraging a range of activities within the team.

The context of restructuring, and the specificity of progressive schools within it is important. In Part One I discussed the analysis of Sharp and Green, which emphasizes the conservative character of progressivism, as an effective mode of social control in an advanced capitalist society. I also noted the existence of, for example Black Paperite criticism, expressed predominantly in terms of standards, but also in explicit references to facilitation of Marxist political activities within progressive schools. I suggested that whilst during a period of expanding economy, and an expanding education system, the development of progressivism in schools was possible, such a development was halted and reversed when an economic crisis precipitated a period of restructuring affecting social relations in the society as a whole. The disjunctures that had opened up and/or expanded between the state form and state apparatus became increasingly volatile, containing oppositional spaces potentially assuming increased significance in rendering restructuring more difficult during a period marked by fragility of the capital-labour relation.

A consideration of progressivism clarified the above analysis; it was seen to contain different strands. The liberal strand was indeed seen to facilitate a new mode of control through humanization and informalization of school practices based on an avoidance of conflict. The libertarian stand was seen to have potential affinities with the socialist strand, combining child-centred practices with a critical perspective on society, and an analysis of the expected functions schools were to fulfil, co-existing with a preparedness to take militant trade union action. Thus there were in existence within the schools groups of teachers, and a small number of students (for example within the NUSS), willing to explore the existence of oppositional spaces within schools, and moreover, prepared to utilize them within the framwork of restructuring. The *potential* significance of this group was more crucial than its actual quantitative and qualitative impact.

Restructuring of education began in the early seventies and preceded the 'Great Debate'; the trend towards centralization and standardization was already in motion (chapter 2). The major avenue through which restructuring has proceeded has been provided by the public expenditure cuts. The impact of the cuts has been qualitative as well as quantitative (chapter 2); such impact reaches progressive schools particularly quickly, because of their dependence on favourable pupil-teacher ratios, resources, flexibility provided by teacher autonomy and control, curriculum-based staffing etc.

Reorganization in Greenfield has occurred in order to accommodate the quantitative impact of reduced resources. The halting or reversal of innovative development in the school is demoralizing to teachers committed to educational change. Vertical teams implied a change involving major organizational and curricular rethinking, and, it is speculated here, could have therefore provided a dynamic around which active, school-based initiatives could have been organized, reviewing the range and nature of work, and relationships, the role of examinations etc. That the introduction of vertical teams might have served as a focal point does not lead to a suggestion that the impact of the cuts could be avoided by school-based action, but assumes significance nevertheless when compared to the alternative of defensive reaction in the context of standardization and centralization of formal education.

I shall now illustrate the paradox of a contradictory mixture of radicalism and conservatism referred to above. Overall, the role of the students in the democratic processes, and their response to the introduction of vertical teams were not often raised by the teachers. During a weekend conference in spring 1980 the question was touched in the following way:

Bill: It's important not to break friendship groups.
Alex: What do the kids think.
Bill: We haven't really thought about that. If you ask kids to have a hole in the wall, you won't get a hole in the wall.[4]
Alex: Yes it's difficult to organize kids. Their initial response is like the one about the hole in the wall.
Phil: Kids don't like any reorganization.
Jonathan: You need to be careful. If Gregg Spencer[5] gets his teeth into something that staff are doing without students ... (general laughter and jokes): the discussion then shifted to another aspect.[6]

In a staffing meeting it was noted that students would cause a problem. Julie stressed that students who would need to move from their teams in the initial changeover were not likely to want to go vertical; a decision ought to be made whether students would be imposed upon in order to avoid a 'hole-in-the-wall' incident. The discussion was not pursued. In a later staffing meeting Sharon initiated a brief discussion:

Sharon: It's not only a question of staff, but also of students. If you think of the hole-in-the-wall you can see that resistance to breaking of teams will be there. The present fourth years expect to stay in the same place for two years. Better to tell in the beginning of next year's fourth year that there will be change. Personally I would like to go ahead. But we got to be aware of what students think.

Julie: We should have no illusions about the fact that it has to be pushed hard, and no illusions about democratic decisions. It could be done on the strength of it being good for the school.

Graeme: Is this the best deal for kids next year in the face of cuts? Various possibilities are open to us. We sometimes look at things from our point of view rather than from the kids' point of view.[7]

These questions were raised in informal discussions, and not pursued partly for tactical reasons — supporters of vertical teams considered the persuasion of other teachers as a priority. The question of student participation was thus not addressed, and problems posed by their potential response were pushed aside. There was an implicit assumption that students do not approve of change and innovation, and would be unlikely to support a major reorganization if they were involved in the decision-making process.

But when vertical teams were initially discussed in the school, students were in fact keen participants. A girl wrote a paper 'Vertical teams for vertical people', arguing that

We don't live in a horizontal world — except when we are at school. It seems ridiculous that school students should be classed into separate groups and labelled fourth, fifth, sixth and whatever ... To stick to the horizontal teams ... would be to stay in the unprogressive rut.

More recently in one fifth year team (the students of which would leave before the reorganization) vertical teams were discussed without teachers trying to secure their support for any particular position. There was no uniform negative response. The student opinions were connected to their educational and political thinking as well as their personal preferences. No clear demarcation lines between teachers and students emerged; the students were aware of differences in teacher approaches to the issue. However, in the process taking place during the interval between the moot deciding to introduce vertical teams and the moot overturning the decision, such battle lines were relatively clearly drawn. I shall explore these, concentrating first on teachers and then on students.

The Teachers

A group of teachers wanted to 'go vertical' for educational and social advantages perceived, as noted above. There were practical reasons too. Vertical teams appeared an attractive solution to problems relating to the working situation of several teachers,[8] and to the internal power balance between fourth and fifth year teams. Mixing staff would provide a new stimulation, and would tackle the demarcation between teams, and equalize them in terms of staffing, resources and physical space. The problems were exacerbated by the cuts and the increased roll; a new team had to be created despite the deteriorated staff/student ratio, and it was difficult to ensure a sufficient mix of skills and aptitudes in each team.

When debating whether the two teams should be allowed to organize vertically others were supportive for several reasons: they agreed with vertical teams in principle, saw them as a solution to practical problems, or did not wish to hinder a group of teachers wanting reorganization. Those opposed raised mainly practical considerations which led them to focus on the disadvantage of vertical teams. The efficiency and the ability of those involved to organize a smooth transition was questioned: 'all the people who were open-minded were also simultaneously organizational nitwits ... they plunge into things without ever seeing ifs and buts'. Particularly the pragmatist teachers were guided by such concerns. The two teams wishing to reorganize vertically contained a considerable proportion of teachers with a relatively strong radical profile, either libertarian or socialist, and/or militant trade unionist.

Practical considerations were in the forefront during the debate, and no clear patterns in terms of educational and political thinking of the teachers emerged. But when the teachers were forced to make a decision in the final moot, a demarcation line emerged. Some blurring of divisions occurred as a few libertarian teachers adopted a position opposing the introduction of vertical teams, along with the liberals and pragmatists. However, in general, the libertarian and socialist teachers voted for going vertical. The radical teachers were thus either supportive in principle, or reluctant to veto the wishes of others. The liberal and pragmatist teachers remained doubtful about the value of vertical teams, about the overall resources of the school and its teachers (during a period of cuts and an increased roll) to support the change, and about the efficiency of the teams in carrying out the experiment.

The question of student response was relatively uniformly related to by the staff — the issue was not often raised, was not pursued, and no decisions were made. The teachers were unable openly to acknowledge their intention not to involve the students, and, also, to discuss how the decision would be imposed upon them. Duncan explains later:

> there was a kind of implicit assumption on the part of a lot of the staff that team[9] would presumably have sorted out some sort of understanding with the kids. I think that was the way it was left.

Wishful thinking was involved — it was assumed that the teaching body would not need to make a decision about the student participation, and the problem could be solved on a small scale by one team. This is indicative of fragmentation in the school, and a tendency towards team-based action, which poses limitations when there is an attempt by the school as a whole to achieve a policy and to implement it.

The teacher-ambiguities related to their difficult position in trying to take into account various contradictory features of their situation, all not clearly visible. It was not easy to formulate a coherent position on the basis of the structural location of the teachers, the school ethos, and the political and educational framework (progressive, ranging from the centre to the left). The structural location of teachers requires them to control and evaluate students; they have to be considered as atomized units without noting their personal, concrete characteristics, in terms of their institutional role as a student, and their capacity to fulfil external criteria related to examinations. The school ethos with its child-centred perspective implies that students are related to in a personalized way, but their particularities taken into consideration. Negotiation and individual potential and motivation, are emphasized. The radical teachers, in the context of their political framework, perceive students as a collective totality divorced from actual single students or groups of students and their action was perceived in terms of external criteria rather than the particularity of the situation of these Greenfield students. The liberal and libertarian teachers aim to overcome institutional constraints, but have no framework within which to theorize and understand student concern with institutional aspects. The pragmatist teachers are most able to address such questions, but find it difficult to introduce their concerns to other members of staff without being labelled as 'plodders' devoid of inspiration and enthusiasm.

In relating to students teachers shift from personal to positional interaction (chapters 7 and 9). In both situations the students remain 'individuals', though differently constituted in teacher practices. The students as a collective appear as unreal to the teachers in general, in two different ways. First, they do not consider students in their totality, but in practice decisions relating to the management of the school involve implicit assumptions about the student body as objects of policies. Second, if the teachers do think of students in collective terms, the collective is ideal, not made up of the actual students in the school with their characteristics, expectations, class position, cultural milieux, and experience shaped by these.

These ambiguities were not brought into the open. The teachers adopted a professional stance when dealing with students, though the implications of imposition it contained were contradictory to their ethos and thinking, because of the element of uncertainty among the teachers, and the student response. The teachers related to the students as an atomized mass, rather than as a collective consisting of 'thinking individuals' able to see beyond the constraints of their life situation. The students were thus likely to respond in terms of their sectional interests in the institution as students; such interests were likely to be diametrically opposed to the institutional interests of teachers. Had the students been able to perceive teachers as a collective consisting of thinking individuals, able to see and act beyond the constraints of *their* life situation, it would have been possible for the students to respond likewise. But, met by teacher-professionals, reluctant to impose upon the students, and uncertain about the legitimacy of doing so, the students reflected this in their own organization by drawing the battlelines. Faced with the challenge to their position in the moot called by the students the teachers adopted a united approach, arguing for the introduction of vertical teams. The course of events, particularly immediately after the moot, was commonly explained by teachers referring to student 'selfishness' and 'conservatism'.

Thus the teachers were unable to carry out the professional strategy of imposition they had adopted despite their ideology. The students gradually became aware of teacher decisions through rumours and speculation. They confronted individual teachers and discussed the issue with them. Teachers reacted to student pressure and requests for information, and were following from behind, not leading the way. When a protest feel was emerging among students, the teachers were unable to respond systematically. Initially teacher reactions were either helpful or hindering, depending on the strength of their support for student democracy.[10]

In the final moot teachers adopted a united line. The sides had been drawn. Necessities imposed by the public expenditure cuts were appealed to, rather than educational arguments. Sarah notes that the staff 'presented a united front with the kids, and also were prepared to use arguments which I thought were quite dishonest really'. The teacher position in the moot was based on false premises in terms of the arguments used, and in terms of the fact that as thinking individuals they were not all favourable to vertical teams. But in the moot they acted as professionals defending their rights and institutional position in the school, and trying to persuade and manipulate the students to accept this position, rather than imposing it upon them. The teachers did not diverge from their position as teachers, and their conduct was conservative in that it contributed to the maintenance of a divided reality, not cutting across it.

The teachers lacked resolution to come to terms with the contradictory elements in their position. They had located a space within the school; it seemed possible to adopt a reorganization which would have entailed a dynamic and active response to the qualitative restructuring affecting the school through the quantitative medium of the cuts. But their lack of resolution either to carry their decision in a professional manner, or to involve the students in the early stages in a participatory process led to an outcome whereby the identified space could not be utilized.

Teacher frustration with the student action subsided, and later they considered the difficulties of student involvement. The uncertainties of teachers posed problems: 'we were very unsure of our own views anyway and we didn't feel we wanted to involve the students at that stage'. The perceptions of students reluctant to accept innovation were repeated: 'the weakness of any kind of student involvement so far has been an unwilling-ness among the students to look really much beyond their own position'. But not all teachers agreed: 'I had very mixed feelings about the student decision ... although they argued superbly — it was an extremely well-informed discussion'. Some teachers emphasized the need to involve students more closely in democracy; their 'selfishness' is an attitude which 'we won't change unless we actually get them to participate more'. But the contradictions in student participation were noted by some socialist and pragmatist teachers. The former point to the cooption involved in the democratic processes, and do not view student participation as positive — autonomous action would be more appropriate. The latter are worried about contradictions and ambi-guities, and are prepared to address these issues, and to adjust the school ethos accordingly. Teachers are able to take a long-term view, and if they feel that something is educationally important, it is a serious problem, argues Shane, if 'students really motivated by self-interest ... can overthrow it'. Teachers' positions are differentiated in complex ways, and particular indi-viduals can shift from views contained within one strand to another, or unexpected overlaps occur when the issue cuts through the interstices of political, educational and practical considerations.

We can now return to the paradox. The teachers made a radical decision which they attempted to implement in a conservative way. Throughout the discussions teachers had shifted their position, and considered arguments for and against vertical teams, and in first votes many abstained. Therefore in the early stages no clear dividing lines were visible among the teachers. How-ever, in the final moot their positions were crystallized, and socialist and the majority of libertarian teachers voted for vertical teams, whilst the pragmatist and liberal teachers tended to vote against them. The socialists and liberta-rians did not necessarily approve of the new organization, but did not wish to deny other teachers the scope of carrying out changes they were dedicated to. The radicalism of socialists and libertarians gained prominence over the caution emphasized by liberals and pragmatists.

But when the implementation of the vertical team decision was dis-cussed, the differences between teachers in terms of their political and educa-tional framework were, if not insignificant, at least invisible. Professionalism united them as a device addressing the ambiguities of student participation. The teachers could not, however, adopt a professional stance openly, and pursue its implications systematically, because of the democratic school ethos. Therefore the strategy of professionalism failed in the face of student resistance. I shall argue below that it was the very professionalism of teachers, clearly communicating itself as a strategy, if not openly expressed in rhetoric, which sparked the students to organize against the introduction of vertical teams.

The Students

The students identified and utilized a space as well — but not in a teacher-defined manner. Their action was radical, but the decision arrived at was conservative. Their role in this process was contradictory and complex, like that of the teachers. The students took cues from, and responded to teacher positions both in a thinking way, as actors with particular political and educational frameworks, and in a way reflecting their structural and 'sectional' position as students within an institution. It was difficult for students to see the issues clearly beyond their own point of view, when the teachers adopted a professional façade in their dealings with students, and their debates and differentiation remained hidden on the whole.

The structural position of students as students is significant. Their class position must be considered, along with the cultural milieux and expectations developed, and their understanding of the labour market and the role of certification within it. Greenfield is an area marked with a high proportion of skilled working class inhabitants with a relatively comfortable material situation. There is also a large proportion of self-employed people, and of those who have experienced social mobility through education, or more commonly through work (chapter 5). Education is seen as an important avenue providing the children with the same position as parents, and it is seen to offer the possibility of adding status to the material position already achieved by the parents. Thus schools are seen to play a vital role. Lenhardt (1978) emphasizes the significance of working class demands in precipitating educational reforms. Mason (1970) refers to the demand for education in the Leicestershire region. Because of these expectations many students have an instrumental attitude towards schools, which are seen to fulfil a particular role through the process of certification. This does not imply simple acceptance of dominant ideology as such — rather it is better explained through the notion of 'fetishism', because the 'surface' reality has, up to now, indeed confirmed student/parent attitudes, as social mobility has been available for large numbers in this relatively affluent area, where recession has taken a long time to penetrate; thus upward social mobility has been an experience close at hand for many students.

Alongside the belief in social mobility is an awareness of structured inequalities, a sense of 'loaded dice'. There is a sense of a need to struggle, to be ambitious; a realization that working class students with high expectations may not float through the schooling system with ease equal to that of middle class students, who are on familiar terrain. Whilst Greenfield College as a progressive school may not be easy to understand for middle-class parents with formal educational background either, through the individualization of the school they are nevertheless able to encourage their child to construct a purposeful career directed towards examinations. Middle-class parents may be too 'pushy', and the teachers frequently comment that the pressures placed on students at home are detrimental to their progress in school, academically as well as socially and emotionally, but middle-class parents can provide help for their children when location in the labour market is considered.

The working class student and parent perceptions of competitiveness co-exist with the acceptance of individualistic solutions to the sense of powerlessness, dissatisfaction and alienation integral to the structural position of the working class in a capitalist mode of production (for example Kevin, chapter 10). This sense of competitiveness in students makes their career construction in the schools difficult, if they lacked the flair which made their instrumental attitude less evident (chapter 10). Students assessed able and capable of achievement, but not instrumentally orientated, also experienced problems. Whilst they may have conducted their negotiations with dignity in the school, they left without the external criteria of success provided by certification (chapter 10 — for example Brian).

The examinations system reinforces the instrumentalism of students. In Greenfield it provides a further problem; it is a mode through which personalization is transformed into atomization. Teachers attempt to relate to each as a concrete individual, with specific characteristics. However, the students take the examinations as units; preparation involves relating the students' achievement and assessed ability to the external criteria provided by examinations. Personalization, and the 'thinking individual' recede to the background by the time each unit is faced with examinations. But the elements of personalization and atomization, both as facets of individualization, have become entangled, and their differential impacts are not easily evident in the day-to-day reality of the school for those participating.

The confusion that can be caused by the transformation that students undergo during their school career is reflected in the comments of Annette, a fifth year girl who was a central figure in the move to overturn the decision to introduce vertical teams. When asked what she thinks about the argument that the students were motivated by self-interest, Annette replies intensely:

> I don't know how they can say we were only thinking of ourselves. You got to don't you to get on in the world. You can't think in the long run all the time, because who's to say you're gonna last that long.

A sense of powerlessness, of a need to struggle, of possible curtailment of ambitions, a confusion of what one is, and what is demanded of one, transforms individualization and imposes a definite timescale. Working class students feel that they have to take their chances now. There is no safety net, no back-up service — things left now cannot easily be taken up in later life. Resistance as a response has been explored;[11] instrumentalism is also crucial.

The student action was concentrated particularly in the team where students would be split and joined by incoming fourth years (to provide two vertical teams). These students were not officially told about the decision to introduce vertical teams, as Annette explains:

> Well I first heard from another person in our pod[12] ... She says have
> you heard that this is going on ... I started asking round, and then
> Charles faced us with it ... he went round it in a sneaky way. He
> said what would you think to us having vertical teams, and we asked
> what they were, and they explained ... A lot of us said no, and he
> was asking why not and we were saying our reasons for not wanting
> it. And then he turns round and says well ... that's what we're
> going to try next term.

Speculation was rife in this situation; but why did it crystallize into organized
action?

Student knowledge of the democratic processes is on the whole limited
(chapter 7). However, it was argued that they have nevertheless 'soaked up'
and internalized the democratic milieu to some extent. The students had
experienced several incidents where they had been involved.[13] Those who
had attended moots may have been confused by the organizational procedures, but nevertheless they had experienced the school rhetoric in action.
Annette explains that 'a lot of it was to do with the fact that we could say
something about it, and I felt enough people wanted to say it, but were afraid
to say it'. The students had developed expectations of involvement. Their
immediate response, therefore, was to feel indignant that something concerning them directly had been decided without discussion or consultation.
Furthermore, there was a sense that students *could* do something. Moreover,
the determination and efficiency of those leading the student organization
must be taken into account. They were prepared to devote a great deal of
their time and energy to acquaint themselves with the procedures they had to
master in order to achieve their objectives. They were also girls, and in
chapter 11 it was noted that ambitious girls were particularly imbued by a
sense of struggle and determination.

Having sensed the scope for action, why did students act? First, student
instrumentalism was significant; the provision of certification was considered
as a major function of schools, and students striving towards qualifications
which they perceived as facilitating entry to specific locations in the labour
market did not want changed circumstances when preparing for examinations in their final year. Such a concern is an integral effect of the structural
and cultural position of many of the students; explanations noting student
'selfishness' interpret this instrumentalism in a narrow way without drawing
attention to the struggle the students experience when attempting to realize
their ambitions.

Second, the student reaction resulted from an internalization of the
school ethos of personalization emphasizing the significance of each individual with a particular set of concrete characteristics. Interaction is based on
personal relationships and negotiations. The introduction of vertical teams,
which would involve the splitting up of these students and their tutors into
two groups militated against the patterns of interactions that had been estab-

lished and the personal importance of each student. The students do not only work with their own tutors — many of them have close working relationships with other tutors as well. Thus, whilst they would remain with their own tutor, they may lose important relationships developed with others. The introduction of vertical teams would disrupt patterns of negotiations, and the construction of the student careers. This militated against the ethos where each student matters as an individual, and can determine the direction of his/her learning within the flexible, but steady, secure framework of the team. Now the framework was going to change, and the students objected.

The reasons the students gave for their action were as follows:

(i)   they had not been told about the decisions, nor had they been involved in making them;

(ii)   the changeover was designed to convenience teachers rather than students;

(iii) the effect of the changeover on the students had not been thought out;

(iv) the students had developed a good base in the team, which they did not want to lose;

(v)   the upheaval would disrupt their concentration on preparation for examinations;

(vi) students from one feeder high school had experienced vertical teams, and their impressions were not favourable.

Teachers gave prominence to practical considerations in their advocacy of vertical teams, both in their own debates, and in the debate with the students in the moot. Educational reasons were given low priority. Institutional needs argued in a professional way were privileged over the importance of any particular students. The latter responded by asserting their own importance, and drawing on the school ethos in doing so. Thus battlelines were drawn, and polarization occurred, students faced teachers as students, interpreting their own interests in a sectional way, in opposition to the teachers. The existence of a small group of alienated students antagonistic to the school reinforced the crystallization of two sides in conflict.

When students began to organize, teachers responded in different ways. Some teachers offered information on the democratic structures, and advice on utilizing them, but others were reluctant to help, or gave undue emphasis to procedural aspects, thereby complicating the task of the students. For example Annette recounts:

(A teacher) stopped me as I was going down to the coffee bar, and started to ask me reasons and in the end I just turned round and said look I tell you when the moot comes and not until then. And he says well the proper way of going about it is to give the reasons — a list of your reasons of why you think you shouldn't have vertical teams.

> So we wrote them down and printed them out for the teachers, as
> they had done for us, but we didn't get them till the moot.

But the students were also given time off lessons to organize their campaign,
and they received guidance from teachers who even if keen to introduce
vertical teams, considered student democracy important.

The debate in the moot concentrated on practical issues put forward by
teachers, and the student objections. All but a handful of students attending
voted against the introduction of vertical teams. Those involved in the
organization of the campaign were pleased with the outcome, and some
students grasped the opportunity to express anti-school sentiments, confirming by their behaviour the sense of the existence of battlelines. The latter
group consisted mainly of boys, whereas girls had adopted an organizational
approach, and carried through the campaign.

The teachers accepted the student decision; some felt bitter or worried
about the power students could wield; others, in the end, welcomed the fact
that students had organized; some raised doubts about the validity of the
'sectional' vote, but there was no serious suggestion of calling the outcome of
the moot into question. Teacher frustration was initially focussed on students, but shifted (generally) to an exasperation with the particular teachers
involved,[14] or to consideration of problems engendered when formal democracy involves students. An interesting feature of the aftermath was the
worry expressed by some teachers about the effect of the campaign on its
central figures; for example Sharon:

> Annette led the battle and she did it very well, and I suppose she
> could have gained quite a lot from that, but I think it made her feel
> very insecure in lots of ways as well. She had actually done it, she
> had actually got herself in that position.[15]

When I talked to Annette, I sensed her satisfaction on having accomplished
something that she and others had felt strongly about. She seemed exhila-
rated by the sense of scope and the ability of students to grasp it: 'before the
moot I'd never realized we had such a say in what happened in the school . . .
we just stepped forward and did it'.

Student organization remained on a one-issue basis. They did attempt to
follow the process particularly as teachers suggested to them, somewhat
bitterly, that they could come to a meeting to tackle problems that the
introduction of vertical teams would have alleviated, and to search for
alternative organizational solutions. Annette recounts:

> You just couldn't think of anything to say, because it was all sort of
> the money situation and everything, and we didn't know anything
> about that. We'd been sort of pushed into going to that, because a
> teacher turned round and says I wonder how many of them will help
> to sort out this mess now that they've won the vote. So we went just
> to show that we weren't doing it for our own good, but we couldn't

say anything, because there were teachers getting all hysterical over things, and teachers were arguing. It was really strange to see them arguing like they were. And in the end there wasn't a conclusion made, and nothing else was said about it.

Immediate issue-based organization is possible for students within the framework of Greenfield College, but their involvement in the democratic processes on a systematic basis is not easy as the processes are not constructed with an attempt to integrate them (chapter 5).

Annette refers to the confusing impact of observing disagreements among teachers who had presented a united approach on vertical teams. An early involvement in debates about vertical teams, exposing students to the issues, and different ways of interpreting them might well have diffused polarization on the basis of institutional positions of teachers and students. Both for the teachers and students their educational framework would have assumed an increasing significance, and support or opposition for an organizational and curricular change should have been found on both sides. Evidence for this possibility is gained from discussions on vertical teams where teachers have not presented a professional stance; I referred to these above (p. 227).

Conclusion

Attempts to utilize spaces within schools are fraught with contradictions, as is indicated by the events in Greenfield. The teachers and students reached an impasse, where the radical features subsided, and conservatism and stifling of innovation with dynamic possibilities assumed predominance. I have argued that whilst the teachers had made a radical decision, they attempted to implement it in a conservative way. They relied on professionalism to solve the problems of ambivalence posed by student democracy, when a resolute tackling of the issues raised by student participation was not considered possible. Thus student democracy continues, with its important legitimating function; it facilitates the ensuring of student consent, whilst at the same time providing a pinnacle on which teacher ambivalences about their thinking and practices are focussed.

The process indicates the way in which personalization becomes transformed into atomization through the mode of professionalism, which enables teachers to place institutional needs of the school and long-term considerations affecting teachers in the context of cuts above the needs of particular concrete students presently in the school. At the same time it is evident that the teachers, because of their educational and political framework, and the school ethos within which they operate, do not find imposition of professional solutions on students easy. Thus whilst professionalism provides solutions, it also creates further problems in school where the majority of students expect that their opinions matter and they matter, and where the democratic atmosphere with all its limitations predisposes them in specific situations to demand that such significance be accorded to them. Such demands, moreover, can be successful, as was the case in connection with vertical teams. Unless pragmatism gains further prevalence in Greenfield, the teachers will not be able to abandon their commitment to student democracy, albeit that they can see the limitations and contradictions contained within it. The events described here frustrated the teachers, and reminded them of the difficulties posed when students do get involved within a framework of detachment from the running of the school on a one-issue basis. In such a situation it is not easy for the students to weigh up the issues without being motivated by self-interest — the actions and decisions of teachers are influenced by considerations of their own position, albeit that they can be persuaded to place these alongside wider interests in the school, brought to them by often intense and lengthy debates.

At the same time the events confirmed to the teachers the significance of student democracy as a reality rather than a mere façade. In practice the students *were* able to overturn a crucial decision, against the advice and opinion of teachers as a whole. For many teachers this confirmed a belief in the importance of student democracy despite its limitations. For Sarah it was 'like a slap in the face which we deserved, because we hadn't involved the students in a proper way, not just over that issue, but over the whole running of the school'. In a progressive school with formal democracy student democracy would be difficult to abandon because of its legitimating role for radical teachers, enabling them to contain ambivalences and contradictions in their practices and thinking when working within a state institution during a period of restructuring. But student participation would be unlikely as a prioritized issue.

In a meeting of radical Greenfield teachers the issues raised by this analysis of the vertical team saga were discussed; the teachers talked about their contradictory position, and Steven noted that they had been aware of these problems for years. But an arrival at a resolution was not imminent. Student democracy was not firmly on the agenda again, but not insignificant either. For example in 1984 students called a moot with a large turn-out which voted tht pupil-teacher ratio should not be more than twenty five — 'a typical Greenfield pie in the sky', cried pragmatists. And indeed the 'world outside' was further encroaching upon the college and spaces were further eroded. Within the school certainly the executive thought that the democratic structures had become 'soft machinery unable to reach hard decisions'.

Notes

1 The team structure in the school is horizontal; each team caters for one age group only. Vertical teams would combine fourth and fifth year students, and, possibly sixth-form students as well.

2 Two current fifth year teams were faced with the problem of splitting into three teams, because of the increased roll. The problems were exacerbated externally by the deteriorated staff-student ratio, and, internally, by an uneven balance of power between fourth and fifth year teams.

3 A situation where in the fifth year the majority of students prepared for GCEs or CSEs would be avoided.

4 Chapter 5 page 74.

5 This student had actively used the democratic processes of the school in order to put forward a number of proposals.

6 From minutes kept by me.

7 From minutes kept by me.

8 A number of teachers had worked together for a long time and felt that they no longer stimulated each other.

9 The fourth year team where students would need to split into two vertical teams in their fifth year, with the incoming fourth years.

10 Thus for example a team teacher who had campaigned for vertical teams helped students to organize, because he was in favour of student democracy. Students were allowed to do their organizational work in lesson time. Hindering consisted, for example, of emphasizing formal democratic procedures — p. 235.

11 For example WILLIS (1977), CORRIGAN (1979), HALL and JEFFERSON (Eds) (1977).

12 This refers to a team area.

13 For example the moot on the mini-bus, discussed in chapter 5.

14 DUNEAN explained: 'we'd been led a song and dance by the staff involved in the vertical team thing ... In the end there was a feeling that the teachers had pissed the school around a bit really by their kind of woolly idealism, which they hadn't thought through'.

15 I showed the transcript of this interview to Sharon after she had left Greenfield College — she was surprised that she had assumed that Annette would have been adversely affected. But at the same time other teachers had expressed similar sentiments.

Chapter 13

The Challenge of the Eighties

The bulk of the preceding chapters has been based on work carried out in the late 1970s and early 1980s. The present situation is described separately, because I wanted to indicate a sense of change. The Greenfield of 1978 was set within an unfavourable climate; there were problems, contradictions, frustrations as well as routine and day-to-day boredom. But there was also a sense of excitement, of liveliness, of engagement with issues, of criticism and self-criticism, debates, action and innovation. The Greenfield of 1985 has, however, become much more demoralized; teachers are dismayed at the internal and external situation. There are resolute and differentiated views on how the College should conduct itself — but the balance of power has changed and radical teachers are 'defending their corners' whilst the executive (supported by the LEA and the governors) are trying to impose new management structures. Democracy has been suspended and the pressure is on; teachers find it difficult to act rather than react. It seems that 'the bells have rung' and 'the playtime is over' as David feared (chapter 6, p. 90).

The internal events in the school are occurring in the context of restructuring which has posed difficulties particularly for progressive schools, which need favourable teacher-student ratios etc. The effects of the cuts were discussed, and the difficulties posed by the Conservative legislation introducing publication of examination results and parental choice of schools have been noted (chapter 5). Standardization and centralization processes within formal education and the increase in training have been referred to (chapter 2). An interesting example is the decision by Greenfield College to participate in the Manpower Services Commission's (MSC) Technical and Vocational Education Initiative (TVEI). The staff debated the issue in 1983. Those interested in the scheme, particularly male teachers of technical subjects, and the Principal, argued for educational advantages of participation; it would provide inspiration for curriculum development and would enable broader learning experiences to be made available to students. But many teachers were interested in participation for pragmatic reasons; TVEI meant more resources and staff which would benefit the whole school. Misgivings about TVEI were expressed; teachers did not want MSC control and impositions because of its bureaucratic nature not in line with the democratic structures and processes in Greenfield. Feminist teachers criticized the male bias of TVEI; resources would be directed to boys, and new staff employed would be male.[1]

The effects of TVEI have not been systematically monitored, but for our purposes significant observations can be made. Though there were considerable misgivings about the scheme about two-thirds of teachers favoured participation, but for many this support was pragmatic. Hence there has not been enthusiasm for implementing TVEI across the College; for example, profiling encouraged by the MSC could not be carried out. But, more importantly, the staff as a whole did not become involved in TVEI through the democratic structures to the frustration of teachers working for TVEI. For them this provided particular reasons for dissatisfaction with the democratic structures; decisions could not be reached and/or implemented. Hence there is support for the executive argument that Greenfield democracy was a 'soft' machinery unable to make 'hard' decisions. Thus staff committed to democracy were prepared to support proposals to reform it, provided that these were going to remain democratic in theory and in practice. The TVEI also focussed recurring disputes about allowances when new staff was appointed without regard to the allowance policy.

The Leicestershire involvement with the MSC is connected to the development of cluster structures, whereby several educational institutions are grouped together to form a cluster, which has to make joint bids for resources in competition with other clusters. Hence the importance of making quick decisions increased, and the democratic structures of Greenfield began to seem to many as something of a dinosaur doomed to extinction in a school seeking to meet the 'challenge of the 1980s' in a positive way.

Many teachers argue that early misgivings about TVEI were ill-founded; Greenfield has been able to implement it in a flexible way, and if more staff were involved, the benefits of the scheme could be spread wider in the school. Nevertheless, I have indicated above that participation in TVEI can be perceived as having opened up yet new inroads for external pressures, and in subtle ways restructuring has been mediated to schools. Staff involved have not been unaware of this; Des notes that teacher unenthusiasm in implementing TVEI has led him closer to the executive, and Colin refers to his radicalism which is compromised by his pragmatic philosophy. TVEI requires swift decisions, and the internal organization of Greenfield did not seem responsive to its needs. The TVEI debate also seemed to crystallize increasingly evident divisions among teachers.

The internal events in Greenfield before and after the suspension of democracy, the 'impasse', have been occurring in the context of restructuring and resistance to it; teachers have been involved in prolonged national trade union action in relation to their pay and conditions of service which has been connected to a debate about standards of provision in schools and criticism of government policies on education. Throughout the focus on Greenfield

College difficulties and contradictions have been evident. In chapter 5 the build-up of the 'impasse' was discussed (p. 80). There was a series of incidents throughout the eighties which increased tensions, crystallized teacher differentiation (chapter 6) and were manifested in personal rows and clashes. But important features can be extricated. First, the executive, now in the Liberal Leicestershire tradition (chapter 5, p. 80 and note 52) and supported by the LEA and the governors, has not been supportive of democratic structures. Their misgivings have been manifested for example in several disputes over allowances. Second, union action has posed difficulties and interfered with democratic structures;[2] Third, participation in MSC controlled TVEI presented new demands. Fourth, the increasing significance of radical-ism in teachers' orientations on the one hand, and pragmatism on the other hand led to further differentiation and conflicts. Fifth, as the school expanded many new teachers joined the staff prepared to accept the executive's right to make decisions.

By autumn 1985 the dispute has not been resolved; the national union action makes negotiations difficult. Many teachers have refused to cooperate in attempts to implement the proposed changes in the management of the school, but the persistence of the LEA and the governors is such that teachers concede that because of these pressures there are going to be changes. There is no framework of support for critical teachers who struggle against further erosion of spaces. A socialist teacher remarked that 'this school is less distinctive now, but it is still distinctive'.[3] The question of 'survival' and its meaning (p. 72) is firmly on the agenda. The teachers have been reminded that 'the LEA determines the general educational character of the school'.[4] Only in the context of a management system endorsed by them could 'irregularities' be accepted.[5] Current challenges could not be met by 'the informal and voluntary infra-structure of the College committees (departing) for the high mountains of resistance'.[6] It was time for people to agree to 'shed what they presume is their power'.[7] The Principal reminded the teachers of a County Council minute stating that their role could only be consultative; a deputy director told the teachers that a changed management system was required; the Principal noted that an inspection by HMI might be the alternative. The Principal insisted that the teachers must not be able to opt out of management decisions during trade union action.

An incident which acted as one of triggers leading to the suspension of democracy illustrates present problems. In the context of humanities work, striking miners were invited to come and talk to students and teachers who wished to attend.[8] Tensions and communication problems were manifested; the Principal decided to ban the meeting on the day it was to take place; the miners had already arrived. An emergency union meeting was called; it decided that the miners' meeting should go ahead. These events led to an LEA enquiry culminating in a formal verbal warning directed at two teachers, and increased pressure to strengthen management structures in the College.

A humanities teacher (who was one of those receiving a warning) explained in his statement how he perceived the context of the miners' visit by explaining the general approach to humanities:

> The humanities staff at Greenfield have always placed major emphasis on using appropriate resources, media, visits and speakers ... There has been a long history in the college of visiting speakers offering a variety of social perspectives, and often speaking on controversial subjects ... The teenagers with whom we work raise the controversial issues themselves. The staff do not shy away from these issues, pretending we did not hear, but aim to deal with them sensitively and responsibly. We hope to develop genuine understanding and critical appreciation of the issues on the part of the students.

More specifically on the particular context for the visit he wrote:

> there were a variety of initiatives around the themes of work, employment, unemployment and trade unionism. These included visits to the major autumn conferences — TUC, Liberal and Labour (the Conservative conference does not accept student groups); visit to Jaguar Cars, Coventry; visit to T.I. Raleigh, Nottingham ... there has been a recent visit to the College by an official from the NCB.

The enquiry considered statements by teachers, and many gave evidence. The NUT formally objected to the warnings received by two teachers:

> The LEA failed to show any due cause why these two teachers should have been singled out from the larger group of staff involved in the humanities forum.[9]

The teachers who received warnings were a socialist and a libertarian, both militant trade unionists and critics of new developments in the College.

The introduction of new management structures was made difficult because of opposition to those structures, and because of trade union action making meetings about implementing proposals difficult. But teachers have not been united in their opposition. Differentiations were noted in chapter 6. Pragmatists and liberals tended to be sympathetic to changes and libertarians and socialists to oppose them; feminist teachers opposed them. Crystallization into pragmatism and radicalism has been considerable, but at the same time the relatively powerless situation of teachers (in the face of external pressures with direct mediations to the school) has led to a range of opinions and difficulties in achieving unity. Thus, for example, Duncan was sympathetic to many of the executive criticisms, whilst Janet did not accept them. Duncan was prepared to consider new structures, but was opposed to the executive approach; Janet did not deny problems in the school, but wanted to tackle them by developing the democratic structures that had existed. Both Duncan and Janet were radicals, but Duncan was increasingly persuaded by aspects of pragmatism. Des, a liberal pragmatist, was critical of militant teachers who had, he thought, contributed to increased pressures through their actions (for example in connection with the miners' meeting). Des perceived the new structures as democratic still, though even supporters of changes such as Colin expressed worries about how the structures would be perceived and developed by the executive. Lisa, a feminist, argued that the new structures would be male-dominated.

The Principal felt that changes were necessary in order for the school to survive and to thrive in the eighties in the midst of restructuring, diminished resources and competition as exemplified in the cluster structures (p. 241). The College had to be able to make 'hard' decisions quickly; thus 'tight control at the centre and clear definitions of roles and responsibilities'[10] were required. But, the Principal noted, his aim was 'to make a virtue' of constraints. In the midst of centralization 'new wave' comprehensives are coming into being, note the deputics. The new Greenfield is considered progressive as is evident in a description of these schools: they 'value relationships; negotiation of the curriculum; more appropriate and personal methods of recording achievements; extensive involvement with the local community whose confidence it will need to have in order to survive'.[11] The Principal has referred to conservatism of Greenfield ethos and structures — in contrast the executive plans are, he believes, innovative.

But the critics of the executive plans also refer to progressivism — they reiterate the links between learning and organization in Greenfield. It is noted that power 'imposed from the outside ... is of little use in a school built around the notion of negotiation',[12] These teachers are convinced that the democratic structures can still work, and several proposals were put forward. But some were converted; Gavin explained that his changed position on democracy was due to 'a creeping frustration and a reluctant and remorseless growing disbelief in our decision-making and implementing ability'.[13] Differences among teachers led to a situation which Duncan bemoaned; 'people will snipe at each other and the ship will go down while they are doing that'.[14]

The new proposals (chapter 5) required all teams and areas to have coordinators.[15] Teachers worry that coordinators will be like heads of departments, and thus hierarchical rather than democratic structures will develop. These worries were expressed even by supporters of changes. What coordination will mean in practice will no doubt be a focus of struggles when the system is implemented. Some teachers resisting changes are looking for new jobs, some bow in front of perceived inevitability, and yet others are subject to individual pressures, as was the case in the incident of the miners' meeting above — any mistakes made by opponents are utilized to press upon them that they should cooperate or leave. The executive believe in progressive education and open debate, but external pressures are such that in practice conformity is sought for and management is emphasized. What coordination might mean in practice can be glimpsed from the Principal talking about a conference workshop which was 'run, organized, coordinated'[16] by a deputy; if coordinators 'run' teams, they may not be different from heads of departments.

There are still debates, discussions and 'sniping'; disagreement, distrust and the continued NUT action render the achievement of a working compromise difficult. Though the impasse continues, it is clear that there will be changes. Confidence of the Education Department and governors could only be achieved in the context of 'clear descriptions of authority and role'; 'it was time', the Principal demanded, for teachers 'to agree'.[17] But there are those who feel that in Greenfield many positive gains are being lost — that several teachers asked me to name the College is symptomatic. After these developments, I would like to return to the general concerns that informed the way in which I have focussed on progressive education.

Conclusion

The left critics have argued that progressivism in the state sector in the 1960s and 1970s is compatible with liberal Conservatism. The study of Leicestershire supports this argument (chapter 4). The right critics of progressivism have, however, noted (and exaggerated) the existence of 'oppositional spaces' within it. The divergence of Greenfield from the local liberal tradition indicates that there have been spaces. The left and right critiques signified that progressivism is best understood as a contradictory constellation consisting of different strands with differing implications for educational and political practice in schools (chapter 3); the debates and tensions in Greenfield convey this (for example chapter 6). Progressive education has been seen to contain possibilities for radical teaching and learning, but these possibilities are limited by the contradictions within progressivism and by the context of formal schooling as a state apparatus and therefore as a microcosm of the struggles and contradictions embedded in the state (chapter 1).

The limitations find expression through the child-centred ethos and practices of progressivism. The personalized content in the school is penetrated by individualization-atomization (chapter 8) as a capitalist and patriarchal (chapter 11) form; modes such as professionalism, certification and compulsory school attendance act as mediations (chapter 9). The question of possibilities and limitations for radical learning assumes particular specificity during restructuring, when any resistance assumes significance because of the greater vulnerability of a society undergoing rapid social change (chapter 2). Thus during restructuring oppositional spaces and the willingness (if not ability) by the left to utilize them within schools, are seen as a source of potential instability for the state and patterns of social relationships. There is less scope for islands of tolerable deviance as increasing pressures on Greenfield indicate.

Reasons for official promotion of progressivism in the 1960s were discussed (chapter 2). There was a drive to recruit male graduates into teaching, and therefore teaching was represented as a profession with high status, remuneration and scope for decision-making — all these were consistent with the liberal progressive rhetoric and practices. But because all progressive practices rely on teacher autonomy, generous resources and a favourable teacher-student ratio, progressivism as a whole becomes inappropriate during restructuring when the aims of centralization and standardization are largely realized through cuts and initiatives such as APU and MSC. Liberal progressivism itself, though contributing to the status quo during a period of expansion, poses problems during restructuring. Its emphasis on informality, choice, diversity of learning etc. is inappropriate when trends in society and in the labour market are towards greater authoritarianism and control (for example initiatives in trade union legislation). In Greenfield we have seen an increased emphasis on 'balance' between teams and 'uniformity' of experiences of students, and the importance of examination results as a criterion of success.

The existence of early comprehensive reorganization and widely renowned progressivism in a Conservative LEA was discussed. The paradox was addressed through a consideration of stable and relative prosperity of Leicestershire, where lack of sudden social changes and political extremism made liberal conservatism possible. Within that framework the relatively autonomous development of education was also possible, directed by officers and directors espousing liberal ideology combined with efficiency and pragmatism. The strand of progressivism prevalent, and encouraged, has been that of liberal progressivism, with its child-centred, apolitical ethos, and a conception of a changing society within which traditional schooling is considered inappropriate.

Attention then turned to Greenfield College, and a further paradox was explored: how was the development of a school widely considered radical, possible within the context of liberalism? The appointment of headteachers whose educational rhetoric was not significantly different from that prevalent in Leicestershire was considered. However, in a new school, with new buildings and new staff, such rhetoric became a guide for practice to a degree hitherto not experienced, particularly the participatory democracy which is unusual in the state sector. The radical and libertarian strands assumed greater significance in the school than in similar community colleges. Thus the implications of the degree of autonomy granted to the schools were visible. However, the limitations could be observed as well, in the crisis of the school, culminating in an early inspection, and then periodically resurfacing, if the school was publicly identified with controversial action and practices. The school, then, contained oppositional spaces, which were, however, delimited, and largely remained a potential rather than a reality. Their identification, however, and the differential relationship to them by teachers of different persuasions, posed a number of contradictions in the school in decision-making about further innovation and trade union action for example. Such contradictions have heightened as the process of restructuring has assumed increasing impact on the school.

This research, and its conception, has in many ways been a political project, though through its historical and theoretical formulations, and the case study undertaken, it is hoped that its relevance and validity exists outside that project. The project involved has been to ask questions important for those practising within education, (these questions have evolved through various experiences within education both as a consumer and as a practitioner). Such questions centre on the scope for socialists, feminists, libertarians, liberals, humanitarians, and all who are interested in education as a transformative activity, and who have embarked on their involvement in teaching and learning through a desire to work towards such a transformation, whatever its goals. The questions have attempted to pose the theoretically and practically sterile problem of schools as determined or determining in a new way, which can conceive of the possibilities for radical practices, and emphasizes the significance of grasping such possibilities whilst noting the limitations which engulf them. The questions have, also, directed attention towards charting some of the efforts that have been occurring within education during the sixties and seventies. But the longitudinal aspect has also resulted in a record of restructuring and the erosion of spaces which led to the crisis of democracy in Greenfield, and to an impasse. In considering the directions of the 'new wave' comprehensives amidst the educational squeeze of the eighties the earlier efforts of those practising within education are looked at in order to note their importance. Many problems and contradictions of progressive education have been referred to; it is not difficult to make connections between the problems caused by these and the rise of Conservative populism. 'The progressives, reformers and idealists ... have taken to whispering'. In this contect it is hoped to be refreshing to look at a school where the nature of 'realism' has been a source of dispute, and a school which has tried to be about education as well as schooling — schooling may be about realism — but is *education*?

Notes

1 Indeed girls have not been getting much out of the TVEI, but because there is an equal opportunities requirement contained within it, there are increasing attempts to spread the benefits of staff and resources to girls.
2 The connections between union and democracy have been discussed in chapter 5 p. 62.
3 From field notes.
4 An open letter by the Deputy Director of Education to the staff of Greenfield College.

5 An internal paper by the Principal 19 April, 1985.

6 An internal paper by the Principal 29 January 1985.

7 *Ibid.*

8 The school bulletin contained this announcement:

> 'Miners in the school Wednesday afternoon: if you have any students researching issues of trade unionism, unemployment, law and order, current political issues etc., there will be a forum on Wednesday afternoon when they can discuss with, question and challenge local miners who will be in College. An opportunity for students to go beyond newspaper reports.'

9 In a letter addressed to the LEA 25 Feburary 1985.

10 An internal paper by the principal 19 February 1985.

11 Development Plan 1984/5.

12 An internal paper, N.D.

13 An internal paper, 4 Feburary 1985.

14 Field notes on a conversation 16 Feburary 1985.

15 How these would be chosen was quite complicated, partly because of the guidelines posed by the equal opportunities code of the LEA. This code was referred to when discussing whether coordinators should be chosen or appointed; it was interpreted to limit the staff freedom for choosing candidates. Criticisms of the effective operation of the code can be found in *Times Educational Supplement* 10 May 1985, p. 12.

16 In an interview.

17 An internal paper.

Methodological Appendix

An underlying question of this research has addressed the relationship between theoretical and empirical work. The thesis set out to consider the usefulness of general theories in terms of their practical application. Thus the articulations between macro- and micro-levels have been explored; the importance of empirical work as well as general theoretical considerations is emphasized. This approach has guided the structuring of the thesis. Part One and Part Two offer separate, if linked, starting points, which are brought together in Parts Three and Four, where concepts bridging Parts One and Two are developed and applied. Thus Parts One and Two are largely horizontally organized, whereas Parts Three and Four introduce concepts which vertically progress through each part of the thesis. The theoretical framework has thrown light on the empirical data; at the same time the fieldwork has illustrated the theory, and led to a development of its applicability.

By discussing the conduct of the case study the methods and procedures, problems and underlying themes are considered. Bottomley[1] notes that social existence is disordered, ambiguous and messy, and adds that this applies to the researchers as well as the researched; attempts to make sense of this world lead to 'sanitized' methods which simplify, order and generalize. I have been concerned to avoid such sanitization, and have tried to account for the complexities in a particular social formation, whilst finding ingress into it through broad theoretical concepts; the multifarious nature of that formation has been explored through a process of *saturation*. Saturation refers to a 'state of mind' of the researcher, *and* a particular formulation of research techniques. Grace uses the term 'theoretical saturation', and defines it in the following way; it refers

> to researcher's attempt to 'take on' the theory and the world-view of another through detailed knowledge of their discourse.[2]

Grace's usage of the term is somewhat different from that of Glaser and Strauss,[3] elaborated in their discussion of 'grounded theories' derived from empirical data. In this study the concept of saturation does not address the question of the grounded nature of the theory, but refers to a particular interplay between theory and data, whereby a process of mutual illustration occurs, and a sanitized ordering of social reality is avoided.

'Saturation' refers to a state of mind as well as techniques. Therefore I shall separately discuss aspects of my approach, and methods used to translate that approach into a procedure in the field. The concept of individualization has been accorded great importance in this research. This concept is linked to the methodological problem of the distinction between natural and social individuals. Where one deals with human beings as concrete individuals in fieldwork, both the necessity and the possibility of considering their existence within social relations is argued. The social relations constitute the forms within which concrete individuals operate as social individuals. However, we are left with a problem. Molina (chapter 8, p. 145) notes the need to search for forms of existence, and not simply the patterns and content of it. But he does not address himself to the existence of concrete individuals as human actors in any satisfactory way. When one talks about a capitalist, one is referring to a social relation; to a function that s/he is accomplishing:

> The fact that his individuality is affected by this is a different problem.[4]

This problem, according to Molina, is not properly considered in a Marxist analysis: social relations are impressed upon people.

> The effects of this impression on individuality as such (individuals as individuals) implies a *production* of specific individuality by these effects: ... In other words, it concerns the problem of that 'individualization in the midst of society' signalled by Marx, and also concerns the problem of 'personal relations flow out of relations of production and exchange'. but this problematic is not Marx's own.[5]

Whilst Molina considers this problem as 'different' and 'not Marx's own', and he is critical of attempts to solve it within humanist theories or through an amalgamation of psychoanalysis and Marxism, he briefly considers how to construct an adequate approach. This resides within an Althusserian framework, employing the concept of ideology, the precise function of which is seen to be to constitute concrete individuals and subjects. In this formulation social relations are reproduced, not produced, and concrete individuals are seen as 'bearers' of these as well as of ideological relations. This formulation remains static, and ahistorical, and thus does not consider the forging and re-forging of social relations through class struggle. Molina does not introduce sufficient dynamism by adding that

> The ideological class struggle is a fight for an effectivity at the level of individuality.[6]

Seve (1978), whose humanitarian theory Molina criticizes, and whose discussion on the human essence indeed poses a number of problems, nevertheless discusses issues which are pertinent to the problem of considering concrete individuals in empirical work, whilst at the same time focussing on social relations. Seve construes individuals as 'temporal topologies'; 'temporarily organized processes' rather than as 'an architechture'. Thus there is no need to aim at an analysis of 'the singular concrete in general', but the focus is on how the singular concrete is produced. Seve points to the possibilities of a dynamic analysis considering concrete individuals in their social relations. Such possibility, in this research, is important, as it allows for the consideration of student careers without constructing theories of personality, but searching for the process of negotiation within the specific and general locations of those individuals.

In the fieldwork, then, we have the problem of considering individuals within social relations and structures they inhabit, whilst at the same time having to concentrate on concrete human actors, with their own biographies as thinking individuals. By drawing heavily on the constructions of individuals, one in a sense ends up looking at the subjectivities of human actors, and privileging them as offering explanations in themselves. The solutions are sought on three levels: first, through saturation and vertical and horizontal disentangling of general trends and tensions caused by contradictions between forms, modes and content; second, following Gerstenberger the search is for constituents of consciousness, not the end-result; and third, noting insights developed by combining feminist, Marxist and psychoanalytic approaches in order to understand individual subjectivity, that is, the shared constituents of subjectivities of individuals.

Thus the participants in the concrete social formation studied are considered actors, and subjects, that is 'thinking' individuals. These actors, during the course of the research, have provided information *and* interpretation; the research has been a collaborative exercise to the extent that their observations have not simply provided data, but have helped to order that data.

The method of participant observation, combined with interviewing, study of documentation and a questionnaire was adopted. Such participant observation was necessarily very intense and longitudinal, in order to allow for the process of saturation and the interplay between the theoretical framework and empirical data. Sharp and Green (1975) note that many crucial insights emerge after leaving the field and crystallize in a negotiation with the theoretical perspective. Because of the importance of saturation, in this research it was necessary that such negotiation would occur in the context of continued contact with the field. The possibility of this is discussed in connection with procedures.

I secured entry into Greenfield College in autumn 1978, having talked to a number of teachers about my research, and having offered to contribute to the teaching of social studies. I was attached to one team, working with seven teachers and 150 students through their fourth and fifth years. During the first year I visited the school once a week/once a fortnight, two days at a time, on fixed days. I was employed as a social studies teacher (part-time) in an ILEA comprehensive school at the time. During the second year I timed my visits according to events in the school, and thus the lengths of my stay varied, the intervals were not of equal length and days of visit were not fixed. Between September 1980 and June 1981 my visits were less frequent, but informal observational contact with students who had stayed on to the sixth-form was kept, and interviews conducted. Between September 1981 and June 1982 a few visits took place, involving observation and informal contacts, and meetings with members of staff and some students, discussing the analysis I was developing. After the autumn term 1982 I did not visit the school till 1985, but maintained contact through meeting teachers, telephoning them, sending papers for teachers to read and comment on, and through written materials from the school. In 1985 I visited the school again (twice) and gathered further documentation and interviewed teachers; this material is presented as updating rather than as part of a continuous narrative, in order to illuminate the process of restructuring.

As well as participant observation in one team (whereby I got to know all the 150 students to varying degrees) sustained contact was maintained with a large proportion of the students. I attended meetings,[7] was engaged in various activities with students and staff,[8] and had informal meetings and discussions with a range of people,[9] visited other team areas and specialist subject areas, collected documents and materials,[10] was in contact with the local education authority, administered questionnaires to students in the team, and conducted semi-structured interviews with thirty-one students, with follow-up interviews a year later, and interviews with all the team teachers concentrating on the students in the team, and interviews with 22 teachers across the school. All the interviews were recorded and transcribed, and transcripts were returned to the interviewees, except the follow-up interviews with students.

A few words about my role in the team are appropriate. The students were told that though I was not employed in Greenfield as a teacher, I was a qualified teacher, and working as such in London, and that I was concerned to help them with their social studies work, as well as discuss other aspects. Thus a great deal of contact with the students was in the context of their work, but because of the informal, individualized setting, and the broad concerns of social studies, it was possible to discuss and pursue a number of issues raised by the students or by me. The students accepted me as a teacher, and, during the first year in particular, expected my presence at certain times, as if I were a part-time teacher — if the interval between my visits was a fortnight rather than a week, I received several queries: 'where were you then?' During this year the teacher aspect of my role was more pronounced, and afforded me a perspective at close hand on realities of teaching in Greenfield, and made participation in daily teacher conversations possible. One student, Ralph, during this year, when talking to me and a teaching practice student, told him 'you can't tell me what to do, you're just a student — she can.' Though my role in control was only very slight, and engaged in only when it seemed evident that help was needed, and though Ralph in particular had on occasions ignored my plea not to disrupt another group of students, his comment was nevertheless significant. However, the ambivalence in my role must not be underplayed, and was mediated to the students with increasing clarity after I had made contacts with them, and was known and accepted as a legitimate prober and interrupter of their activities. The ambivalence was, however, important, so that I would not be too closely identified with the teachers. Thus a gradual reduction in the teacher role occurred throughout the second year, when the interviews were conducted. Philippa noted in the interview:

> I look on you as — I don't know — a person. I think I've seen you as a teacher in a way that I can turn round and ask you a question about something and you'd know it, that sort of way (laughter). But I can speak to you freely. I'm — depending on the subject I'd probably watch what I was saying a bit more 'cause you're an adult, not because you are a teacher, because you're older. I think that's about all. I just treat you as an adult (laughter).

Andrew's comments explicate some of the ambivalence, and the way in which it was overcome through extended contact — he focusses on one aspect that I am not a native of this country:

> when you first came here and said your name was Tupu it sounded really weird you know; after a bit it's just another name isn't it . . . me mum and dad were going . . . there's some strange woman ringing you up . . . oh it's Tupu, and it seems normal to me, but they were sort of — who's this then, that's a funny name, you know. I said 'no it's not, what's wrong with it' you know. They thought it was strange, but I'm used to it.

The conduct of the research was characterized by informality. This partly expressed the informality at Greenfield College. The administration of questionnaires to all students in the team during the fifth year indicates the difficulties encountered in any other type of work. The number of returned questionnaires was eighty-four — 60 per cent. The figure is relatively low. Each student had to be contacted individually in order to hand out and collect the questionnaire — it was not possible to get groups of students to complete the collectively. Thus, whilst only two students refused to answer the questionnaire, a number lost them or forgot them, having taken them home.

The fragmentation of the school also posed problems in the conduct of the research. The existence of informal networks and channels of communication meant that intensive and longitudinal participation was necessary in order to become familiar with such networks and channels. As a teacher commented 'this place exists in people's heads' — this indicates the need to participate in a great deal of discussion with teachers across the school, as well as participation in meetings and affairs of one team. The flexibility of the structures and organization in the school meant that following up of decisions and initiatives required a great deal of work in contacting various members of the school —

thus the method of 'triangulation' (Elliott and Adelman, 1975) was automatically built into the research methods.

The practical problems that led to the informality of the research exist alongside an approach which questions the usefulness of 'sanitized' methods, as discussed above. An extensive use of quantitative methods was considered inappropriate for the concerns about oppositional spaces, possibilities and limitations for radical teaching and learning, and questions about contradictions and tensions within progressivism crystallized into differing strands within it. Thus I have inclined towards 'interpretive' sociology, and away from positivism, defined by Giddens (1974) as

> depending upon the assertion that the concepts and methods employed in natural sciences can be applied to form a 'science of man', or a 'natural science of society'.[11]

However, a distinction exists between the approach adopted here, and that within an interactionist perspective, such as Ball (1981) and Woods (1979), in that the case study conducted here is more firmly located in a macro-context. The distinction can be conceptualized through the term 'saturation', and procedurally described through the possibility of interplay between theoretical and empirical parts of the study.

A few chronological comments are appropriate here. The first year of the research was spent in formulating the theoretical framework explored in Part One. The second year of the research was spent in the field, and as I was simultaneously employed as a teacher in London, little new theoretical development took place during this year. I was, during this year, immersed in the field, and whilst foci were provided by categories such as spaces, restructuring, cuts, strands of progressivism, etc., at the same time I attempted to be as non-selective as possible when collecting materials and recording observations. A field diary was kept throughout the research which gave detailed descriptions of students, their work, teachers, conversations heard and conversations conducted, minutes of meetings etc., even though all the detail did not seem to signify any particular point. Through this diary I attempted to absorb preoccupations of the field, and the hundreds of pages of it figure very little in the finished product of this book, but served as a background in attempting to 'understand' the social reality of the particular social formation as interpreted by actor-participants. The interviews were conducted during the second and third years of the field work; they were semi-structured, and relied considerably on the knowledge developed during the course of participant observation. The choice of interviewees also depended on this background information — this involved theoretical sampling according to the criteria which afforded a mixture of pupils in terms of class, sex, range of attainment in school, of career aspirations, of political and educational thinking and of identities within the school (as assumed by the students themselves, and as perceived by the teachers). The teachers were chosen to form a mixture of teams, subjects, sex, number of years taught in the school, educational thinking as perceived by the researcher in the course of participant observation, and related political thinking, as observed particularly in the various meetings, and a range of positions within the school, from Principal to probationer.

During these two years further theoretical work was also undertaken, and the analysis of the chapters contained in Part One was developed. This made the interplay between the theoretical and empirical concerns possible, and the development of concepts to bridge the two sets of concerns, discussed in Part Three and applied in Part Four, develped during a period when they could be 'tested' in the field by confronting the participants with them, and by focussing observations through them, thus experimenting with their explanatory capacity. Particularly the discussion of vertical teams in chapter 12 exemplifies this process.

The research has been characterized by longitudinal contact, varying in its intensity. Thus virtual participation shifted towards a greater degree of observation, and application of developed concepts; from considerable involvement to greater detachment. Both phases have been crucial for the way in which this book is conceived, theoretically and methodologically, allowing for the emphasis on the significance of general theories, as well as the privileging of fieldwork; they have also been crucial in the way in which I, as a researcher, have been able to open myself up to the social realities of the participants as thinking subjects, as well as detaching myself from them on the basis of my pre-existing theoretical and practical interests and concerns. The research was considered collaborative in many ways, but divisions of labour between the researcher and teachers nevertheless remained, though they were reduced.

There was an attempt to avoid a construction of clear hierarchies (Bartholomew, 1974) and what Oakley (1981) calls 'masculine paradigms', and the emphasis was on alternatives constructed on the basis of equality, shared experiences and 'giving voice'. Hence the problem of 'going native' was posed. During the first year of the fieldwork, with its immersion in the field, participation was intense, but the aim was to increase the observational content subsequently. Moreover, during that year the employment in London acted as a stepping stone in repeatedly rendering the practices and organization of Greenfield College 'strange'. The research diary was a further distancing device. Awareness of problems was maintained, and the longitudinal nature of the study afforded the possibility of increased detachment, whilst maintaining insights gained through immersion.

A few comments are appropriate about the choice of case study, participant observation and an ethnographic presentation of data in the descriptive Part Two. All these present problems to work outside the interactionist perspective (for example, Pearson and Twohig, 1977; Butters, 1977). Such choices were dictated by a number of reasons. The elusiveness of progressivism, and the contradictions it entailed, rendered the case study an appropriate method through which to conduct an in-depth investigation to illuminate such concerns. A case study also enabled the longitudinal perspective, necessary because it allowed the consideration of effects of restructuring, and because it allowed for the specific interplay between theory and fieldwork, which helped to overcome problems of participant observation in providing insights into the object of study beyond the micro-level. The methods and mode of presentation were also influenced by the evident uniqueness of Greenfield College, affording us an opportunity to observe a particular instance in formal schooling, both in its discontinuities and continuities. The uniqueness assumed further significance because of the context of the local education authority, the educational policies and practices which are of interest in their specificity. Not many studies have been conducted of schools, and particularly of progressive schools, in the sociology of education. Thus ethnographic presentation was considered valuable in adding to the information we have of different kinds of schooling. Willis explains his choice of such presentation:

> In particular, the ethnographic account, without always knowing how, can allow a degree of the activity, creativity and human agency within the object of study to come through into the analysis and the reader's experience.[12]

Part Two, then, is lengthy for two reasons. First, there was an intention to portray the uniqueness of Greenfield College, as well as patterns within it — thus not all the data presented in that part is mobilized in the analysis in Part Three and Four. Second, such presentation stems from an attempt to have two separate starting points so far as is possible, by emphasizing the importance of the theoretical framework whilst also privileging empirical data. The concept of saturation indicates that the study of the school had to be made more internally complex than the theoretical discussion in Part One initially signposted.

How was the analysis of the data conducted? No clear-cut procedures were followed; the specificity of the approach arose theoretically from the wish to combine macro- and micro-levels, where the theories would focus the data, but where the data also illuminated the theory, and enabled the construction of 'intermediate concepts' to bridge the gap between the general concepts and empirical observations. The longitudinal conduct of the case study facilitated the interplay between analysis and fieldwork. With each new hunch the data collected could be reviewed, but also new observations could be made, and participants in the field could be confronted in the search for their interpretations. Such a process is difficult to explicate through neat formulae and outlines of procedure. I shall therefore try to illustrate how the analysis was conducted with one particular example, which, appropriately, concerns individualization, a central theme of the thesis.

In Part One I discussed the implications of formal schooling as a state apparatus. This guides our attention to examinations, mediating external influences to schools enjoying a relative degree of autonomy. The concept of restructuring gives a dynamic dimension to such concerns — we can note the increased importance of examinations in a concern for standards and accountability, expressed in trends towards centralization and standardization.

Discussion of examinations at the school level includes consideration of teacher assessment — what is the teacher's orientation towards examinations in the case of individual students in a school with child-centred ethos and practice?

Meritocratic student comments emphasize importance of examination success, link it to individual efforts and motivation, and conceptualize certification as a gateway to the labour market.

The concern for social differentiation vis-à-vis structured inequalities was dictated by the general theoretical approach. Student comments indicated an existence of a surface structure of choice, whereby students were seen to choose their future directions through their attitudes and efforts at school. This was linked to an awareness of a deep structure of limitations, which became evident in interviews through deeper probing.

The theoretical framework led me to consider individualization as an effect of the labour process and state practices.

Organization of teaching and learning in Greenfield drew my attention to individualization as a descriptive category in the school.

Discussion of assessment focussed on the importance of professionalism. Comments about students vis-à-vis examination standards indicated that now we were not considering concrete, whole persons, but units with specific performance and attainment vis-à-vis external criteria.

Individualization was developed into a form, and a distinction between atomization and personalization was made to account for the differences observed in teacher discourses. Professionalism was developed into a mode, which mediated atomization to bear an imprint on the content of the school, according to its ethos and teacher thinking based on personalization. The effectivity of mediations could be considered vis-à-vis content — student observations on examinations and individual effort, combining liberal, libertarian and conservative notions of individualism, reinforcing the general conservative ethos of the local area, and stripping the framework within which students could conceptualize and express their sense of social differentiation and 'loaded dice'.

At the same time, observations of shifts in teacher-student interaction, frequently evident, could be understood by referring to personalization of the school ethos, and the atomization embedded in the form of individualization mediated through professionalism.

The increased occurrence of such shifts in situation where the participants, particularly the teachers, experienced the pressures of time, could be related to the qualitative effects of the public expenditure cuts, mediating restructuring to the level of school content.

In this way chains of analysis took place, linking empirical observations to general theories through development of concepts, and vertical scanning from macro- to micro-level and back again. During the course of such interplay observations such as that of shifts in teacher-student interaction, recorded without a consistent explanation of its significance, could later be linked to the chain of mediations, providing a concrete observable index of a process linking general theory, analytical tools and empirical data, noting the mediation of forms through modes to content, allowing us to build bridges between macro- and micro-levels.

The second example concerns the identification of strands of progressivism. Within the school a distinction between political and educational radicals has been made.[13] The former are those prepared to take industrial action and to adopt stances of solidarity rather than isolationism, with a preparedness to be militant. The latter are concerned for child-centred teaching and autonomous self-direction of students within non-authoritarian relationships, aim to abandon teachers' preconceived notions of curriculum and learning, and tend to oppose industrial action not discussed in moots. Such a distinction does not imply poles of moderation and radicalism, but criss-crossing strands related to various issues. Such an ordering of reality was powerful for me as a researcher as well; it seemed that a progressive school contains institutional realities and ethos which cut across any classification and analysis in terms of strands (chapter 3) as distinct frameworks used to analyze and explain schooling as informing practices.

However, through observation in meetings over a period of four years it was possible to begin to build a picture of divisions in terms of people involved and arguments put forward, crystallized in voting patterns. These pictures were reinforced through informal discussions, interviews and participation in practices. This was not a straightforward process for several reasons. The thinking and practices of teachers in experimental, innovative schools are necessarily contradictory, as they find themselves in a complicated position with conflicting demands and dilemmas without final solutions, as has been demonstrated for example in the discussion on examinations.

Moreover, the assumption of a unitary subject characterized by cohesion in his/her thinking and behaviour is, generally, argued not to be tenable. This is developed further in chapter 8 on individualization, which pursues themes introduced in chapter 1, arguing that lives of people are structured in fragmented ways which make the totalities of social structures relatively invisible. Thus the teachers' educational and political thinking may shift and change, depending on whether they see themselves as educationalists, trade unionists, teachers, parents, political activists etc. in specific situations.[14] Further, teachers may consider an issue on the basis of its impact on them and their location within the school; thus a team and a subject teacher with similar political perspectives can disagree on a matter of internal organization because of their differential relation to it.

Another difficulty in the disentangling of strands within the school relates to the libertarian strand — the libertarian teachers align themselves with the radicals for example in connection with trade union action, but also align themselves with the liberals, for example in connection with curriculum issues. Moreover, within the school exists a group of teachers whom I was unable to identify with any strand — I am describing them as 'pragmatists', referring to their tendency to begin a discussion on issues by saying 'well as I am a pragmatist really ...'.

I have tried to indicate the close connections between the theoretical approach, methods of study and mode of presentation of this thesis. These have been guided by underlying epistemological assumptions about relationships between theory and empirical data, emphasizing the interplay between them in constructing a picture of social reality of a given formation; ideological assumptions about relationships between the researcher and the researched, linked, however, to a theoretical and methodological unwillingness to engage in 'sanitized' accounting; by personal concerns created through participation in formal education as a pupil, a student, a teacher and a researcher; by a political interest in exploring the relationship between schooling and education; and by an academic concern for the small number of studies in sociology of education developing a mode of analysis connecting macro- and micro-level, and by deepening understanding of progressive education in the context of restructuring. Meeting such multifarious concerns is a tall order; I hope I have achieved some success in my attempt to do so.

Notes

1 BOTTOMLEY, B. (1978) 'Words, deeds and postgraduate research' in BELL and ENCEL (1978).
2 GRACE (1978) p. 240, note.
3 GLASER, B. and STRAUSS, A. (1969) *The Discovery of Grounded Theory*, London, Weidenfeld and Nicolson.
4 MOLINA (1978) p. 238.
5 *Ibid.* p. 238.
6 *Ibid.* p. 256.
7 Such as moots, standing committees and its sub-committees, (one of which, the Staffing Committee, was followed closely for one year), resources meetings, team meetings, NUT meetings, miscellaneous staff meetings, and meetings outside the school with teacher involvement.
8 Visits with pupils (for example, to courts), out-of-school activities with students and teachers, participation in events organized by the community side of the college, organisation of a two-day visit of the school by four pupils from the ILEA comprehensive I was teaching in, following an exchange of recorded tapes between pupils of the two schools; visit to another community college in Leicestershire, etc.
9 Teaching practice students, visiting academics, prospective parents, ancillary staff, ex-teachers, ex-students, feeder-school teachers, tutors in charge of community activities, governors and an LEA representative.
10 Minutes of meetings (dating back to the first year of the school), papers written by staff and students; student magazines, newspaper articles relating to the college and other Leicestershire schools and colleges, student work, examples of school resources, examination results, feeder school reports on students, published mate-

rial (books and articles) relating to the school (and other Leicestershire schools).
11 GIDDENS (1974) p. 3.
12 WILLIS (1977) p. 3.
13 *C.f.* MINCHIN (1975).
14 Thus a teacher as a parent responsible for a family may adopt a different position on allowances than another teacher with similar political thinking, but no such responsibilities.

Bibliography

ABERCROMBIE, N. and TURNER, B.S. (1978) 'The dominant ideology thesis', *British Journal of Sociology*, 29, 4, October.

ALTHUSSER, L. (1971) 'Ideology and ideological state apparatuses' in ALTHUSSER, L. (Ed.) *Lenin and Philosophy*, London, New Left Review Books.

ANDERSON, P. (1977) 'The antinomies of Antonio Gramsci', *New Left Review*, 100, November 1976–January 1977.

ANTHONY, W. (1979) 'Progressive learning theories: The evidence', in BERNBAUM, G. (Ed.) *Schooling in Decline*, London, Macmillan

ARMSTRONG, M. (1973) 'The role of the teacher', in BUCKMAN, P. (Ed.) *Education Without Schools*, London, Souvenir Press.

ASHTON, D and MAGUIRE, M. (1980) 'Young women in the labour market' in DEEM, R. (Ed.) *Schooling for Women's Work*, London, Routledge and Kegan Paul.

ASSOCIATION FOR SUPERVISION AND CURRICULUM DEVLEOPMENT (1972) *A New Look at Progressive Education*, ASCD.

AULD, R., Q.C. (1976) *William Tyndale Junior and Infants Schools Public Inquiry*, London, Inner London Education Authority.

BALL, S.J. (1981) *Beachside Comprehensive: A Case-Study of Secondary Schooling*, Cambridge, Cambridge University Press.

BARKER, C. (1978) 'A note on the theory of capitalist states', *Capital and Class*, 4.

BARRETT, M. (1980) *Women's Oppression Today*, London, Verso.

BARRETT, M. and MCINTOSH, M. (1979) 'Christine Delphy: Towards a materialist feminism' *Feminist Review*, 1.

BARTHOLOMEW, J. (1974) 'Sustaining hierarchy through teaching and research' in FLUDE, M. and AHIER, J. (Eds) *Educability, Schools and Ideology*, London, Croom Helm.

BECHHOFER, F, ELLIOTT, B. and McCRONE, D. (1978) 'Structure, consciousness and action: A sociological profile of the British middle class', *British Journal of Sociology*, 29, 4.

BEECHEY, V. (1979) 'On patriarchy', *Feminist Review*, 3.

BELL, C. and ENCEL, S. (Eds) (1978) *Inside the Whale*, Oxford, Pergamon Press.

BENINGTON, J. (1976) *Local Government Becomes Big Business*, London, Community Development Project Information and Intelligence.

BENNETT, N. (1976) *Teaching Styles and Pupil Progress*, London, Open Books.

BERNBAUM, G. (1973) 'Countesthorpe College, Leicester, United Kingdom' in Centre for Educational Research and Innovation *Case Studies of Educational Innovation, III, At the School Level*, Paris, OECD.

BERNSTEIN, B. (1971) *Class, Codes and Control, Vol. 1*, London, Routledge and Kegan Paul.

BERNSTEIN, B. (1975) *Class, Codes and Control, Vol. 3*, London, Routledge and Kegan Paul.

BEST, R., JARVIS, C. and RIBBINS, P. (1980) *Perspectives on Pastoral Care*, London, Heinemann.

BLAND, L., BRUNSDON, C., HOBSON, D. and WINSHIP, J. (1978) 'Women "inside and outside" the relations of production' in Women's Studies Group, *Women Take Issue*, London, Hutchinson.

BOURDIEU, P. (1976a) 'The school as a conservative force', in DALE, R. *et. al.* (Eds) *Schooling and Capitalism*, London, Routledge and Kegan Paul Open University

BOURDIEU, P. (1976b) 'Systems of education and systems of thought', in DALE, R. *et. al.* (Eds) *Schooling and Capitalism*, London, Routledge and Kegan Paul Open University

BOWLES, S. and GINTIS, H. (1976) *Schooling in Capitalist America*, London, Routledge Kegan Paul.

BROCKINGTON, W.A. 'Short review 1925–1928', *Education Committee of the Council of the County of Leicester*.

BROWNE, S. (1977) 'Curriculum: An HMI view', *Trends in Education,* 3

BRUNSDON, C. (1978) 'It is well known that by nature women are inclined to be rather personal' in Women's Studies Group, *Women Take Issue*, London, Hutchinson.

BUTTER, S. (1977) 'The logic of enquiry of participant observation: A critical review' in HALL, S. and JEFFERSON, T. (Eds) *Resistance through Rituals*, London, Hutchinson.

CALLINICOS, A. (1976) *Althusser's Marxism*, London, Pluto Press.

CARNOY, M. (1975) *Schooling in a Corporate Society*, New York, David McKay.

CASTLES, S. and WUSTENBERG, W. (1979a) 'A polytechnic community workshop based on marxist education principles', paper presented at the annual conference of the CSE.

CASTLES, S. and WÜSTENBERG, W. (1979b) *The Education for Future*, London, Pluto Press.

CASTLES, S. and WÜSTENBERG, W. (1979c) 'The education ideas of Marx, their development by N.K. KRUPSKAYA and their application in the early Soviet Untion', paper presented at the annual conference of the CSE.

CHANAN, G. and GILCHRIST, L. (1974) *What School is For*, London, Methuen.

CHANDLER, E.M. (1980) *Educating Adolescent Girls*, London, George Allen and Unwin.

CLARKE, S. (1977) 'Marxism, sociology and Poulantzas' theory of the state', *Capital and Class*, 2.

CLARRICOATES, K. (1978) 'Dinosaurs in the classroom', *Women's Studies Int. Quart.*, 1.

COCKBURN, C. (1977) *The Local State*, London, Pluto Press.

COCKSHOTT, P. (1978) 'The crisis of capital accumulation', paper presented at the annual conference of the CSE.

COHEN, S. (1973) *Folk Devils and Moral Panics*, Harmondsworth, Penguin.

COLE, M. and SKELTON, B. (Eds) (1980) *Blind Alley: Youth in a Crisis of Capital*, Ormskirk, G.W. and A. Hesketh.

CORRIGAN, P. (1979) *Schooling the Smash Street Kids*, London, Macmillan.

CORWIN, R. (1965) 'Militant professionalism, initiative and compliance in public education', *Sociology of Education*, 38, 4.

COX, C.B. and DYSON, A.E. (Eds) (1971) *The Black Papers on Education*, London, Davis-Poynter.

CSE STATE GROUP (1979) *Struggle Over the State*, London, CSE Books.

DALE, R. (1978) 'The politicization of school deviance: Reactions to William Tyndale' in BARTON, L. and MEIGHAN, R. (Eds) *Schools, Pupils and Deviance*, Nafferton, Nafferton Books.

DALE, R. (1979) 'From endorsement to disintegration: Progressive education from the golden age to the Green Paper', *British Journal of Educational Studies*, XXVII, 3, October.

DALE, R. (1981) 'Accountability and William Tyndale' in DALE, R. *et. al.* (Eds) *Education and the State Vol. II: Politics, Patriarchy and Practice*, Lewes, Falmer Press.

DAVID, M.E. (1980) *The State, the Family and Education*, London, Routledge and Kegan Paul.

DAVIES, L. (1978) 'Deadlier than the male? Girls' conformity and deviance in school' in BARTON, L. and MEIGHAN, R. (Eds) *Schools, Pupils and Deviance*, Nafferton, Nafferton Books.

DEEM, R. (1976) 'Professionalism, unity and militant action', *Sociological Review*, 24, 1.

DEEM, R. (1978) *Women and Schooling*, London, Routledge and Kegan Paul.

DEEM, R. (Ed.) (1980) *Schooling for Women's Work*, London, Routledge and Kegan Paul.

DELPHY, C. (1977) *The Main Enemy: A Materialist Analysis of Women's Oppression*, London, Women's Research and Resources Centre Publications.

DELPHY, C. (1980) 'A materialist feminism is possible', *Feminist Review*, 4.

DENT, H.C. (1976) 'Legend of urbanity and tact', *Education*, 9 January.

DEPARTMENT OF EDUCATION AND SCIENCE (1967–1976) *Education and Science*, annual reports, London, HMSO.

DEPARTMENT OF EDUCATION AND SCIENCE (1975) *Education Survey 21 — Curricular Differences for Boys and Girls*, London, HMSO.

DEPARTMENT OF EDUCATION AND SCIENCE (1977a) *Educating Our Children: Four Subjects for Debate*, London, HMSO.

DEPARTMENT OF EDUCATION AND SCIENCE (1977b) *Education in Schools: A Consultative Document*, Cmnd. 6869, London, HMSO.

DEPARTMENT OF EDUCATION AND SCIENCE (1977–1980) *Annual Report*, London, HMSO.

DEPARTMENT OF EDUCATION AND SCIENCE (1979) *Aspects of Secondary Education in England: A Survey by H.M. Inspectorate of Schools*, London, HMSO.

DOMINELLI, L. (1978) 'Female labour: Its centrality to the class struggle', paper presented at the annual conference of the CSE.

DONALD, J. (1978) 'Media studies: Possibilities and limitations', paper presented at the annual conference of the CSE.

DONALD, J. (1979) 'Green paper: "Noise of Crisis"', *Screen Education*, 30.

DOUGLAS, J.W.B. (1971) *The Home and the School*, London, Panther.

EDUCATION GROUP, CENTRE FOR CONTEMPORARY CULTURAL STUDIES (1981) *Unpopular Education*, London, Hutchinson.

EGGLESTON, J. (1965) 'How comprehensive is the Leicestershire plan', *New Society*, 25 April.

ELLIOTT, B. (1970) 'The implementation of the Leicestershire plan', *Forum*, Summer.

ELLIOTT, J. and ADELMAN, C. (1975) 'Teachers' accounts and the objectivity of classroom research', *London Educational Review*, 4, 2/3.

ELLIS, T. (*et. al.*) (1976) *William Tyndale: The Teachers' Story*, London, Writers and Readers Publishing Cooperative.

ENTWISTLE, H. (1970) *Child-centred Education*, London, Methuen.

FAIRBAIRN, A.N. (1971) *The Leicestershire Community Colleges*, London, National Institute of Adult Education.

FAIRBAIRN, A.N. (1978) *The Leicestershire Community Colleges and Centres*, Nottingham Working Papers in the Education of Adults, University of Nottingham, Department of Adult Education.

FAIRBAIRN, A.N. (Ed.) (1980) *The Leicestershire Plan*, London, Heinemann.

FAY, B. (1975) *Social Theory and Political Practice*, London, George Allen and Unwin.

FINN, D., GRANT, N. and JOHNSON, R. (1977) 'Social democracy, education and the crisis', *Working Papers in Cultural Studies*, 10, CCCS, University of Birmingham.

FIRESTONE, S. (1979) *The Dialectic of Sex*, London, Women's Press.

FLETCHER, C., CARON, M. and WILLIAMS, W. (1985) *Schools on Trial: The Trials of Democratic Comprehensives*, Milton Keynes, Open University Press.

FREIRE, P. (1972) *Cultural Action for Freedom*, Harmondsworth, Penguin Books.

FRITH, S. (1978) 'Notes for a discussion of trade unions and training', paper presented at the annual conference of the CSE.

FRITH, S. (1980) 'Education, training and the labour process', in COLE, M. and SKELTON, B. (Eds) *Blind Alley: Youth in a Crisis of Capital*, Ormskirk, G.W. and A. Hesketh.

FRITH, S. (1981) 'Dancing in the streets', *Time Out*, 20–26 March.

FULLER, M. (1980) 'Black girls in a London comprehensive school' in DEEM, R. (Ed.) *Schooling for Women's Work*, London, Routledge and Kegan Paul.

GALTON, M. and SIMON, B. (Ed.) (1980) *Progress and Performance in the Primary School*, London, Routledge and Kegan Paul.

GAMBLE, A. and WALTON, P. (1976) *Capitalism in Crisis*, London, Macmillan.

GARDINER, J. (1977) 'Women in the labour process and class structure', in HUNT, A. (Ed.) *Class and Class Structure*, London, Lawrence and Wishart.

GERAS, N. (1973) 'Marx and the critique of political economy', in BLACKBURN, R. (Ed.) *Ideology in Social Science*, London, Fontana.

GERSTENBERGER, H. (1977) 'Fetish and control', paper presented at the annual conference of the CSE.

GIDDENS, A. (Ed.) (1974) *Positivism and Sociology*, London, Heinemann.

GINSBURG, M.B. *et. al.* (1980) 'Teachers' conceptions of professionalism and trades unionism' in WOODS, P. (Ed.) *Teacher Strategies*, London, Croom Helm.

GIROUX, H.A. (1983) *Theory and Resistance in Education: A Pedagogy for the Opposition*, London, Heinemann.

GLEESON, D. and WHITTY, G. (1976) *Developments in Social Studies Teaching*, London, Open Books.

GOODSON, I. (1975) 'The teachers' curriculum and the new reformation', *Journal of Curriculum Studies*, 7, 2, November.

GORDON, T. (1985) *Progressivism and the Changing Educational Climate — A Case Study of a Community College in Leicestershire*, PhD. thesis, University of London Institute of Education.

GRACE, G. (1978) *Teachers, Ideology and Control: A Study in Urban Education*, London, Routledge and Kegan Paul.

GRAHL, J. (1978) 'Restructuring in West European industry', *Capital and Class*, 19, Spring.

GRIBBLE, D. (1985) *Considering Children: A Parents' Guide to Progressive Education*, London, Dorling Kindersley.

GROSS, B. and R. (Eds) (1971) *Radical School Reform*, London, Victor Gollancz.

GUMBERT, E.B. and SPRING, J.H. (1974) *The Superschool and the Superstate: American Education in the 20 Century, 1918–1970*, New York, John Wiley and Sons.

HABERMAS, J. (1976) *Legitimation Crisis*, London, Heinemann.

HALL, S. (nd) 'Drifting into the "Law and Order" Society', Cobden Trust.

HALL, S., CRITCHER, C., JEFFERSON, T., CLARKE, J. and ROBERTS, B. (1978) *Policing the Crisis: Mugging, the State, and Law and Order*, London, Macmillan.

HALL, S. and JEFFERSON, T. (Eds) (1977) *Resistance Through Rituals: Youth Subcultures in Post-war Britain*, London, Hutchinson.

HALSEY, A.H. (1978) *Change in British Society*, Oxford, Oxford University Press.

HALSEY, A.H. (1980) *Origins and Destinations*, Oxford, Clarendon Press.

HANNAN, A. (1975) 'The problem of the unmotivated in an open school' in CHANAN, G. and DELAMONT, S. (Eds) *Frontiers of Classroom Research*, Windsor, NFER.

HARGREAVES, A. (1982) 'Resistance and relative autonomy theories', *British Journal of Sociology of Education*, 3, 2.

HARGREAVES, D. (1967) *Social Relations in a Secondary School*, London, Routledge and Kegan Paul.

HARGREAVES, D. (1980) 'The occupational culture of teachers' in WOODS, P. (Ed.) *Teacher Strategies*, London, Croom Helm.

HARTMANN, H. (1979) 'The unhappy marriage of Marxism and feminism' *Capital and Class*, 8.

HEWITT, R. (1982) *The Abuse of Power*, Oxford, Martin Robertson.

HEXTALL, I. (1980) 'Up against the wall: Restructuring state education', in COLE, M. and SKELTON, B. (Eds) *Blind Alley: Youth in a Crisis of Capital*, Ormskirk, G.W. and A. Hesketh.

HIRST, P.Q. (1975) *Durkheim, Bernard and Epistemology, Part Two: Durkheim's Rules of Sociological Method*, London. Routledge and Kegan Paul.

HOARE, Q. and NOWELL SMITH C. (Eds) (1971) *Antonio Gramsci: Selections from the Prison Notebooks*, London, Lawrence and Wishart.

HOBSON, D. (1978) 'Housewives: Isolation as oppression', Women's Studies Group, *Women Take Issue*, London, Hutchinson.

HOLLOWAY, J. and PICCIOTTO, S. (1977) 'Capital, crisis and the state' *Capital and Class*, 2., Summer.

HOLLOWAY, J. and PICCIOTTO, S. (1978a) 'Education and the crisis of social relations', paper presented at the Socialist Teachers Alliance Conference.

HOLLOWAY, J. and PICCIOTTO, S. (1978b) *State and Capital*, London, Edward Arnold.

HOLLY, D. (1974) *Beyond Curriculum*, Frogmore, Herts, Paladin.

HOLMES, B. (1973) 'Leicestershire, UK', in Centre for Educational Research and Innovation, *Case Studies of Educational Innovation II, At the Regional Level*, Paris, OECD.

HOLT, J. (1969) *How Children Fail*, Harmondsworth, Penguin.

HOLT, J. (1973) *Freedom and Beyond*, Harmondsworth, Penguin.

HUNTER, C. (1980) 'The politics of participation', in WOODS, P. (Ed.) *Teacher Strategies*, London, Croom Helm.

HUSSAIN, A. (1976) 'The economy and the educational system in capitalistic societies', *Economy and Society*, 5, 4.

HUSSAIN, A. (1977) 'Crises and tendencies of capitalism' in *Economy and Society*, 6, 4.

JACKSON, B. and MARSDEN, D. (1966) *Education and the Working Class*, London, Routledge and Kegan Paul.

JACKSON, R.A. (1979) 'Schools and industry — A view from the TUC', *Trends in Education*, 2.

JESSOP, B. (1977) 'Recent theories of the capitalist state', *Cambridge Journal of Economics*, 119.

JESSOP, B. (1982) *The Capitalist State*, Oxford, Martin Robertson.

JOHNSON, C. (1980) 'The problem of reformism and Marx's theory of fetishism' *New Left Review*, 119.

JOHNSON, R. (1976a) 'Educational policy and social control in early Victorian England', *Past and Present*, 49.

JOHNSON, R. (1976b) 'Notes on the schooling of the English working class 1780–1850' in DALE, R. *et. al.* (Eds) *Schooling and Capitalism*, London, Routledge and Kegan Paul Open University.

JOHNSON, R. (1976/77) 'Really useful knowledge', *Radical Education*, 7 and 8.

JOHNSON, R. (1979a) 'Histories of cultures/theories of ideology: Notes on an impasse' in BARRETT, M. *et. al.* (Ed.) *Ideology and Cultural Production*, London, Croom Helm.

JOHNSON, R. (1979b) 'Three problematics: Elements of a theory of working-class culture', in CLARKE, J. *et. al.* (Eds) *Working Class Culture: Studies in History and*

Theory, London, Hutchinson.
JOHNSON, T.J. (1972) *Professions and Power*, London, Macmillan.
JONES, K. (1983) *Beyond Progressive Education*, London, Macmillan.
JONES, K. and WILLIAMSON, K. (1979) 'The birth of a schoolroom', *Governing the Present, I and C*, 6, autumn.
KARIER, C.J., VIOLAS, P. and SPRING, J. (Eds) (1973) *Roots of Crisis: American Education in the 20th Century*, Chicago, Rand McNally.
KEDDIE, N. (Ed.) (1973) *Tinker, Tailor ... the Myth of Cultural Deprivation*, Harmondsworth, Penguin.
KEIL, T. and NEWTON, P. (1980) 'Into work: Continuity and change' in DEEM, R. (Ed.) *Schooling for Women's Work*, London, Routledge and Kegan Paul.
KUHN, A. (1978) 'Structures of patriarchy and capital in the family', in KUHN, A. and WOLPE, A.M. (Eds) *Feminism and Materialism*, London, Routledge and Kegan Paul.
LACLAU, E. (1975) 'The specificity of the political', in *Economy and Society*, 4, 1.
LARSON, M.S. (1977) *The Rise of Professionalism*, University of California Press.
LASCH, C. (1981) 'The Freudian Left and cultural revolution' *New Left Review*, 129.
LAWTON, D. (1984) 'The tightening grip: Growth of central control of the school curriculum', Bedford Way Papers 21, Institute of Education, University of London.
LEGGATT, T. (1970) 'Teaching as a profession' in JACKSON, J.A. (Ed.) *Professions and Professionalism*, Cambridge University Press.
LEICESTERSHIRE COUNTY COUNCIL, (1973) Leicestershire Education 1973–1983, Ten Year Policy, FAIRBAIRN, A.N.
LEICESTERSHIRE COUNTY COUNCIL (1974) Reorganization of Secondary Education, Report of the Chief Officers' Management Team, June.
LEICESTERSHIRE COUNTY COUNCIL, The Leicestershire Experiment — the Next Phase, Council Minutes and Reports, May 1959 — February 1960, pp. 24–7.
LENHARDT, G. (1978) 'On limits of educational reform: The case of West Germany', paper presented at the annual conference of the CSE.
LEONARD, P. (1984) *Personality and Ideology: Towards a Materialist Understanding of the Individual*, London, Macmillan.
LIGHTFOOT, S.L. (1975) 'Sociology of education: Perspectives on women', in MILLMAN, M. and KANTER, R.M. (Eds) *Another Voice*, New York, Anchor Books.
LONDON EDINBURGH WEEKEND RETURN GROUP (1980) *In and Against the State*, London, Pluto Press.
LUKES, S. (1973) *Individualism*, Oxford, Basil Blackwell.
McDONALD, M. (1980) 'Socio-cultural reproduction and women's education' in DEEM, R. (Ed.) *Schooling for Women's Work*, London, Routledge and Kegan Paul.
McDONNELL, K. (1978) 'Ideology, crisis and the cuts', *Capital and Class*, 4, spring.
McFARLANE, A. (1978) *The Origins of English Individualism*, Oxford, Basil Blackwell.
McMULLEN, T. (1968) 'Flexibility for a comprehensive school', *Forum*, 10, 2, spring.
McMULLEN, T. (1972) 'Countesthorpe College, Leicestershire', *Forum*, 14, 2, spring.
McPHERSON, C.B. (1962) *The Political Theory of Possessive Individualism*, Oxford, Clarendon Press.
McPHERSON, C.B. (1972) 'Politics: Post-Liberal democracy?' in BLACKBURN, R. (Ed.) *Ideology in Social Science*, London, Fontana.
McROBBIE, A. (1978a) 'Jackie: An ideology of adolescent femininity', Stencilled Occasional Paper, SP No. 53, Centre for Contemporary Cultural Studies, University of Birmingham.
McROBBIE, A. (1978b) 'Working class girls and the culture of femininity', in Women's Studies Group, *Women Take Issue*, London, Hutchinson.
McROBBIE, A. and NAVA, M. (Eds) (1984) *Gender and Generation*, London, Macmillan.

MANN, M. (1973) *Consciousness and Action Among the Western Working Class*, London, Macmillan.

MARDLE, G. and WALKER, M. (1980) 'Strategies and structure: some critical notes on teacher socialization' in WOODS, P. (Ed.) *Teacher Strategies*, London, Croom Helm.

MARKS, P. (1976) 'Femininity in the classroom' in MITCHELL, J. and OAKLEY, A. (Eds) *The Rights and Wrongs of Women*, Harmondsworth, Penguin.

MARX, K. (1970) *The German Ideology*, edited and with an introduction by ARTHUR, C.J., London, Lawrence and Wishart.

MARX, K. (1974) *Capital, Volume One*, London, Lawrence and Wishart.

MARX, K. and ENGELS, F. (1970) *Selected Works*, Lawrence and Wishart.

MASON, S.C. (1963) *The Leicestershire Experiment and Plan*, London, Councils and Education Press, 1957, 1960, 1963.

MASON, S.C. (Ed.) (1970) *In Our Experience*, London, Longman.

MEIKSINS WOOD, E. (1981) 'The separation of the economic and the political in capitalism' *New Left Review*, 127, May/June.

MILIBAND, R. (1969) *The State in Capitalist Society*, London, Weidenfeld and Nicolson.

MILIBAND, R. (1978) 'A state of de-subordination', *British Journal of Sociology*, 30, 4, December.

MILLETT, K. (1971) *Sexual Politics*, New York, Avon Books.

MINCHIN, M.F. (1975) 'Countesthorpe College — Problems and Possibilities of Radical Innovation', unpublished Special Study, University of Nottingham School of Education.

MINISTRY OF EDUCATION, *Education*, annual reports 1960 to 1966, London, HMSO.

MITCHELL, J. (1975) *Psychoanalysis and Feminism*, Harmondsworth, Penguin.

MOLINA, V. (1978) 'Notes on Marx and the problem of individuality' in Centre for Contemporary Cultural Studies, *On Ideology*, London, Hutchinson.

MONTESSORI, M. (1948) *The Discovery of the Child*, India, Kalakshetra Publications.

MOON, B. (Ed.) (1983) *Comprehensive Schools: Challenge and Change*, Windsor, NFER-Nelson.

MOORE, R. (1978/9) 'The value of reproduction', *Screen Education*, 39, winter.

MUSGROVE, F. (1971) *Patterns of Power and Authority in English Education*, London, Methuen.

MYRDAL, G. (1968) *Value in Social Theory*, London, Routledge and Kegan Paul.

NAIRN, T. (1979) 'The future of Britain's crisis', *New Left Review*, 113–114.

NATIONAL UNION OF TEACHERS (1977) *Education in Schools: The NUT's Response to the Recommendations in the 1977 Green Paper*, London, NUT.

NEILL, A.S. (1971) *Talking about Summerhill*, London, Victor Gollancz.

OAKLEY, A. (1981) 'Interviewing women: A contradiction in terms', in ROBERTS, H. (Ed.) *Doing Feminist Research*, London, Routledge and Kegan Paul.

OFFE, C. and RONGE, V. (1981) 'Theses on the theory of the state' in DALE, R. et. al. (Eds) '*Education and the State, Vol. One, Schooling and the National Interest, Open University*'. Lewes, Falmer Press.

OVERBEEK, H. (1979) 'Finance capital and crisis in Britain', paper presented at the annual conference of the CSE.

PANITCH, L. (1978a) 'Profits and politics: Labour and the crisis of British capitalism', paper presented at the annual conference of the CSE.

PANITCH, L. (1978b) 'The state and the future of socialism', paper presented at the annual conference of the CSE.

PARRY, N. and PARRY, J. (1974) 'The teachers and professionalism' in FLUDE, M. and AHIER, J. (Eds) *Educability, Schools and Ideology*, London, Croom Helm.

PEARSON, G. and TWOHIG, J. (1977) 'Ethnography through the looking glass', in HALL, S. and JEFFERSON, T. (Eds) *Resistance through Rituals*, London, Hutchinson.

PHILLIPS, A. and PUTNAM, T. (1980) 'Education for emancipation', *Capital and Class*,

10, Spring.

PICCIOTTO, S. (1972) 'Myths of bourgeois legality', paper presented at the annual conference of the CSE.

PIVEN, F.F. and CLOWARD, R.A. (1972) *Regulating the Poor*, London, Tavistock Publications Ltd.

PLASKOW, M. (1985) *Life and Death of the Schools Council*, Lewes, Falmer Press.

PLATT, J. (1981) 'On interviewing peers', *British Journal of Sociology*, XXXII, 1, March.

POULANTZAS, N. (1972) 'The problem of the capitalist state', in BLACKBURN, R. (Ed.) *Ideology in Social Science*, London, Fontana.

POULANTZAS, N. (1973) *Political Power and Social Classes*, London, New Left Books.

POULANTZAS, N. (1978) *State, Power and Socialism*, London, New Left Books.

PRANDY, K. (1979) 'Alienation and interests in the analysis of social cognitions', *British Journal of Sociology*, 30, 4, December.

PRICE, R.F. (1977) *Marx and Education in Russia and China*, London, Croom Helm.

PUNCH, M. (1977) *Progressive Retreat*, Cambridge University Press.

PURVIS, J. (1981) 'Women and teaching in the nineteenth century', in DALE, R. *et al.* (Eds) *Education and the State, Vol. 2: Politics, Patriarchy and Practice*, Lewes, Falmer Press.

PYE, N. (1972) *Leicester and Its Region*, University of Leicester Press.

ROBERTS, H. (1981) *Doing Feminist Research*, London, Routledge and Kegan Paul.

ROGERS, T. (Ed.) (1971) *School for the Community*, London, Routledge and Kegan Paul.

ROSE, N. (1972) 'Fetishism and ideology', *Ideology and Consciousness*, 2, Autumn.

ROSENTHAL, R. and JACOBSON, L. (1968) *Pygmalion in the Classroom*, London, Holt, Rinehart and Winston.

RUBIN, G. (1975) 'The traffic in women: Notes on the "political economy" of sex', in REITER, R.R. (Ed.) *Toward an Anthropology of Women*, New York, Monthly Review Press.

RUBINSTEIN, D. and SIMON, B. (1973) *The Evolution of the Comprehensive School 1926–72*, London, Routledge and Kegan Paul.

RUSSELL, D. (1981) *The Tamarisk Tree: Vol. 2 My School and the Years of War*, London, Virago.

SARGENT, L. (Ed.) (1981) *The Unhappy Marriage of Marxism and Feminism*, London, Pluto Press.

SEARLE, C. (1975) *Classrooms of Resistance*, London, Writers and Readers Publishing Cooperative.

SELLECK, R.J.W. (1968) *The New Education, 1870–1914*, London, Sir Isaac Pitman and Sons.

SELLECK, R.J.W. (1972) *English Primary Education and the Progressives 1914–39*, London and Boston, Routledge and Kegan Paul.

SEVE, L. (1978) *Man in Marxist Theory and the Psychology of Personality*, Hassocks, the Harvester Press.

SHARP, R. and GREEN, A. (1975) *Education and Social Control*, London, Routledge and Kegan Paul.

SHARPE, S. (1976) *Just Like a Girl*, Harmondsworth, Penguin.

SHARPLES, A. (1979) 'The industrial strategy — State intervention in the mid-seventies', paper presented at the annual conference of the CSE.

SHAW, J. (1979) 'School attendance — Some notes on a further feature of sexual division', paper presented at the University of London Institute of Education.

SHAW, J. (1981) 'In loco parentis: A relationship between parent, state and child', in DALE, R., et. al. (Eds) *Education and the State, Vol. II, Politics, Patriarchy and Practice*, Lewes, Falmer Press.

SILVER, H. (1965) *The Concept of Popular Education, A Study of Ideas and Social*

Movements in the Early 19th Century, London, Macgibbon and Kee.

SIMON, B. (1965) *Education and the Labour Movement, 1870–1920*, London, Lawrence and Wishart.

SIMON, B. (1972) 'Education in Leicestershire', in PYE, N. (Ed.) *Leicester and Its Region*, University of Leicester Press.

SIMON, B. (1974a) *The Two Nations and the Educational Structure 1780–1870*, London, Lawrence and Wishart.

SIMON, B. (1974b) *The Politics of Educational Reform 1920–1940*, London, Lawrence and Wishart.

SIMON, B. (Ed.) (1972) *Education in Leicestershire 1540–1940*, University of Leicester Press.

SMITH, D.E. (1978) 'A peculiar eclipsing: Women's exclusion from man's culture', *Women's Studies Int. Quart.*, Vol. 1.

SOMERVILLE, J. (1980) 'Poulantzas, class and power' in *I and C*, 7, autumn.

SPRING, J. (1972) *Education and the Rise of the Corporate State*, Boston, Beacon Press.

SPRING, J. (1977) *A Primer of Libertarian Education*, New York, Free Life Editions.

STEBBINS, R.A. (1980) 'The role of humour in teaching: Strategy and self-expression', in WOODS, P. (Ed.) *Teacher Strategies*, London, Croom Helm.

STEPHENS, J.D. (1979) 'Class formation and class consciousness' *British Journal of Sociology*, 30, 4, December.

STEWART, W.A.C. (1979) 'Progressive education — Past, present and future' *British Journal of Educational Studies*, XXVII, 2.

TAPPER, T. and SALTER, B. (1978) *Education and the Political Order — Changing Patterns of Class Control*, London, Macmillan.

THERBORN, G. (1971) 'Habermas: A New Eclectic' *New Left Review*, 67.

TURNER, B. (1971) 'An inspired reformer: Author of Leicestershire plan retires', *Times Educational Supplement*, 1 October, p. 13.

VIRTANEN, L. (1973) 'Tapiolan School, Tapiola, Finland', in Centre for Educational Research and Innovation, *Case Studies of Educational Innovation, III, At the School Level*, Paris, OECD.

WALKER, R. and GOODSON, I. (1977) 'Humour in the classroom' in WOODS, P. and HAMMERSLEY, M. (Eds) *School Experience*, London, Croom Helm.

WALKERDINE, V. (1981) 'Sex, power and pedagogy' *Screen Education*, 38, spring.

WALKERDINE, V. (1984) 'Some day my prince will come' in McROBBIE, A. and NAVA, M. (Eds) *Gender and Generation*, London, Macmillan.

WATTS, J. (1973) 'Tell me what to do and I'll do it', in TURNER, B. (Ed.) *Discipline in Schools*, London, Ward Lock.

WATTS, J. (1976) 'Creative conflict' in MACBETH, J.E.C. (Ed.) *A Question of Schooling*, London, Hodder and Stoughton.

WATTS, J. (Ed.) (1977) *The Countesthorpe Experience: The First Five Years*, London, George Allen and Unwin.

WATTS, J. (1980) *Towards an Open School*, London, Longman.

WHITE, J. (1975) 'The end of the compulsory curriculum', in The Doris Lee Lectures, 1975; The Curriculum, *Studies in Education 2*, University of London Institute of Education.

WHITESIDE, T. (1978) *The Sociology of Educational Innovation: Contemporary Sociology of the School*, London, Methuen.

WILLIAMS, R. (1961) *The Long Revolution*, Harmondsworth, Penguin.

WILLIS, P. (1977) *Learning to Labour: How Working Class Kids Get Working Class Jobs*, Farnborough, Saxon House.

WINSHIP, J. (1978) 'A woman's world' in Women's Studies Group, *Women Take Issue*, London, Hutchinson.

WINSHIP, J. (1981) 'Woman becomes an "individual"', Stencilled Occasional Paper,

S.P. No. 65, Centre for Contemporary Cultural Studies, University of Birmingham.

WOLPE, A-M (1974) 'The official ideology of education for girls', in FLUDE, M. and AHIER, J. (Eds) *Educability, Schools and Ideology*, London, Croom Helm.

WOLPE, A-M (1977) *Some Processes in Sexist Education*, London, Women's Research and Resources Centre Publications.

WOLPE, A-M. (1978) 'Education and the sexual division of labour' in KUHN, A. and WOLPE, A-M. (Eds) *Feminism and Materialism*, London, Routledge and Kegan Paul.

WOOD, J. (1978) 'Dealing with disaffection: New policies in education', paper presented at the annual conference of the CSE.

WOODS, P. (1979) *The Divided School*, London, Routledge and Kegan Paul.

WOODS, P. (Ed.) (1980) *Teacher Strategies*, London, Croom Helm.

WRIGHT, N. (1977) *Progress in Education*, London, Croom Helm.

YEO, S. (1974) 'On the uses of "Apathy"', *European Journal of Sociology*, XV, 2.

YOUNG, I. (1981) 'Beyond the happy-marriage: A critique of the dual systems theory', in SARGENT, L. (Ed.) *The Unhappy Marriage of Marxism and Feminism*, London, Pluto Press.

YOUNG, M. and ARMSTRONG, M. (1965) 'The flexible school' *Where*, Supplement Five, autumn, Advisory Centre for Education.

YOUNG, M.F.D. (1971) (Ed.) *Knowledge and Control*, London, Collier-Macmillan.

YOUNG, M.F.D. and WHITTY, G. (1977) (Eds) *Society, State and Schooling*, Lewes, Falmer Press.

Index

anarchist libertarianism, 37–8
Anti-Nazi League, 134
APU
    see Assessment of Performance Unit
Assessment of Performance Unit (APU),
    21, 246
Assisted Places Scheme, 23
atomization, 144, 148, 151–2, 155, 156,
    157–8, 159, 161, 162, 165, 169, 173–5,
    178, 179, 180–204, 214, 219, 221, 223,
    229, 233, 237, 245, 257
    see also individualization
Auld enquiry, 44
Auld Report, 44
autonomy
    in schools
    see Greenfield College, autonomy in

Bennett, N., 30
Bernstein, B., 41, 46
Big Flame (collective), 42
Black Papers, 3n3, 17, 18, 26, 30–2, 33,
    34, 45, 69, 70, 225
Boyson, R., 22, 69
Britain
    and imperialism, 12–13
    'new education' in, 28
    progressive education in, *passim*
    restructuring in, *passim*
Bullock Report, 21
bureaucratization, 14
    see also centralization
Burnham Committee, 76

Callaghan, J. (Prime Minister), 18, 19,
    20, 21
capital-labour relations, 2, 8–9, 10, 11,
    12, 15–16
capitalism, 7–9, 10, 206–7, 208, 219,
    221n4, 245
    see also capital-labour relations
careers
    see also student careers
    definition of, 179
    methodology in study of, 179
Carlisle, M., 22
CBI (Confederation of British Industry),
    21
CCCS (Centre for Contemporary
    Cultural Studies)
    Education Group of, 7, 45, 47
central government
    see centralization; restructuring
centralization, 2, 3, 14, 21, 23, 26, 33–4,
    44, 46, 47, 81, 88, 108, 143, 149, 156,
    174, 221, 223, 226, 240, 244, 246
    see also standardization
Centre for Contemporary Cultural
    Studies
    see CCCS
certification
    see examinations
child-centred approach, 27, 31, 32, 33,
    38–41, 47, 61, 76–7, 81, 85, 88, 104,
    106, 112, 116–17, 147, 162, 172, 178,
    229, 245, 246, 258
'Children's Houses'
    and Montessori approach, 39
class struggle, 9, 10, 13, 14–15
    see also social class
Classrooms of Resistance, 19, 43–4
community colleges, 55–6, 57–139,
    246–7
    see also Greenfield College

271

comprehensive schooling, 17, 31–2, 39–40, 46, 53, 246, 247
Conservative government, 13, 14–15
   see also centralization; restructuring; Thatcherism
Conservative party
   and local level, 52–9
corporatist strategy, 13–14, 21
correspondence principle, 6
Crosbie, Eileen, 23
curriculum, 20–3
   see also Greenfield College

Dale, R., 34–5, 47
Dartington Hall, 37
Department of Education and Science (DES), 20
desubordination, 15, 47, 148
Dewey, J., 27
Disruptive Pupils Scheme, 20

Ecology Party, 131
economic factors
   and schooling, 7–8
   see also expenditure cuts
education
   see also formal education; Greenfield College; schooling
   and autonomy, 19, 57–8
   and corporate state, 6
   development in Leicestershire of, 53–4
   distinguished from schooling, 42–3
   equal opportunity in, 41
   and liberalism, 38–41
   and libertarianism, 35–8
   and social relations, 6–11
   and socialism, 42–6
Education Act (1944), 23, 39
Educational Priority Areas, 17
ethnography, 255–7
examinations, 88–90, 117–19, 137, 147, 151–2, 162–5, 174, 186–8, 190–202, 219, 232–3, 234, 240, 245, 246, 256–7
expenditure cuts, 3, 21–3, 34, 57–8, 71–2, 78–80, 81, 102–3, 226, 240

femininity, 207–9, 213, 214–15, 217–18, 220
   see also feminism; sex-gender
feminism, 1, 2, 8–9, 100–1, 197–202, 220, 221, 221n5, 241, 243, 244
   see also femininity; sex-gender
formal education

   see also education; Greenfield College; schooling
   analyses of, 6–7
   definition of, 11n2
   and expenditure cuts, 21–3
   and qualitative effects of expenditure cuts, 22
   in 1960s, 16–24
   in 1970s, 16–24
   and restructuring, 23, 26; *see also* restructuring
   as state apparatus, 2, 6–11; *see also* state apparatus
Foucauld, 1,
Freire, P., 42–3

gender
   see sex-gender
Great Debate, 3n13, 18, 20, 21, 33, 226
Green, A.
   see Sharp and Green
Greenfield College [pseudonym], 2, 52–139
   allowances policy in, 75–6, 80, 169, 210, 241
   autonomy in, 62, 67, 70, 85–8, 92, 95, 111, 127, 178, 246
   case studies of students at, 189–202
   collaboration between students and teachers at, *see* Greenfield College, teacher-student relationships in
   conflict in, 68–72
   consensus in, 64–5
   context of, 246
   control in, 67, 126, 165–7, 211–13
   curriculum in, 62–3, 85–90, 111–19
   democracy in, 61–81, 90–5, 102, 104, 113, 119–22, 127, 150, 153, 171, 211, 223, 224, 231, 234, 235–8, 239n10, 240–4, 246
   described, 60–84
   divisions among teachers at, 76–7
   examinations at, 88–90, 102, 117–19, 137, 162–5, 174, 186–8, 190–202, 219, 232–3, 234, 240, 246, 256–7
   and expenditure cuts, 71–2, 78–80, 81, 102–3, 226, 240
   formal structures in, 63–6, 240–3, 244–5, 246–7
   fragmentation in, 77, 80, 92, 150–1, 229, 253–4
   gender differentiation at, *see* Greenfield

College, sex-gender at
and governors, 66
group work at, *see* Greenfield College,
  team system in
headteacher at, 65, 68
hidden curriculum in, 206
history of, 68–81
humanities at, 242–3
impasse in, 80, 95, 241–2
individualization at, *see*
  individualization
informal relationships in, 153
innovation in, 60–81, 95, 102, 108–9,
  226, 230–1, 237, 244, 247
and local area, 61
and local education authority, 241–2
masculine 'tone' at, 211–12, 222n14
in mid-1980s, 240–8
Mode III examinations in, 165
moots at, 63–6, 73–4, 80, 82, 119–20,
  150, 223, 227, 228, 230, 231, 234,
  235, 236, 238
National Union of School Students
  (NUSS) in, 74–5, 95
opening of, 61
organization in, 61–2
and parents, 66, 69, 81, 82n18, 83n28
  and n29
participation in, *see* Greenfield College,
  democracy in
and progressivism, 60–84; *see also*
  progressivism
and racism, 100–2, 133–5, 153
relationships in, *see* Greenfield College,
  teacher-student relationships in
research at, 60–1, 251–60
sex-gender at, 100–1, 135–7, 188–9,
  210–21
sexism in, 210–21
social class in, 98–100, 125–31, 132–
  3, 155–6, 218, 232–3
social context of, 61
staffing in, 71–2
student careers in, 178–204
student strike in, 73, 216–17
teacher-student relationships in, 62–3,
  67, 78–9, 81, 89, 93, 95–7, 102,
  111, 112, 122–7, 154–5, 168, 209–
  14, 226–7, 228–31, 235–6, 238,
  257–8
teachers in, 66, 70–1, 75–7, 85–110,
  210–14, 228–31
team system in, 62–3, 77, 86–8, 111,

156, 157, 223–39
and Technical and Vocational
  Education Initiative (TVEI), 240–1,
  242
and trade unions, *see* trade unions
vertical teams in, 223–39; *see also*
  Greenfield College, team system in
grounded theory, 249–50

Hadow Report, 29
Hailsham, Lord Chancellor, 16
Hartmann, H., 207
Heath, E. (Prime Minister), 13
hidden curriculum, 41, 206
HMI (Her Majesty's Inspectorate), 20,
  23, 242
Holloway, J. and Picciotto, S., 8–11
Home Office, 20
Houghton Committee, 18
humanitarian libertarianism, 35–8

individualism, 37, 143–4, 161–2
  see also individualization
individualization, 2, 56, 77, 81, 85–90,
  97, 98–9, 106–7, 111–17, 127, 137,
  142–58, 159, 161, 162, 165, 166, 169,
  171, 173–5, 178, 180–1, 203, 206,
  207–9, 214–21, 232–3, 245, 250,
  256–8
  see also personalization
  as atomization, 148–9
  as control, 146–9
  as form, 143–6
  as gender-specific, 207–9
  in Greenfield College, 149–57
  and schooling, 145–9
  and social class, 145–6
  and students, 151–6
  and teachers, 149–51
individuals
  and social relations, 250–1
imperialism, 12–13
Industrial Relations Act (1971), 13
Inner London Education Authority
  (ILEA), 20, 23
innovation
  see Greenfield College, innovation in
interactionist tradition, 1–2, 254

Jackie, 208–9, 217
Joseph, Sir Keith, 21, 22

Keynesian techniques, 13

Kidbrooke School, 20
Krupskaya, 42

Labour government, 13
Labour party
  and centralization, 23
  different tendencies within the, 45
Lane, H., 28
Leicester, University of
  School of Education at, 30
Leicester Mercury, 71
Leicestershire
  community colleges in, 55–6
  development of education in, 53–4
  educational rhetoric in, 246
  expenditure cuts and education in,
    57–8
  Greenfield College in, *see* Greenfield
    College
  progressive education in, 52–139
Leicestershire Experiment and Plan, 53
'Leicestershire Scheme for Further
  Education and Plan for County
  Colleges', 55
libertarianism
  see also progressivism, libertarian
    strand of
  in independent schools, 35–8
  and social structures, 36–7
Little Commonwealth, 28
local education authorities (LEAs), 241–2
  see also Inner London Education
    Authority
London
  political activism in schools in, 44–5
  see also Inner London Education
    Authority

Macmillan, H., 13
McRobbie, A., 208–9, 217
Manpower Services Commission (MSC),
  20, 24, 81, 240–1, 242, 246
Mapledene School, 32–3, 39, 45
marriage
  students' attitudes to, 136
  and women's dependency, 207–8
Marx, K., 142
  see also Marxism
Marxism, 1, 2, 7, 17, 38, 145, 206, 250
  see also neo-Marxism
masculinity, 211–13, 217–18, 220
  see also sex-gender
Mason, S., 61

materialist analysis, 8–11
  see also Marxism
methodological issues, 249–60
Miliband, R., 15
miners, 13, 242–4
Molina, V., 250–1
Montessori, M., 38–9, 45
Montessori schools, 38–9, 45
Morris, H., 55
MSC
  see Manpower Services Commission
Murray, L., 14

National Front, 101, 133, 134
National Union of School Students
  (NUSS), 17, 20, 74–5, 95, 154, 172,
  226
National Union of Teachers (NUT), 61,
  71, 73, 76, 80, 102, 243, 245
Neill, A.S., 35
neo-Marxism, 1, 6, 32–4
  see also Marxism
Newsom Report, 17
Norwood Report, 39
NUSS
  see National Union of School Students
NUT
  see National Union of Teachers

'oppositional spaces', 10, 11, 12, 46, 59,
  88, 90, 108, 147, 148, 153, 156–7, 162,
  171, 223, 224, 225–6, 230, 232, 237,
  238, 245–7
ORACLE research, 30

participant observation, 251–6
participatory democracy
  see Greenfield College, democracy in
patriarchy, 6, 7, 9, 10, 206–7, 208, 209,
  212, 219, 221n4, 245
pedagogy
  see also teachers
  invisible, 41, 99
  oppositional, 43
  visible, 41
personalization, 148–9, 151–2, 156, 157–
  8, 161, 162, 165, 167–8, 173–5, 178,
  179, 180–204, 214, 217, 219–21, 223,
  233, 234–5, 237, 257
  see also individualization
Picciotto, S.
  see Holloway and Picciotto
Plowden Report, 17, 41

political development
   materialist theory of, 8–11
Poulantzas, N., 144–5
professionalism, 2, 159–76, 178, 180,
   206, 209–10, 219, 223, 224, 229–30,
   231, 237–8, 245, 257
   see also teachers
   and atomization, 159, 161, 162, 257
   cultural, 159–60, 163, 168, 169, 170,
      173–4
   definition of, 160–1
   as gender-specific, 206, 209–10, 219
   in Greenfield College, 162–75, 178,
      180, 206, 209–10, 219, 223, 224,
      229–30, 231, 237–8, 245, 257
   and individualism, 161–2
   and individualization, 159, 161–2, 180,
      245, 257
   and progressivism, 162
   structural, 159–60, 168, 169, 170, 171,
      173
   and teaching, 159–61, 224, 229–30,
      231, 237–8
progressive education, *passim*
   definition of, 29–30
   ideal type of, 29–30
progressivism, 1, 2, 6, 7, 16–17, 19, 22,
   23–4, 25n31, 26–46, 47, 52–139, 143,
   147–9, 156, 162, 178, 223–9, 240, 244,
   245–7, 258–9
   see also Greenfield College
   and autonomy, 54–5, 143, 246
   and child-centred approach, 38–41,
      178, 245
   and concept of whole child, 54
   conservative critique of, 30–2
   in a Conservative local authority, 52–
      139;
   see also Greenfield College
   and control, 19
   crisis in, 16–17, 23–4, 223–9, 240, 244
   development in America of, 6, 26–8
   development in Britain of, 28–9
   and discipline, 27
   and emphasis on the individual, 54
   and expenditure cuts, 22, 71–2, 78–
      80, 81, 102–3, 226, 240
   and integration, 55
   liberal strand in, 25n31, 38–41, 44, 47,
      56–9, 71, 106, 225, 246
   libertarian strand in, 35–8, 47, 71, 107,
      225, 246, 258–9
   neo-Marxist critique of, 32–4

and personalization, *see* personalization
   and professionalism, *see*
      professionalism
   radical, 1, 147–9, 246
   and restructuring, *passim*
   and science and technology, 27
   and social control, 33
   socialist strand in, 42–6, 47, 71, 225–6
   society-centred, 38–41
   and standards in schools, 30–1
   strands of, 34–46, 47, 60, 108, 223,
      245, 258; *see also* progressivism,
      liberal strand in; libertarian strand in;
      socialist strand in
   studied in one community college, *see*
      Greenfield College
Punch, M., 37, 96
pupils
   see students

racism, 100–2, 133–5, 153
radicalism, 1, 3n4, 10, 46
raising of the school leaving age
   (ROSLA), 17
Red Rebel, 20
research
   chronology of, 254–5
   methodology of, 249–60
researcher
   role of, 251–3
restructuring, 1, 2–3, 12–16, 23–4, 46,
   47, 53, 57, 58, 60, 69, 72, 81, 85, 87,
   88, 102, 108, 143, 148, 154, 156–7,
   165, 220, 223, 224, 225–6, 238, 240,
   241, 244, 245–7, 259
Robbins Report, 17
routinization, 161, 168–9, 174
Ruskin College, 18

'saturation', 249–50, 251, 254, 256
School for Community, 56
school organization, 61–2, 223–39
schooling
   see also education; formal education;
      Greenfield College
   and capitalism, 7–8
   distinguished from education, 11n2,
      42–3
   and economic factors, 7–8
   and inequality, 30–1
   and patriarchy, 207
   and restructuring, 12–25
   and social relations, 6–11

and socio-economic conjuncture, 6, 8
schools
  see also Greenfield College
  and autonomy, 53–4, 57
  and industry, 24
  progressive, *passim*
  traditional, 29, 30
Schools Council
  changes in, 21
  closure of, 21, 23
  projects of, 17
Searle, C., 19, 43–4
self-government
  in schools, 36–7
  see also Greenfield College
Selleck, R.J.W., 28–9
Seve, L., 250–1
sex-gender, 6, 8–9, 10, 100–1, 135–7,
  153, 164, 165–6, 178–204, 205–22
  see also femininity; masculinity
sex-stereotyping, 197–202, 215–16
  see also sex-gender
sexism, 100–1, 135–7, 154, 205–22
  see also sex-gender
sexual morality
  student discussions of, 218
sexuality, 176n14
Sharp, R. and Green, A., 26, 32–4, 35,
  39, 46, 56, 160, 225
social change, 245
social class, 12–14, 31–2, 98–100, 128–
  31, 155–6, 164, 165–6, 178–204, 218,
  232–3
social control, 39, 40, 59
social mobility, 129–31, 153, 180–203,
  232–3
social relations, 1, 6–11, 12–16, 17, 46,
  58, 60
Socialist Workers Party, 20
society-centred approach, 27, 76–7
sociology
  interpretive, 254
sociology of education
  'new', 1
  'old', 1
standardization, 2, 3, 23, 26, 44, 46, 47,
  81, 88, 108, 143, 149, 156, 174, 221,
  223, 226, 240, 246
  see also centralization
state
  see also centralization; restructuring;
    state apparatus; state form
  and education, 2, 6–11

as form of capital relation, 9
  and gender-specificity, 8–9
state apparatus, 2, 6–11, 12, 46, 60, 147,
  148, 245
state form, 2, 9–11, 12, 46, 147, 148
student careers, 178–204, 209–10, 218
  see also students
  construction of, 180–203
    and attitudes to education, 185–8
    biographical aspects of, 183–4
    case studies of boys and, 189–97
    case studies of girls and, 197–202
    cultural aspects of, 182–3
    structural aspects of, 180–2
    and worldviews, 184–5
    negotiation of, 180–202
    and sex-gender, 197–202, 218
    and social class, 180–202
students
  see also Greenfield College
  and achievement, 98–100
  apathy of, 120
  and atomization, 151–2
  attitudes to democratic procedures of,
    120–1
  attitudes to education of, 185–8
  attitudes to marriage of, 136
  attitudes to other adults of, 123–4
  attitudes to teachers of, 122–4
  and behavioural difficulties, 20
  careers of, 178–204, 209–10, 218
  case studies of, 113–15, 189–202
  and competitiveness, 233
  and conformism, 127–8
  and conservatism, 184–5
  and control, 126
  and creative writing, 116–17
  and curriculum, 111–19
  and democracy, 119–22, 127
  and deviance, 216–17
  differentiation among, 89, 97–102,
    205–22
  and discipline, 19–20
  and equality of opportunity, 132–3,
    181
  and examinations, *see* examinations
  family background of, 98–9
  and first names convention, 67, 123,
    127, 154–5
  and individualization, 151–6
  and instrumentalism, 116, 190–202,
    233, 234
  and libertarianism, 36–7

and moots, 119–20
and participation, 119–22, 127, 223–39
and pedagogy, 115–16
and personalization, 112–13, 151–2
and politics, 131–2, 184–5
and powerlessness, 131–2, 137, 153, 181, 233
and racism, 100–2, 133–5, 153
and radicalism, 127–8, 184–5
and resistance, 19–20
and self-determination, 137, 152, 153, 154
and self-direction, 178, 181
and sex-gender, 100–1, 135–7, 153, 214–21
and sexism, 219–21
and social class, 98–100, 128–31, 132–3, 155–6, 190–202, 218, 232–3
and social differentiation, 128–37
and social inequality, 129–31
and social mobility, 153
and social studies, 112
and strikes, 20
and subject choice, 111–19, 205, 215–17
and teacher-student relationships, *see* Greenfield College, teacher-student relationships in
and truancy, 19–20
and vertical teams, 232–7
viewed as collective, 229–30
and violence, 19–20
and youth unemployment, 20
Students Action Union, 20
subordination
and resistance, 15
Suggestions (Board of Education guide), 29
Summerhill (school), 35, 36

teacher shortage, 18–19, 47, 162
teacher-student relationships, *see* Greenfield College, teacher-student relationships in
teachers
see also Greenfield College
and accountability, 18
and autonomy, 47, 160, 171, 210, 246
biographies of, 172, 174
and careers, 18–19, 60, 170
and caring, 210
and changes in education, 18–19
and child-centred approach, 76–7
and control, 96, 126, 155, 165–7, 171, 174, 210, 211–13, 215
and curriculum, 85–90
and democracy, 90–5, 102, 104
and deviance, 216–17
differentiation among, 85–7, 90–2
and differentiation among students, 89, 97–102, 215–17
and examinations, 88–90, 97–102, 117–19, 162–5, 174
and expenditure cuts, 102–3
and expertise, 159
at Greenfield College, *see* Greenfield College
and impersonality, 160
and individualization, 149–51
and informal structures, 92–3, 121, 151, 153
liberal, 106, 172, 243, 259
libertarian, 107, 173, 228–9, 231, 243, 258
marginalization of, 93
and militancy, 19
pay of, 23
politics of, 172–3, 174
and positional interaction, 166–7, 229
pragmatist, 107, 172–3, 228–9, 231, 242, 243, 259
and professionalism, 18, 47, 69, 76, 89–90, 105, 156, 159–76
profiles of, 103–6
and promotion, 169
and racism, 100–2, 133–5, 153
radical, 106–7, 228–9, 231, 242, 243, 258
role of, 28, 170–1
and routinization, 161, 168–9, 174
and self-development, 170
and sex-gender, 136, 153, 210–14
and sexism, 219–21
and social class, 98–100, 172, 174
socialist, 172, 173, 228–9, 231, 242, 243
socialization of, 170
and society-centred approach, 76–7
and standards, 18
status of, 47, 246
and subject teaching, 77
and students' subject choices, 216
and teacher-student relationships
see Greenfield College, teacher-student relationships in

and team teaching, 77
and trade unions, 3, 23, 44–5, 47, 64, 71–2, 73, 79, 92, 102–3, 104, 106–7, 149–50, 160, 172–3, 210, 216–17, 226, 241–3, 258
and vertical teams, 223–39
teaching
and expenditure cuts, 22
and professionalism, 159–61
teaching careers
and gender, 209–10
Teaching London Kids, 43
Teaching Styles and Pupil Progress, 30
Technical and Vocational Education Initiative (TVEI), 81, 240–1, 242, 247n1
Thatcher, M. (Prime Minister), 14, 22–3, 58, 69
Thatcherism, 14–15, 22–3, 69
trade unions, 3, 13, 14, 15, 23, 44–5, 47, 64, 71–2, 73, 79, 92, 102–3, 104, 106–7, 149–50, 160, 172–3, 210, 216–17, 226, 241–3, 247, 258
and corporate strategy, 13
and desubordination, 15
and militancy, 23, 47
reform of, 15
and shop stewards, 14
and teachers, *see* teachers, and trade unions

tripartite system, 39
TUC (Trades Union Congress), 21
TVEI
see Technical and Vocational Education Initiative

United States of America (USA)
progressivism in, 26–8
Unpopular Education, 7

vandalism, 47
vertical teams, 223–39
advantages of, 224–5
disadvantages of, 225

Waddell Report, 20
William Tyndale School, 1, 44–5, 46, 47, 162
Williams, S., 19
Willis, P., 162, 178
women
see also femininity; feminism; sex–gender
subordination of, 207–8
working class
see social class

youth cultures, 16, 47
youth unemployment, 20, 47